Dream Reachers

Kiara Hunter

Only those who stretch to reach their
dreams find themselves living them

Celebrity interviews by Chase Von
Celebrity anecdotes by Betty Dravis

VonChase Publishing Company

ISBN: 09766787-8-0

LCCN: 2009923347

Copyright © 2009 by Chase Von and Betty Dravis

Dream Reachers (Vol. 1) manufactured in the USA

An original publication by -

VonChasePublishing Company
P.O. Box 623
Winchester, CA 92596

Cover design by Chase Von, Betty Dravis, Audrey Michelle
© 2009, Cover photograph by Mara

Editors: Betty Dravis, Chase Von, Sara McDonald

Parental advisory, this publication does include some
adult content.

Dedication

This compilation is dedicated to all those included and to a very special soul who did reach for her dreams, and her surviving family members

DEBRA D. GRIFFIN
(interview on page 435)

A portion from the profits of this book will be given to the Breast Cancer Care Research Fund, a cause this "Dream Reacher" so very much believed in and for stem cell research, a cause Betty, Judyth and Chase believe in as well

Betty Dravis also dedicates this book to her beloved daughter MARY LEE FRANCIS who went to be with the Lord on August 30, 2007. Mary Lee is reunited in Heaven with her sister DENYCE "NEECEE" DRAVIS ...Both left us too young, too soon.

Other books by Betty Dravis

1106 Grand Boulevard
The Toonies Invade Silicon Valley
Millennium Babe: The Prophecy

Other books by Chase Von

Your Chance to Hear the Last Panther Speak
Pink, Blue and Green

Acknowledgements

As Walt Disney once said, "It's kind of fun to do the impossible." And I'm certain the talented artists featured in this book agree with him. Through hard work, determination and faith in themselves, they have done the impossible, achieving beyond their wildest dreams. They are the ultimate *"Dream Reachers,"* and I'd like to thank them for making this book possible and for inspiring others to reach for their dreams.

When Chase Von interviewed me for the author's section of *Student Operated Press* his casual manner and natural gift-of-gab relaxed me, making the process a joy. I'd like to thank him for including my interview in this book and for putting up with my quirkiness as we created *"Dream Reachers."* Surprisingly, rather than alienating him, my nitpicking had the opposite effect and we've become great friends. (Yes, he's still speaking to me!)

I'm also grateful to Judyth Piazza, CEO of *Student Operated Press* and radio-talk-show moderator, for mentoring Chase and encouraging this book from its conception.

Another *"Dream Reacher"* who's not in this book (but will be in a future one, I'm certain) is my best friend Linda Bulger. She encouraged me through many post-midnight sessions working with Chase on this dreamy, yet demanding project.

Corresponding between California and her cottage in rural Maine is not easy, but with e-mail all things are possible.

Heart-felt gratitude for the uplifting chats and your expert advice, Linda.

Warm thanks to my beloved children and grandchildren whom I've thanked in all my books. Yes, they've survived a lifetime of long, drawn-out sessions of Mom's "Deadline Dramatics." Thanks for your patience and help. You're rockin' fine kids!

- Betty Dravis

I want to thank Judyth Piazza or as I call her, 'Mighty J,' creator of *The Student Operated Press,* and Betty Dravis because without them, none of this would be possible. I'd also like to thank my family and friends for their steadfast support, as well as all the wonderful people that have let me harass them into doing an interview. (Heh, Heh.)

But foremost, I want to thank God because I have little doubt that my meeting Willard Barth and Willard, in turn, introducing me to Judyth Piazza and all the other great and inspiring people I've met as a result, is totally to be credited to the Lord.

- Chase Von

Foreword by Chase Von

I recently interviewed Betty Dravis, acclaimed author of three novels and a seasoned journalist. During our communication, Betty suggested that I should publish my interviews in a book.

After discussing it with my boss Judyth Piazza, celebrity interviewer and host of the popular radio show The American Perspective, we decided to go for it! Incidentally, Judyth is the first person to recognize that I might have a "knack" for interviewing. (Smile.)

This is the outcome of that idea, and Betty graciously accepted when I invited her to co-author this book and include behind-the-scenes memories of several of her celebrity interviews from "back in the day." Among the few she's releasing for this book are: her interviews with "Living Legend" Clint Eastwood and the unforgettable movie star/icon of the '40s & '50s era Jane Russell.

Note from Betty Dravis:
My Celebrity Interviews

When I was a starry-eyed young journalist dreaming of writing books, I was fortunate to be granted interviews with some of the world's most famous "movers and shakers" in the entertainment and political fields.

Those interviews were published in various California newspapers, including one I owned for fifteen years (refer to my interview by Chase Von for more information on my career). Later, with dreams of writing for a wider audience, I wrote the behind-the-scenes stories, detailing how I landed the interviews and my personal feelings about the celebrities.

I was an impressionable young woman when I interviewed these icons and was overwhelmed by seeing them on the big screen and television one day, being in their presence the next. But I had a job to do and was determined to do it properly, so I put on my best front and became Ms. Cool right before their eyes. My kids would have been so proud of my nonchalant attitude; I pulled it off like a real pro.

And, yes, because I eventually published three novels with more on the way, I am a "Dream Reacher" too. Woo-hoo!

I hope you enjoy reading the following vignettes from my past as much as I like sharing them. May this book inspire you to go for your dreams, and enjoy your life while doing so.

Only those who stretch to reach their dreams find themselves living them. Go for it!

Dream Reachers

Willard L. Barth

Only those who stretch to reach their
dreams find themselves living them

by Chase Von and Betty Dravis

VonChase Publishing Company
http://bettydravisauthor.googlepages.com/

Contents

Special Thanks

****

*Grateful acknowledgment to the following
for permission to reprint photos and movie stills:*

****

The Weinstein Company; Genius Entertainment;
Avi Lerner, movie producer/founder and co-owner of
Nu Image and Millennium Pictures;
Michael Regen, Vice President, Marketing/Acquisitions,
Melee Entertainment; Gus Van Sant, film
director/writer/author/producer; DreamWorks Pictures; Apatow
Productions; Herzog-Cowen Entertainment; Billy Somoa
Saleebey, director, co-producer of acclaimed movie, Rolling;
World-renowned photographer Jim Marshall; David Ford,
Maureen Lamberti and Jodi Peckman of Rolling Stone magazine;
Alex Simon, Editor-In-Chief, Venice magazine; Italiana Eleganza
magazine; Chaunce Hayden, CEO and owner of Steppin' Out
magazine; Connect Savannah magazine; Alan Grey, CEO of
NewsBlaze; Darcy Donavan, CEO of Reel Vision Entertainment;
Willard Barth Enterprises; Armed Forces Entertainment;
Songs from Shenzhen, China;
Steven Zale, CEO of the Zalemark Jewelry Company

****

"Lose your dreams and you might lose your mind."
- Mick Jagger, Rolling Stones

****

Interview with Clint Eastwood

Betty Dravis with Actor Clint Eastwood

A BAD HAIR-DAY
by Betty Dravis

In the late sixties, I wrote a weekly newspaper column for the *East San Jose Sun* where I also specialized in human-interest stories and profiles of prominent local citizens.

For a Halloween feature story, in the late sixties I profiled a woman named June Cheim who was the delight of trick-or-treaters in her rather exclusive neighborhood.

Every year, this gracious woman transformed herself into a frightening witch, acting the part to perfection.

And June--headlined as "The Good Witch of the East Foothills"--brewed a fantastic witch's brew. Topped by roiling clouds of evil-looking, foul-smelling gray smoke, the mixture looked more lethal than Bette Midler's in *Hocus Pocus*. June's brew was apple cider, of course, and it was delicious. The children loved it, and the Cheim home was a favorite haunt on Halloween.

Shortly following publication of the story, I was at home doing laundry when June phoned to thank me for the story, commenting that her friends, neighbors, and family enjoyed it tremendously.

She went on to tell me that a popular movie star was visiting them for a few days and asked if I would like to interview him. She explained that she had gone to school with him and she and her husband Leo had maintained their friendship throughout the years.

The Cheims' friend was one of the world's top box-office draws, rapidly overtaking Charles Bronson. *Wow! Interview that hunk! Ohmigod ... ohmigod!* I thought, but I managed to stammer, "Y-yes, of course."

****

"Go ahead, make my day." - Clint Eastwood, in the fourth Dirty Harry movie "Sudden Impact," 1983

****

I--a low-paid, part-timer at a small weekly--was the only newsperson in San Jose getting a shot at the star. It was my chance to scoop the large daily paper. By no stretch of the i-m-a-g-i-n-a-t-i-o-n was I a career journalist; I was just starting out part-time, not even thinking of going full-time yet. Primarily, I was a mother, struggling to raise six children alone.

I was completely dazzled at the thought of interviewing

that man...and a little frightened. In those days, I had no tape recorder and was concerned that I might write too slowly, botch the interview, and make a fool of myself. Could I do the job properly? Would I be professional enough?

"Take Pride" spokesman Clint Eastwood in Boekel, Holland, 2005

The thrill of meeting such a famous, handsome hunk overcame my professional doubts, and I was hot to trot. *After all*, I told myself, *he's only a man.*

But then, being as vain as the next woman, personal doubts crept in. I began worrying about my appearance. I had always been a natural blonde, but as it faded, I'd started touching it up. Well, that day--of all days--my roots needed touching up and I needed a cut and a style.

In other words, it was a woman's worst nightmare...a

bad hair-day. A very bad hair-day.

Even more frustrating was that June had set the interview for five o'clock that afternoon, and since the star was leaving the next day, it was my only chance.

Time was short, so I called the *Sun* to schedule a photographer to meet me at the Cheim residence, but none was available. Damn!

Next I phoned my hairstylist only to find that she was booked solid. Double damn!

In desperation, I called a friend, Josie.

Yes, Josie had experience! Yes, Josie could do it! And yes, Josie could even baby-sit.

Yes! Yes! Yes!

I thought things were finally going to work out, but that thought was a little premature. Josie thought ash-blonde Clairol worked the same as light blonde; you know, the longer you leave it on, the lighter it becomes? Well, ash-blonde works the opposite. She let it develop too long, and *voila*...brown hair! And to make matters worse, she plastered flirtatious little Spanish sideburns to my cheeks, fashioned a curly topknot and a lopsided cut.

"Definitely not me," I moaned, since I considered myself more the girl-next-door, cheerleader type. *Could Josie be jealous of my lucky break?* I asked myself. Then: *Na-ahh ... she's not that mean-spirited.*

After staring ice-picks at Josie for ruining my looks, I kissed the kiddies good-bye, swallowed my pride, and toodled on to the big interview.

My self-confidence had gone down Josie's drain right along with my hair, but at least I liked my outfit. It was a yellow-and-white-polka-dotted number with a slightly-flared skirt. The dress--and white, high-heeled pumps--set off my tan; not much consolation, but it helped a little.

And, as if that weren't enough, with no cameraman in tow, I felt like a complete amateur. *Oh-h, well, one lucky break a day is all one can hope for,* I told myself as I pulled into the Cheims' circular driveway, hopped out of my clunky old Mercury and sashayed up the walkway.

From somewhere deep within I summoned my usual bravado, and knocked.

Several rapid heartbeats later, the door opened and there he stood--Clint Eastwood! The star gazed at me with his gorgeous bed-room eyes, flashed a devastating smile, took my trembling arm and escorted me into the den for the interview...which went great.

Eastwood was so charming and down-to-earth, he put me at ease immediately. And afterward--when he graciously invited me along for dinner at The Fog Horn-- he made a fan for life. Regretfully, I declined because Josie could only baby-sit till nine o'clock. Triple damn!

As I was leaving, June took several photographs of me with Eastwood, and although I have never liked my hairdo, to this day I adore the way that sexy, all-male hunk gazed down at me. And, God, the way he cupped my neck with those long, strong fingers still gives me goose bumps.

My best friend was the first to tease me about the picture. "Wow, Clint's looking at you like he's in love with you."

"Yeah, he's a great actor, isn't he?" I smugly replied, but I was thinking, *I should be so lucky!* Then I modestly added, "I was just in the right place at the right time."

Now, it's thirty-plus years later, and Eastwood's a mega-star, mega-producer...mega-everything. And another young journalist--Dina Ruiz, TV co-anchor of Action News Eight (Salinas/Monterey/Santa Cruz)--interviewed him a few years ago...and he ended up marrying her. (Small world, but Dina's an acquaintance of my youngest daughter Allison.)

That's one journalist who was really in the right place at the right time. It must have been a great hair-day for her.

But with Dina's beauty, charm, talent...and that gorgeous mane of thick, dark hair, how could she miss?

****

"I have to keep challenging myself and try something I haven't done before. The studios aren't always happy with that... But playing it safe is what's risky, because nothing new comes out of it."
- Clint Eastwood, Actor, Director, Producer

****

"Take Pride" spokesman Clint Eastwood in Boekel, Holland, 2005

****

"As for me, I like being behind the camera instead of in front of it. I can wear what I want. Will I act again? I never say never. I like doing things where I can stretch and go in different directions."
- Clint Eastwood, Actor, Director, Producer

****

Interview with Senator Edward "Ted" Kennedy

Betty Dravis with Sen. Ted Kennedy

A TREASURED MOMENT IN TIME
by Betty Dravis

Like the rest of the world, when our beloved President John Fitzgerald Kennedy was assassinated on November 22, 1963, I remember where I was and what I was doing at that exact moment. I was sitting in a dentist's office when another patient arrived, bearing the tragic news. I rushed home to find that my husband had left work, picked the kids up from school and they were sitting on the couch watching the dreadful event unroll right before their eyes.

I joined them and we hugged our children close as tears welled in our eyes. We were stunned into silence.

Thirty-five years later, I was stunned in a more joyful way when I was seated beside JFK's brother, Senator Edward "Ted" Kennedy, at a banquet, enjoying a brief conversation.

Before I tell you the story of how I met Kennedy, I'd like to express my sorrow that in May of 2008, he suffered a seizure and was airlifted to a Boston hospital, where doctors discovered a malignant tumor in his brain.

I doubt if he will ever read this or even that he will remember me after all this time, but that doesn't matter. What matters is that he touched my life for a brief, memorable moment and I have not forgotten him. And now that he's ill, I'd like for him to know that my thoughts are with him and his family as I pray for complete recovery. May God be with you, Senator Kennedy.

I met Kennedy back in the mid-seventies. At that time I owned and published *Construction Labor News*, a regional newspaper for members of the Building Trades Council. Headquartered in San Jose, California, *CLN* was recognized by the AFL-CIO International as an official labor publication. Our slogan was: *The Voice of Labor in Silicon Valley and Beyond.*

In that capacity we published news of interest to working people and their families along with some national and international news. But our main focus was on local news. Since unions endorse political candidates, mostly Democratic, and contribute to their campaigns, *CLN* staff naturally attended many political fundraisers...from rallies to picnics to fancy dinners.

Since Congressman Norm Mineta, former San Jose Mayor, was a popular local politician and was running his second campaign for Congress, Senator Kennedy came to the Valley to "stump" for him. He was Mineta's guest speaker at a dinner at San Jose Hyatt House, one of the usual dining establishments with banquet facilities utilized by area politicians, unions and other businesses.

If I recall properly, the dinner was the usual $150 per person, with proceeds going towards Mineta's campaign. As a member of the Press, however, *CLN* received several press passes, as is traditional with the media.

In order to write an interesting account of the dinner for *CLN* and to meet Senator Kennedy, I attended. As usual, I sat at the press table situated up front near the speaker's podium, adjacent to the head table.

Mineta's press secretary had arranged for me to meet with Kennedy following the dinner, so as he approached, I rose to greet him, we chatted for a while, and the campaign photographer snapped the above photo.

After our preliminary conversation, Kennedy sat beside me and I interviewed him for the *CLN* article. I found him to be quite polite and open, but, truthfully, he was a little more aloof than others I had interviewed. I took that in stride, reasoning: *After all, this is a KENNEDY sitting beside me, a member of THE Kennedy family, raised with a silver spoon in his mouth, so it's just his way.*

Even though I was a "seasoned professional" by then, I was much more overwhelmed than I pretended, but I put my best foot forward and turned the charm up a volume. And I got my scoop, while my photographer took some great shots of Mineta at the podium and later as he greeted his guests. It was a successful evening.

And, yes, Norm Mineta won the Congressional race again, and in 2001 was appointed by President George W. Bush to be Secretary of Transportation, Department of Transportation. In 2006 Bush appointed him to be a member of the AMTRAK Reform Board, for a five-year term. He is still in Washington, D.C.

Since *CLN* and the Building Trades Council endorsed

*Official Portrait of U.S. Senator from
Massachusetts Edward "Ted" Moore Kennedy*

all of Mineta's campaigns, he was a part of my life until 1992 when I retired.

As for Senator Ted Kennedy, he has had a long, illustrious career, one that I follow with interest, as most people do. He's become known as one of the last lions of liberalism, a full-throated defender of the policies the Democratic Party pursued in the 1960's and 1970's. But within the Senate he has a reputation as one of the most effective members at building bipartisan coalitions.

True to form, Kennedy remains strong and persistent. Following an operation for brain cancer at the Duke University Medical Center in June, he expressed to family members his intention to give a speech at the Democratic National Convention in August 2008. When he arrived in Denver, he was sidetracked with debilitating kidney stones, but that didn't stop this dedicated man. He made it to the convention––doctor and paramedics in tow––and delivered a highly acclaimed opening-night address. May he continue to triumph!

I never again saw Senator Kennedy in person, but I have a fond memory of that night at the Hyatt House...a memory I treasure along with many others in my life. Thanks for the memory, Senator, but most of all, thanks for your dedication to the working people of our great country.

President Kennedy and his brothers. Attorney General Robert F. Kennedy,
Senator Edward "Ted" Moore Kennedy, President John F. Kennedy.
White House, Outside of Oval Office, 08/28/1963
- Photo credit: Stoughton/National Archives via pingnews

Interview with Jane Russell

Betty Dravis with Actress Jane Russell

LOBSTER, ANYONE?
by Betty Dravis

One day in the early seventies I was sitting at my editorial desk at the *Gilroy News Herald* when the publisher burst into my office, grinning as though he had just won a Pulitzer. "Lucky you!" he said, "Guess who you get to interview tomorrow."

"Clint Eastwood? Tom Selleck?" I asked hopefully.

"Not exactly! Someone more my type. That give you a clue?"

Uh-oh, Gordon's got that Playboy centerfold look, I thought, but I said, "Must be Miss July, for you to get so steamed up. Now give....Who is it?"

"Jane Russell--in the flesh."

"Jane Russell...the movie star? When and where?"

"San Francisco...Trader Vic's. Ten AM sharp! Can you make it?"

I assured him I'd be there on time, but was delayed by a chemical spill on Highway 101. I couldn't believe my bad luck, but continued on my way, hoping for the best. I thought I'd been assigned a personal interview with Miss Russell, so was worried about the repercussions of being late.

Like a movie star always gets her man, an editor always gets her story. *But would I get mine this time? Or would I be too late?*

Movie stars Marilyn Monroe and Jane Russell putting signatures in cement at Chinese Theater in Los Angeles, California,1953 (photo from Los Angeles Times photographic archive, UCLA Library; public domain)

Cropped screenshot of Dorothy Lamour, Bing Crosby,
Jane Russell and Bob Hope in Road to Bali, 1952, public domain

When I arrived at Trader Vic's––an hour late––I was relieved to learn it was a round-table interview with representatives of both major dailies and small weeklies present, so nobody had even noticed my absence.

Feeling highly unprofessional, I glanced sheepishly around, then took a seat, placed a tape recorder alongside a notepad on the table and waited for a fellow-journalist to finish speaking so I could ask a few questions. But the minute he finished, the actress's agent ended the session.

"Damn!" I muttered under my breath as I scooped up the tools of my trade, lowered my head and rushed out the nearest exit. I passed a shiny, black Cadillac limo I assumed was Miss Russell's transportation and was standing beside my little white Vega when someone called my name.

I turned to see Miss Russell's agent scurrying after me.

"Betty Dravis...the Gilroy paper?"

"Ye-es," I stammered, reaching into my pocket for a business card.

"Well, Jane didn't want you to be scooped, so is giving you an exclusive," he whispered.

"Give the others time to leave, then meet us back in the conference room."

"Sounds wonderful. Press deadline's tomorrow and my publisher will be thrilled."

I had recovered and was back in business.

The interview went smoothly and afterwards a photographer took several photographs of me with the famous star. My publisher was so pleased with the story, he ran one of the photos, too, and after we put the paper to bed, he treated me to dinner.

Thanks to the generosity of the fabulous Jane Russell, I was a minor celebrity in Gilroy for a few days, and instead of eating crow that day, I ate lobster.

Movie Star Jane Russell; photo from an unregistered trailer of "Gentlemen Prefer Blondes"; photo listed/registered public domain; Wikipedia Commons

The late San Francisco Mayor Joseph Alioto

San Francisco Mayor Joseph L. Alioto - served from 1968-1976

STALKING ALIOTO
by Betty Dravis

When I edited the *Gilroy News Herald*, a small California city newspaper, I was often assigned to cover political fund-raisers...dinners, picnics, rallies, etc. The shorter articles were incorporated into a column I wrote, "The Gilroy Gadabout."

The rallies and picnics were exhilarating, red-white-and-blue parties, the excitement contagious. Those events were fun because my children could attend and get some insight on what Mom did for a living. But I especially enjoyed the dinners because I got to exchange my more conservative business attire for fancy dresses and nights on the town, dining in posh restaurants from Silicon Valley to San Francisco.

I welcomed the opportunities to meet--and sometimes interview--many popular politicians and other noted celebrities. But I found the media push at these affairs very distasteful as photographers and reporters hustled to get better camera angles, better quotes, more recognition. So whenever the publisher assigned a photographer to assist me, I was grateful because it left me free to table-hop, searching out the "movers and shakers."

I was always a polite person, but good manners had little to do with newspaper work, so I learned to hustle with the best of them--when I saw something I wanted bad enough.

And what I wanted one evening at a political dinner in San Francisco's Fairmont Hotel was then-Mayor Joseph Alioto.

There was a huge crowd that evening and whenever I got near His Honor, some bigger, bolder, meaner newsperson elbowed past me. I had never acquired the knack of getting down enough, dirty enough, or mean enough, so I lost Alioto in the crowd.

Then when the speeches ended and dinner was served, I knew time was running out.

The Mayor would be a captive audience, but I couldn't approach him while he was dining, could I? That would be a major faux pas even for a crass newsperson, wouldn't it?

In a last-ditch effort, I climbed onto a chair to try to locate him, and when I did, I jumped off the chair and dashed over. Oh, God, Alioto had a sliver of steak on his fork and was bringing it to his mouth.

But if he hasn't taken a bite, I reasoned to myself,

technically he isn't eating, is he?

I felt like I was running a race with that fork as I boldly closed the space between us. "Mayor Alioto, I'm Betty Dravis from the *Gilroy News Herald*," I breathlessly said. "I hate to interrupt your dinner, but—"

He cut me off by sticking out his large hand, grasping my own smaller one and pumping vigorously. "Well, 'The Gilroy Gadabout.' Your boss and I go way back--but what are you doing in The City?"

"Following politics...and stalking you, it looks like." I gave a small, nervous laugh, then honesty won out. "Actually I'm trying to scoop the *Gilroy Dispatch* with a few good candids."

"They've been around forever. About time they had some competition. I hate monopolies, so go ahead--take your best shots," Alioto said. "And the next time I go to Monterey, I may stop off in Gilroy and give you a hand." Then with his famous big-toothed smile and an airy swoop of his hand, he beckoned my photographer.

Mayor Alioto was a real charmer, a master of political rhetoric. Even though the food was getting cold, he took time for some candid shots, then posed with his dinner companions.

Later, when I told Herald owner--San Jose Attorney Robert Morgan, now deceased--how brazen I'd felt by interrupting Alioto's dinner, he gave me one of his rare half-smiles. "Get the news anyway you can, Miss Betty. And always remember there's nothing a politician likes better than having his picture taken...not even eating."

I thought that was a cynical statement, but have since learned my boss was absolutely right. But that doesn't lessen the gratitude I have for the late-great Joe Alioto who turned what could have been a major *faux pas* into a minor victory for a young editor/writer of a small-town newspaper.

Mercy! Odd place to meet actress Ann Sothern

*1939 promotion photo of Ann Sothern for movie
"Hotel for Women" - public domain; Wikimedia*

THE SWEET LITTLE OLD LADY
by Betty Dravis

In 1961, when my daughter Debbie was six, she underwent open-heart surgery to repair a defective ventricle. Thank God, the surgery was an immediate success, so my parents--who had flown in from Ohio to care for our other children--could return home. After they were gone, with no other child-care and only one automobile, my husband and I took turns visiting Debbie during the hospital recovery period.

It broke my heart to be able to see my daughter only once daily, but she seemed content. She had found a mother-substitute: a "sweet little old lady" who came in to read to her each day. She was hospitalized at Mercy Hospital.

I assumed the woman was a hospital volunteer, but on the day of Debbie's release the woman explained that she was visiting her sister who was recuperating from neck surgery. To pass the time, the woman had visited the children's ward where she saw Debbie, and "fell in love with that beautiful angel at first sight." She said Debbie reminded her of her sister when she was that age.

She went on to say that her sister had a special gift for Debbie and requested that I bring Debbie to her room before we left.

****

"I'd been playing these dames like Rosie and Katy, and Susie and Maisie for over twenty-five years. I thought it was time for me to go back to being Annie."
- *Ann Sothern, Actress, Singer, Comedienne*
****

I was anxious to get Debbie home, but could not refuse that kind-hearted woman. A short while later, the nurse wheeled Debbie to the sister's room, and when she opened the door, I was stunned to learn that Debbie's lady's sister was Ann Sothern, a famous movie and TV actress of those days. I especially enjoyed her TV sit-coms "Private Secretary" (1953) and "The Ann Sothern Show" (1958).

Debbie's sapphire eyes lit up the room when Ann Sothern gave her a hand-crocheted Barbie-doll dress. *How sweet,* I thought. *Not many little girls could boast of a doll dress made by a movie star.*

Although I was delighted to meet Ann Sothern, it's the memory of her kind, caring sister Marian that makes my soul smile. She saw a lovely, lonely, little girl in the hospital recovering from serious heart surgery and took the time to brighten her days and make her feel special.

Time has dimmed my memory and I can't remember Marian's last name, but my gratitude remains eternal.

Cropped screenshot of Ann Sothern from the trailer for
the 1937 film "Dangerous Number" - public domain, Wikimedia

****

*"The best comedienne in this business,
bar none, is Ann Sothern."
- Lucille Ball, personal friend and
beloved star of "I Love Lucy"*

****

Screenshot of the main cast members of the 1943 film "Cry Havoc," clockwise from top left : Margaret Sullavan, Ann Sothern, Ella Raines, Joan Blondell, Frances Gifford, Connie Gilchrist, Diana Lewis and Marsha Hunt; from the trailer; public domain

****

"Ann Sothern died of heart failure in 2001 at her home in Ketchum, Idaho; she was ninety-two. When I read the sad news, I whispered, 'Good night, Ann'... in memory of what she often told her fans when closing her 'Ann Sothern Show': 'Good night...and stay happy.'"
- Betty Dravis, Author, Journalist

****

Celebrating with Tanya Tucker

Betty Dravis with Singer Tanya Tucker

TANYA'S LUCKY THIRTEEN
by Betty Dravis

I met the young singer Tanya Tucker when I was editor of the *Gilroy News Herald* (CA) and was invited to a celebration honoring her for her first three Country Billboard hits. Following is a portion of what I wrote for the *Herald* in my "Gilroy Gadabout" column:

My weekend was dominated by a delightful family from Henderson, Nevada—Jesse "Bo" Tucker and his beautiful daughters, Tanya and La Costa. Tanya, as you all know by now, is the girl who turned the terrible thirteens into the lucky thirteens. She became a teenager and a recording star all in a year. Her very first record "Delta Dawn," which she recorded for Columbia Records, is a tremendous nationwide hit.

And now it looks as though her second recording will make musical history. "The Jamestown Ferry" with "Love's the Answer" on the flip side, are both on the record charts and are rapidly working toward the top of the list. If they do as well as "Delta Dawn," it will be the first time that anyone ever had three hits out of three tries.

That's phenomenal! But then Tanya is quite phenomenal herself. This five-foot-two, eyes-of-blue gal is a natural beauty with a natural talent. And she hails from a down-to-earth, unassuming family. I hope she stays as wholesome as she is now.

Well, the world knows *that* didn't happen, any more than my writing style remained the same. Tanya developed the usual teenage angst, multiplied by sudden fame and fortune and...

But I'm getting ahead of my story. First I'd like to talk about how I met Tanya and the fun my family and I had with her and her family at the Gilroy ranch of their hosts A.C. and Dolores Bowman:

It was A.C. who phoned the *Herald* to invite us to Tanya's Victory Celebration near Thanksgiving that year, so my children and I trekked on over to his ranch to meet the talented, much-touted singer who was already being compared to the great Brenda Lee.

Tanya had just turned fourteen and I found her to be a delightful, precocious teenager. *Herald* photographer Robert Isenberg captured many photos of her with all of us, including the one of Tanya and me inside a barn (above). Tanya showed off her roping skills in some photos, while posing on a horse with her father "Bo" and her older sister La Costa in others.

Following hors d'oeuvres, the Bowmans served a delicious cake that was decorated with the titles of Tanya's three hit songs and a plug for La Costa who was also a singer.

Teens being teens, my kids weren't impressed at the time; they ran around the ranch, playing with Tanya and jabbering as only kids can. Tanya--already a little minx-- even flirted and teased around with my eleven-year-old son Bobby...but her eyes seemed to be on a tall, lanky cowboy, one of Bowman's ranch hands--an older boy who appeared to be around seventeen. *But that's teens for you!*

At one time, Tanya remarked that she could be one of my kids. "Yes, you'd fit in," I replied. "You have the same fair coloring...and the same independent gleam in your eye."

Tanya chuckled at that, then talked about the reason she was in town: for a gig to perform at a popular country-western night club called Bobby McGee's in Morgan Hill.

The following evening, I accompanied her family and the Bowmans to that event and it was a special treat to hear her sing "Delta Dawn" in person. She wore a red-and-white polka-dotted dress, long and loose with a conservative neckline. She looked beautiful, and she stunned the audience with her big voice. *What an incredible talent!*

Tanya's cute little figure was already blossoming, so her father fretted about cleavage. We all laughed at him then, and years later--when she began wearing Elvis-like outfits that clung to her like second skins--I often wondered what kind of "hissyfit" her father threw then. *Well, that's parents for you!*

That was Tanya at fourteen, and by age fifteen she had a "Greatest Hits" album, several #1 records and a million-dollar recording contract!

The rest is history: She now has sold over fifty million records worldwide, sixteen gold and platinum certifications and is one of the top ten most successful female country artists of all time. If that isn't enough, she's the youngest female artist ever to have a box set released and the first country artist ever on the cover of *Rolling Stone Magazine*.

She's also written seven books including an autobiography, performed in five movies, innumerable TV shows and is the first country artist to have her own reality TV series: *Tuckerville*.

From the humongous talent and streak of independence I saw in that young girl I met way back then, I knew she would do big things with her life. If I listed all the Halls of Fame and Walks of Fame Tanya is on, named all her hit records and other accomplishments, this book would never get finished, so on with my thoughts:

Yes, I met this talented, determined woman at age fourteen when she was in the first throes of her magical life. I'm still dazzled that her very first three records made the charts, a fete that even King Elvis didn't accomplish with his first releases. *Unbelievable!*

The last time I saw Tanya was in a re-run of *Tuckerville*. As my daughter Mary Lee and I watched the show together, she remarked, "Mom, do you remember when you wrote in the *Herald* that you hoped Tanya would remain wholesome? Well, she looks wholesome now, but a lot has happened to her since we met her. Like the rest of us, she's had a roller-coaster life. She had her rebellious years and I'll never forget how the media slapped her photos all over the front page when she started drinking...and dating Glenn Campbell."

"Well, all that fame's bound to get to anyone," I responded. "Remember when she crossed over into pop music and got even more famous. Well, I read somewhere that Tanya said she started drinking out of loneliness. That's when she performed two shows a night, received all that on-stage adulation and then went home to an empty motel room. Poor thing."

Mary Lee and I reminisced about Tanya's "Outlaw" image too. She's one of the few and best-known female country singers to be classified as an "Outlaw" in the outlaw country movement, which was most popular in the late 70s. As Tanya matured by the end of that era, her outlaw image grew. She was able to combine qualities of country and rock music into voice to make the outlaw sound, like my favorite outlaws, Willie Nelson, Hank Williams Jr. and Waylon Jennings. These qualities could be heard on some of her biggest hits at the time, including 1978's "Texas (When I Die)."

That spirit of independence that I spotted in the teen Tanya Tucker was another outlaw quality. She ranked #9 on *CMT's Dozen Greatest Outlaws*, the only woman to appear on that list.

I'm in awe of this mega-talented sensation, and happy to say, "I knew her when!"

****

"I don't know what keeps me going. Sometimes I wonder... I think it's just pure perseverance and wanting to succeed and having that burning desire to always have success."
- Tanya Tucker, Singer, Actress, Songwriter
****

Cover photo by Doug Metzler from Rolling Stone, September 26, 1974
© Rolling Stone LLC 1974
All Rights Reserved, Reprinted By Permission

Interview with Darcy Donavan

THE NEW EMINEM
by Chase Von

Photo by Mara

ANCHORMAN

Starring Will Ferrell With Supporting Actress Darcy Donavan

Producer DreamWorks Pictures; Apatow Productions;
Herzog-Cowen Entertainment; director Adam McKay

Chase Von: Hey, Darcy! On behalf of myself and *The Student Operated Press*, I truly appreciate you finding the time in your hectic schedule to share yourself with our readers. You are someone that is taking Hollywood and the world itself by storm. And you have done so very much in your life it truly is incredible. I can`t possibly ask you about it all. Before we speak of your new CD, your many television and movie appearances, your stellar great looks and--yes, I`m married but not visually impaired. (Smile.)--can you tell our readers more about your growing up years in Nashville, Tennessee and whether you always knew you were destined for stardom. And once again, thanks so much for sharing yourself with us here!

Darcy: LOL...You are too kind. Thanks so much, Chase, you really made my day. I think I am going to take your interview, download it, frame it and put it on my wall so it puts me in a good mood when I am having a bad day. (Wink, wink.) Now as far as being destined for stardom you can ask my feisty German grandmother who said when I came home from kindergarten that I would say, "Grandma when I grow up I am going to be a big star and take care of you, granddaddy and mom and daddy and buy us a big house where we can all be happy and I can take care of you all." She got a real chuckle out of it because my parents were divorced....LOL. But at a very young age I was always singing, acting in plays and was always the class clown. I secretly wanted to grow up and be a comedian since I loved to make people happy and laugh.

Chase Von: Before you were an "internationally known star," what other kind of jobs had you held in your life? I`m thinking that even *you* once had to do some things you didn`t want to do to get where you are today.

Darcy: Well, to say I had a Paris Hilton life would be a real joke. It was hard because my mother worked two jobs to support me. When I was in high school I was working two jobs to buy things that I wanted and needed. I worked at Burger King which I hated, then at a men`s clothing store called D.J`s and at Olan Mills Portrait Studios. It was hard for me, being raised by a single mother who worked all the time, going to school to get good grades and working. The girls in school were also mean to me, so I was basically a loner, staying in the teachers' classrooms and cleaning them up to stay away from the girls who would throw food at me because they were jealous. (That is what my mom thought.) Jealous of *what*, I really don`t know. A lot of them had a better life than me and did not have to work at all. I felt I really never had a childhood and working at a young age was just instilled in me. I think it's because my mother was such a strong, independent woman who worked hard so she could give me the best she could.

Chase Von: Really? Wish I could have stopped by a few of those places...well, when I wasn't married. (Smile.) I also wanted to ask you, since you are what "The Commodores" sang about, an actual "Brick House" with measurements of 36-24-36. (I had to stop myself from writing the words that immediately follow. Heh-Heh.) But were you a girly girl? You are exceptionally beautiful, but I get the sense you might have been a "tomboy": athletic, climbing trees, jumping ramps on bikes and maybe even taking part in a pick-up football game every now and then. Considering you are one of the most beautiful women in the world, it would be easy to assume you were pampered and protected and all hell would break loose if you fell and skinned your knee. So were you out and rampaging through the neighborhoods where you lived? Or were you basically under guard and prepared to be the beauty you have emerged to be?

Darcy: LOL! You are too funny! In all actuality, I was a mixture of both. I liked to play with my dolls, have fun cheerleading and wearing pretty girly outfits, but I also played in the dirt, rode my bike and jumped ramps with the boys and collected worms and frogs. I also loved to play basketball and football. I know more about football than my half-brothers. I want to tell you a funny story about me when I was very young: my grandmother took me to church, and in my little coin purse I had all my worms that I collected for fishing. When the money-offering plate came around my grandmother reached in to get out my money and nearly had a heart attack when the worms came out when she was getting my money. I was in so much trouble, but I didn't care. I loved boy-stuff like that. I always felt I fit in more with the boys then I did the girls. I used to have more guy friends than girlfriends, 'cause I was like one of the boys. I was definitely not pampered; my father was a football coach and he definitely treated me more like one of the boys then a girl.

Chase Von: Now that gives new meaning to "Keep The Change," Darcy! ... LOL. I also read about how you were the former Miss Nashville, Tennessee and how hard you worked in the very place that launched the careers of the King himself, Elvis Presley, and also the incredibly famous, talented and lovable Dolly Parton and scores of others. You even formed your own band while there and were on the brink of stardom yourself when a series of tornados came through and took out not only the recording studio but your dreams with it. We know now you went on to Hollywood, but few--who haven't experienced the devastation tornados and hurricanes can wreak--know how much they can destroy things that have existed for so very many years in a single day. More know now, of course, after the horror delivered by Katrina, but how were you able to rebound from seeing all you had worked for leveled? And where did you find the will to push on after seeing how unmerciful Mother Nature can sometimes be? Because the truth is that after such a traumatic event there are a lot of people that would have seen it as an ending point...not something to overcome.

Darcy: Honestly, Chase, it was really hard, and there were times I really thought, *How can I go on?* But I am very resilient. I've always been a fighter, ever since I was a little girl. I got bullied and teased when I was growing up, as other people have experienced. I thought, *How can I go on having to face these people anymore?* At one point it got so bad that my mother wanted me to transfer to another school but I wouldn't do it because I wasn't going to let them win. That same attitude is what I've had with my career. No matter what life throws at me, a tornado, earthquake, etc., I am going to keep pushing forward. The entertainment business has been in my blood since I was a child, and I feel like a lot of people don't realize that if you want to be in this business, you have to be resilient and a fighter. Think of all the people that turned down Madonna and are now kicking themselves. It's happening right now with my career...just for the simple fact that people are prejudiced because of the way I look. They don't realize that there is a big brain under this blonde hair and a big heart under these boobs. One of the things that I've always wanted to do is to help people. Being in the business is one of the best ways for me to help the masses. It's funny you say how "unmerciful Mother Nature can be," because people can be just as unmerciful and cruel. I've always wanted to help people and do things for people who needed my help. That is one of the reasons why I take a portion of the proceeds from my album sales to help out victims of natural disasters, as well as some of my other charities.

Chase Von: How appalled were you by the response to the victims of Katrina--or better put, *lack of a timely response*--considering you yourself have been through similar events?

Darcy: I think it's ridiculous! The government has billions of dollars that they are putting into war, when we could be putting some of that money towards helping people going through these terrible times due to Mother Nature...not to mention we need money going to health care, social security, better schools, law enforcement and to help our own country...period! I'm so sick of us helping other countries when our country is in such need itself. Don't get me wrong, I definitely think helping these other countries is a good thing, but how can we help someone if we can't help ourselves?

Chase Von: I'm publishing a book by a friend called *Whispers, Tears, Prayers and Hope;* Ed Roberts is a phenomenal poet! A student read one of his poems and then took it to her father who she thought was contemplating suicide because he had lost *all* during Katrina. He cried, but the poem helped him to regain focus and to move on. You also use your platform to inspire, educate and encourage others, as well, and I was really taken with you on sight. (Smile.) But you are also a lover of words! You're also accomplished in so many areas: acting, singing, modeling and rapping. But how important are words to you? And how does a girl from Nashville, which is known for "country music," become a rapper compared to one of the greatest rappers of all time? *The one and only Eminem!* But also one who makes sure her music is something people can learn positive things from to better enhance their lives?

Darcy: Well, in all honesty, I don't know where all this comparison to Eminem is coming from, but I do believe that Eminem and I have a lot of similarities. It's funny because my nickname in LA is "Southern Thug," and I think because of my blonde hair and curvy body people don't know what to expect when they hear all the hype about me. But I promise you, people don't want to cross me when they see me get upset. I think that I have a very strong personality and my intensity can go either way. I feel as if Eminem has that same intensity. That is where all the comparison's coming from. I also think because Eminem is this blue-eyed, blond-haired "pretty boy," people didn't expect him to rap out his lyrics with an intensity not heard before from a white boy. You can see that I'm getting the same kind of slack because of my similar look with the added boobs. Ha-ha!

Chase Von: Kim Kline is a friend of mine, as well. She's from Texas and you are from Nashville. Texas is another place that is associated with country music, but she's a rocker. She won the "Best Top 40 New Artist of The Year for 2007" and beat out people like Colbie Caillat and Amy Winehouse, to name just a few. Do you ever plan in the future to tackle some country music? I imagine it was part of your upbringing, being from where you are from. Personally, I prefer "R & B" mostly, but I`ve written a few country song lyrics myself. (Smile.) I`m what you call eclectic. In my view of things, it matters little which vein it is said to be in; if I like it, I like it, and if I don`t, it doesn`t matter what they`re calling it.

Darcy: Well, first and foremost, tell Kim congrats on all her outstanding achievements. Secondly, who knows whether I`ll go back to Nashville? I still have a house there...which is the funny thing, because at this point in my life, I like where I am. I just didn`t fit in Nashville. My look at the time wasn`t acceptable. It is now, since Shania Twain started showing skin. The executives there wanted to make me the "Madonna of Country," and there was a lot of politics in the business. It just seemed to me that they didn`t think outside the box--and not only that, they would choose people not based on their talent. It was like a clique! It made me really angry and that`s why I decided to change my path. It was funny because I was actually going to get out of the music business. I couldn`t believe that I was going to do that because I am a fighter. I was on my way to Los Angeles to visit a friend at that time and it`s funny how God puts people in your path to steer you back on track for what you are supposed to do. I just happened to sit next to a man who was a motivational speaker on his way to speak to a seminar for a hundred thousand people or more. It`s funny how we tell strangers our stories rather than our own family and friends. Well, I proceeded to tell him my story of all the hardships I had endured and how it was tearing me apart. I would not compromise my morals by sleeping my way to the top. He then told me an inspirational story about how I was a sailboat, and even though a sailboat may be going to its destination and trying to stay straight on course, winds or storms may try to throw it off its course. So this sailboat may have made detours along the way, but it eventually reaches its destination.

Chase Von: Comedy seems to come so naturally to you when you're on the screen, but you can do it all: serious parts, comedic and even horror. On the real tip, are you as funny in person as you are on the big screen? (Smile.)

Darcy: Actually, I'm told I'm a big jokester by my friends and family. They tell me that I remind them of Lucille Ball. My mom says that when I was little I was a big ham and would get up on the fireplace and perform. When I was growing up I secretly wanted to be a comedian. I like to make people happy and make them laugh. As for your other question, I *can* do it all. I never set limits to anything I do. Our minds are the only thing that can get in the way of achieving our goals and dreams. I have a horror film that I will start filming the end of January/February 2009. I have the female lead. I read the script and was amazed at how well written it was. The Weinstein Company has already picked the film up for major distribution. There is also another movie that is in the pre-production stage. The film will be a paranormal drama that will really have people talking. I feel that it will make a huge impact on the world and open people's eyes to things they may not have known or thought of. I can't go into specifics on that, though, so let's keep it on the hush-hush:)

Chase Von: Miss Tennessee--who then goes on to star in *Anchorman* with comedic genius Will Ferrell! I have to tell you, when I was doing my research I didn`t realize that, initially, but then later I remembered seeing you in that movie. And I particularly remember that part where he walks away from you, because you are simply gorgeous! (How could any sane man walk away?) But that`s just barely scratching the surface when it comes to your many accomplishments. You are in the National Seagram`s Calendar with such known stars as Pamela Anderson, Nikki Ziering, and Gina Lee Nolan! You`re the "brunette beauty" on the internationally distributed "AC/DC Tribute" album cover titled, *We Salute You* that won the prestigious "Cleo Award" for best album cover. You have a four-page, exclusive interview appearing in *Elite Fighter* magazine (October 2007); that cover is graced by none other than the incredible fighter, Chuck Liddell, better known as *The Ice Man*. You`ve appeared on *Nickelodeon* in "Uh-Oh" and shared more of your comedic talent as well on *Spike TV Foxxy News*. You are also starring in the psychological thriller written by Jack Sawyers called *Devil's Gold* and *My Name is Earl*, opposite Craig T. Nelson from the series *Coach*— joining a long list of celebrities who have made guest appearances on *My Name is Earl*, including Jaime Pressly from *DOA: Dead or Alive* and *Charmed*, John Leguizamo from *Love in the Time of Cholera* and *ER*, and Page Kennedy from *Roots* and *CSI, Crime Scene Investigators*. Your beautiful and dance-oriented CD *Distraction* is even being promoted in "Grappling," and you yourself have appeared as a ring girl in *Elite Fighter!* You also have quite a few songs that are being far more than well-received, such as "Come Get Love," "Gold Collar Diamond Ring," "Helping Karma Along" and "Here We Go Again." I also saw where you don the costume of Wonder Woman, and might I say you look wonderful? But could Wonder Woman even keep up with you? Because we both know that isn't all that you have done. Or are you really the real Wonder Woman? Because if you said you were, I wouldn't argue with you. Unless it would lead to you tying me up with that special rope she—I mean you— carries. Heh-heh.

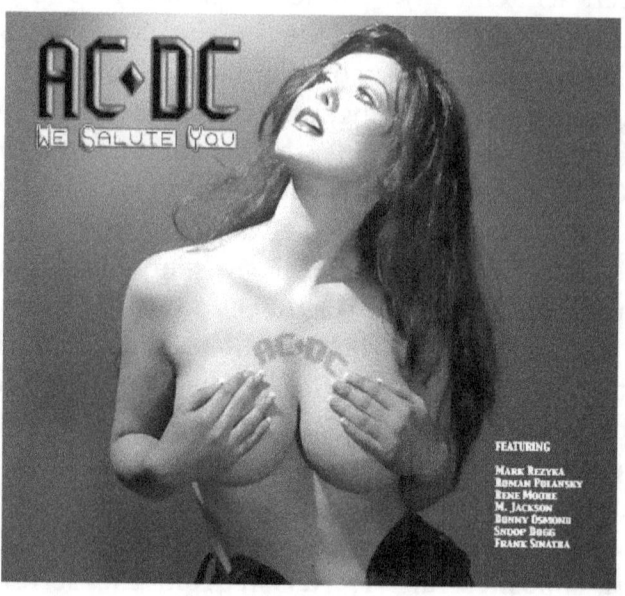

Darcy: Wonder Woman learned all her moves from me, and she came by my house to borrow the rope and headband. But in all seriousness, I do juggle a lot of things: the modeling, acting, music, and running a company. I also have a new clothing line that will debut very soon, an energy drink I developed, and a natural flea repellant I created. I'm also in the process of writing a book, co-writing a screenplay and developing several television series. Should I stop there? Are you tired just hearing all this stuff? I'm tired from just typing it...LOL.

Chase Von: I also read where you are a strong advocate against domestic violence. I have another fellow-author friend, Michele Green, who has a book called *The Passion*

Within, which is a compilation of several authors, and a portion of the proceeds goes to those who find themselves in that situation. Is there a personal reason why you are so deeply touched by this, and what are some other causes you support?

Darcy: Yes, my mother was in an abusive relationship when I was growing up and it really had an impact on me. Because of what happened, I didn't respect my mother for a long time. Then later in life I dealt with a similar situation of my own that almost killed me. I always thought of myself as a strong woman, but sometimes these things can happen to even the strongest of us. God always has his ways of teaching us lessons. I have learned a great deal from everything I experienced, and because of that I have a very deep respect for my mother now...and what she went through. She was a very strong person to deal with that and try to keep her child safe. With the knowledge that I have gained from my experiences in life, I can now help people all over to become stronger, give them the knowledge on how to deal with it and move on in their lives. Just as the saying says: *Knowledge is Power.* There are several other causes that I support, such as: The Brittany Foundation which helps abused animals, Safe Passage for domestic violence, PETA, and I've also helped with some other organizations that give care packages to our soldiers overseas. I'm also an advocate for breast-cancer awareness and one day I will be starting the Donavan Foundation For Families.

Chase Von: What's the likelihood that we will see you and Eminem performing together in the future, and who are some of the rappers, singers, actors and just "people in general" you admire and respect yourself?

Darcy: Now as far as Eminem goes, only time can tell. I've heard a lot of rumors recently, but who knows what the future holds. In regards to artists that I admire, I really admire all of the ones that have worked hard to achieve their successes. I have such a broad range when it comes to my admiration, such as God, who has steered my career, my wonderful mother, grandmother and grandfather for all their support. And the team of people I have right now that are some of the most amazing people I have ever met. I admire Dolly Parton, Garth Brooks, Madonna, Pink, Gwen Stefani, Fergie, P. Diddy, Ludacris, Will Smith, LL Cool J, Missy Elliot, Pavarotti, Neal E. Boyd, Justin Timberlake, Eminem, Tina Turner, Shirley McClaine, Jack Nicholson, Robert Williams, the late Heath Ledger, Angelina Jolie, Tom Cruise, Brad Pitt, Denzel Washington, Lawrence Fishbourne, Anthony Hopkins, John Travolta, Jodie Foster, Angela Basset...the list goes on and on.

Chase Von: Who are some of the people you consider mentors? And since you've become accomplished at so very many things, what would you say to people about expanding and trying different things, or in other words, stretching out their comfort zones?

Darcy: Actually, that's an easy one. I have the best mentor anyone could imagine: *God!* Other than Him and my angels, I've done it all myself through prayer. Now don't get me wrong, I've had people who have taught me things along the way, but as far as mentoring me, *No!* I always thought outside the box and I did not listen to people's negativity. For most of the celebrities I have worked with, the majority of them have experienced rejection but never gave up on their goals. So if I was to give a bit of advice to others, it would be to never give up on your dreams or let people derail you from what you want to achieve in life. So many people walk around in a box throughout their lives and let people bring them down by the things they say or do. So, step outside the box and see the world through new eyes.

Chase Von: Well, Darcy, I have to tell you, I am a man that loves women. I, personally, think they are the most beautiful of all God`s creations. However, different women have different kinds of beauty. I think Mother Theresa was beautiful, I think Maya Angelou is beautiful, I think Rachael Bell is beautiful—and Judyth Piazza and Alina and Barbara Evans and Kimberly Prendez and Audrey Michelle and Dawn Huffaker—because quite a few I`ve actually spoken to and know both the inner as well as outside beauty. I also think Lucille Ball, Bibi McGill and Kathy Bates (of the movie *Fried Green Tomatoes*), the one that played *I Dream of Jeannie*, Barbara Eden, Thelma from *Good Times* or Bern Nadette Stanis. My mother is also beautiful, as well as my wife. But again, as a man, I have to share this with you also: there are women I think are so beautiful just physically, that they are in a category where I feel as if it`s...*like-it-matters* beautiful. (Smile,) Halle Berry or Darcy Donavan? Angelina Jolie or Darcy Donavan? Vanessa Williams or Darcy Donavan? Darcy Donavan or Barbara Evans? Shawn Richardz or Darcy Donavan? Sade or Darcy Donavan? Darcy Donavan or Alicia Keys? Darcy Donavan or Christina Aguilera? Darcy Donavan or Ziyi Zhang? Darcy Donavan or Mary Christina Brown? Darcy Donavan or Noemi Lenoir? Darcy Donavan or Aishwarya Rai? Darcy Donavan or Kirsten Haglund? And I could go on, but at that level of beauty it`s like... Well... *Like it matters!* Gorgeous is gorgeous, and you are right up there with the most beautiful women to ever draw breath. And trying to decide at *that* level is like: *Does it really matter? They are all gorgeous!* You're again *that* kind of beautiful! But you are also compared to the classic beauties of old: Norma Jean Baker, known the entire world over as Marilyn Monroe! Katherine Hepburn, Bette Davis... And you can switch from blonde to brunette to whatever hairstyle you wish to wear and still be a knockout...as you proved with your album cover for AC/DC. So now that I`ve stated that you are *that kind of lovely*--which is something that would hurt a man's brain if he really had to try and decide--what are some of your favorite meals and how do you stay in such great shape?

Darcy: Don`t get me started on that. I love food! However, I strongly believe that a good diet of vegetables and fruit mixed with the occasional splurges are good for you. I also believe in "juice fasting" and I love my juicing machine. I take it with me everywhere. Your body is your temple and engine for life, so what you put in it is what you`ll get out. I also run, bike-ride, and do yoga. Just rehearsing for my tour gets me in shape.

Chase Von: Who are some of the people you truly loved working with? And who are some that you haven`t worked with as of yet, but you would love to in the future?

Darcy: Honestly, there are too many people to name, but I really enjoyed working with Will Ferrell and Paul Rudd, as well as the director Adam McKay, I`ve worked with so many people in the business and each person has brought a different experience. I`d love to work with Shirley McClaine, Goldie Hawn, James Earl Jones, Will Smith, Chris Rock, Anthony Hopkins, Lawrence Fishbourne...just to name a few.

Chase Von: What would you say if you were standing in front of a microphone that could be heard by every child on the planet and regardless of what language they spoke, they would understand you? What positive advice would you give the children, if that were possible?

Darcy: I would tell them that God always hears us, even in our darkest moments. In your heart you have to believe and have faith. If you ask him, he will always be there to help you. Also remember to treat others as you would like to be treated; we will all meet our maker one day. Because when it's all said and done, "there are no luggage racks in a hearse."

Chase Von: Where can our readers learn more about the variety of things you are doing? Your websites, YouTube links and movie and music links? I also know you've formed your own entertainment production company. Are there any things you are producing there or in the near future you can give our readers a heads up to look out for?

Darcy: The best places to see what's going on with me at any given moment would be the sites listed below:
www.darcydonavan.com
www.myspace.com/darcydonavanmusic
www.myspace.com/officialdarcydonadonavan
www.reelvisionentertainment.com
As for projects in the works, we've got a few movies we are working on, a couple books, television series, clothing, jewelry, and perfume line, music tours, celebrity events and many more. I could go on and on, but I would rather you see for yourself. We also have several other celebrities that we work with and promote, such as Cylk Cozart, Brian Krause, Percy Daggs, Tara Paige, Maddy Curly and

some up-and-comers such as celebrity artist Cosandra Calloway, Corey Johnson, celebrity choreographer and up-and-coming celebrity producer Ryakin Rip...just to name a few.

Photo By: Marc Sacro, Design Edit: Rebecca Vincent

Chase Von: On behalf of the *Student Operated Press* and myself, Darcy, I`m truly honored you took out the time from your schedule (that might wear out the actual Wonder Woman herself) to share yourself with our readers. You are not only a beautiful, multi-talented lady with a great mind, as well, but one that is also very down-to-earth and lovable. I guess being raised in a place like Nashville can, in some cases, give a person the ability to relate at a level that is truly human and where the majority of us find ourselves. You're a huge star, but what shines ever so brightly is your sweetness and your genuine concern for humanity as a whole, and your ability to relate to the younger generation and your respect for the older generations. Dana Owens, better known as Queen Latifah, made her first CD--which has the remake of "California Dreamin'" originally done by the Mamas and Poppas with quite a few other songs from an earlier time. I think in so doing, she bridges a gap between generations, and that is something I feel you are doing, as well. I also think that surviving the tornados and all is a horrible thing for anyone to have to endure. But despite the level of stardom you have achieved, it has kept you from becoming one that feels a distance from your fellow human beings. So thanks so much again, Darcy. I wish you continued success, love and light and all things good because you are certainly a blessing to all who learn of you.

Darcy: Thanks so much for that wonderful compliment. (Smile.) I think I'm going to cry. You are so sweet. Chase, again thank you for your kind words and for being a sweetheart and making this interview one of the best I have had the pleasure of being a part of. Much love and success to you, also, and I wish you all the best in your future endeavors.

****

"So if I was to give a bit of advice to others, it would be to never give up on your dreams or let people derail you from what you want to achieve in life."
- Darcy Donavan, Actress, Model, Rapper, Singer
****

****

*"Also remember to treat others as you would like to
be treated; we will all meet our maker one day.
Because when it`s all said and done,
there are no luggage racks in a hearse!"
- Darcy Donavan, Actress, Model, Rapper, Singer*

****

DARCY DONAVAN

Photo by Shane Sato

Interview with Shawn Richardz

LOVELY, FAMOUS ACTRESS
by Chase Von

Chase Von: Hi, Shawn, and on behalf of myself and the *Student Operated Press*, thank you so very much for finding time in your hectic schedule to do this interview.

You are one of the most sought-after actresses in all of Hollywood, so I know fitting this in wasn`t easy. Thank you so much again.

Shawn: This is an extreme pleasure and very much an honor. I would make sure this interview is *squeezed* into whatever I was doing!

Chase Von: Before we talk about your truly amazing career, I would like for our readers to learn more about you yourself. How old were you when you decided acting was your calling, and since making that decision, have you ever had any regrets?

Shawn: I can recall my first "doe-eyed" moment was when I saw some Cable special of Marilyn Monroe. I had to have been about seven years old. I believe it was Marilyn`s birthday and I had watched every movie she ever did. My grandmother made me go to bed; it was a Saturday night around 10:30 pm. I had no clue of the plot to any of the many films she starred in from her first walk-on role to her last incomplete film. I just knew whatever she did was what I wanted to do. Can you believe the power of television? I saw nothing as an obstacle as a kid, and I probably had no idea how to articulate being an actress. It was my little secret until maybe high school.

Chase Von: Were there any lean periods you went through where you weren`t sure if you would reach the levels you are at now? And as for that level, you are now acting opposite "A" list actors and actresses all the time. I`m sure your resume makes even famous actors and actresses we all know do double takes. Acting, however, is certainly one of those professions where many try but few are chosen. You are succeeding and excelling in an incredibly difficult and challenging occupation. So was there ever a time when you thought, *Maybe I`ll just go on and be a full-time model or something else like that?*

Shawn: Well, modeling is something that became a career path in the last few years since I relocated to Los Angeles. Growing up in New York where the models are our skyscrapers and superheroes, it was really not an option at all. But most of my family members were not really supportive. I didn't indicate this is what I really wanted to do, so it was a *huge* surprise. My Dad, however, handed me an amazing book about the life of actor Montgomery Clift. I was about thirteen...yes, thirteen years old at the time. My Dad is, and was, such a non-traditional parent, and I love him for it. That was again a tragic superstar's life cut short. Between Marilyn, Montgomery... and then I went and bought Jayne Mansfield's biography with my weekly allowance. *Why, you ask, would anybody want to be an actress after reading about those three?*...lololol... I believe that was the real reason I could never tell any authority figure my dreams. I had many diaries and I made up what my life would be like for me when I grew up. I would cut out pictures and hide them. My senior year in high school I took acting classes...in the summer at the famed and well-respected HB acting studios. I was in awe! I knew from the moment after I left my last class for the day I was *hooked and this was my career!*

Chase Von: So you were certain all along you would reach where you are? I've interviewed Jason Seitz of the acclaimed movie *Elephant* and Kimberly Prendez who starred in and wrote her own movie, *Until Next Time*. Both are accomplished actors in their own right, but I know they would consider it a part of heaven to be able to act alongside of you, and each has told me how difficult it can sometimes be.

Shawn: *I knew!* And my certainty came and never left

me. I just wasn't comfortable letting anyone else know except my father, and even though he had an idea, I don't think even he knew how deep my passion truly was.

Chase Von: I've read that your father truly was a huge part of encouraging you to pursue your dreams though. And from here, you took it upon yourself to study about all the other legendary actresses and actors yourself. But how much do you think your taking the time to really analyze the "greats" before you, helped you to become a great actress yourself?

Shawn: There is no business like show business, and being raised by my grandparents I watched older programming more than most. I knew legends existed and it seemed tragedy was a part of the road to success but only if you allowed it. How I knew *that* I don't have any idea. Maybe because my grandparents were mere mortals...lololol

Chase Von: Aren't we all? (Smile.) How much did reading the greats influence you?

Shawn: Everyone and everything influences an artist, from family, friends, life and even something they heard as a child once can change a destiny. *Very difficult to pinpoint,* I embrace everything.

Chase Von: Do you really like Cool Whip whipped cream?

Shawn: *I love Cool Whip and always have.* I remember there was Cool Whip in the fridge back when I was in junior high. I opened the container and ate a little each day with a spoon and I got in trouble because the dessert my grandmother was going to make needed that. She

laughed as I was scolded. Now look at the irony of that!
I thank you, Kraft.

Photo by Vivien Sainz

Chase Von: Since you`re in that commercial that is being
aired all the time, I figured I would ask. (Smile.) And also,

you're very attractive and thoughts of you and whipped cream are... Let me stop before I say something wrong here. (If I already haven't ... Heh-heh :) But how, seriously, do you stay in such great shape?

Shawn: Thank you, Chase. *Mom and Dad! It's genetics!* I don't go to the gym. I hike, that's it. I don't lift weights at all. My family is slim on both sides, so I am truly blessed! I also love outdoor activities, though, but I have never been a member of a gym or a gym rat. I haven't eaten red meat, beef or whatever since I was a kid. I have eaten chicken and fish since I can remember. I never liked hamburgers really, or junk food like ice cream and chocolate are just not really something I ever crave. I came up in the age of frozen yogurt so that was on the grocery list almost always. I am a self-proclaimed "foodie," but food and crap are two different things. Alcohol's not my thing, either.

Chase Von: Okay, just for curiosity's sake, what are some of your favorite meals and how often do you get to enjoy them? Or do you have to sacrifice having them to stay in such great shape, or hike more if you do have them?

Shawn: I love sushi, Caribbean, rice, bread. I'll put it like this: I rarely pass up a meal. My workout regimen is hiking Runyon Canyon daily or at least four times a week. I need to start doing yoga like I used to do a while ago, but I am afraid that... That's it! No secret to a better body. ...lololol

Chase Von: You have appeared opposite James Russo who has starred in over ninety films over three decades, one of which being *Beverly Hills Cop,* and you've also played in *Donnie Brasco,* with Dana Carvey, Blair

Underwood, the living-legend, actress Holland Taylor, and also appeared in a video with none other than music-legend and superstar Keith Urban. Women reading this would be touched perhaps for the remainders of their lives if they just met Blair Underwood! Dana Carvey of *Saturday Night Live* fame and the all-time classic *Wayne's World* is one of the best comedians alive today. James Russo is also an incredible, sought-after actor, and Holland Taylor has worked with just about every actor or actress in Hollywood. She is an Emmy-award-winning actress, definitely a living legend, and certainly one of the best actresses to ever live. How much has working with people of the caliber you have, enhanced your own acting skills? And each time you do, do you think that makes you an even better actress?

Shawn: Working with the people you named makes you step your game up. The professionalism that this business requires gives you longevity and a calling card. The actors you named were the most helpful, humble, grateful people you would ever want to meet.

Chase Von: Is there any one in particular you would like to work with in the future or would love to work with again?

Shawn: I want to work with Dirk Craft, director of Nip/Tuck more. The writers, the crew, the creator Ryan Murphy are all geniuses. I have to say I have been blessed, and every person from makeup, to casting directors, to even craft services that have been a part of my journey has helped me prepare for living my reality. I can learn something from whomever, so bring the work on! *I want my TV contractual role...thank you!*

Chase Von: In some of your pictures, you resemble Whitney Houston. I hope you take that as a compliment--and she does, as well, because you are both beautiful. To my knowledge, though, as of yet no one has done an actual autobiography of her life. If one were done, though, would that be a role you would be willing to play?

Shawn: I get that we-resemble comment frequently, and she is beautiful. Whitney Houston is someone I would love to play. She has had a journey that so many people have been intrigued by, and everyone wants her to succeed.

Chase Von: Your hair is like a trademark. :) How do you do your hair, so our women readers that might want to try that style, as well, will know? Or is that a secret? (Smile.)

Shawn: I had a bad reaction to a product some time ago to make my hair straight. Well, it fell out...*straight to the floor!* I have been natural ever since. This isn't a style; it is 100% percent natural. With my favorite products: Mixed Chicks Bumble and Bumble leave-in conditioners, and Biolage.

Chase Von: You yourself have been in the videos "Every Day" by Rascal Flatts, "Somebody Like You" by Keith Urban, "Nip/Tuck," "Knife To a Gun Fight," and "Bros." You've been in the film "Tic, Back From Reality," and "The Invincible Scripture." You've guest-starred *on Saturday Night Live* and, to be honest, I would rather put a link here to your resume because it's seemingly endless and that is such a small portion of it. (Smile.) You have also hosted the Golden Globes in 2007, *The Stream TV* as a guest host, and the Oscars 2007 as the host. One thing that I also saw

Photo by Vivien Sainz

was Nuyorican Poets Cafe, which of course interests me because I am a poet. I also just published a friend that has been many things, but she is also a professional model and is now not only a poet but a spoken-word artist. Her books title is *Vanity? The Pieces of Audrey Michelle.* She is doing something another friend of mine, Willard Barth, teaches, and that is expanding her comfort zones. She can't yet see it, but I wouldn't be surprised at all if she herself ventures into acting. But expanding one's comfort zone is something I believe all successful people learn to do. I am an author, then I learned to publish, as well. You obviously have expanded yours from modeling to acting to dancing to all your many credits in theater and hosting shows, doing voice-overs, being a spokesmodel and... well, your list of accomplishments is mind boggling, to say the least. What I wanted to ask, though, is do you ever see yourself directing?

Shawn: Maybe! I wouldn't rule it out. What a responsibility, though. I see it maybe way down the line in the future. So not now... My plate is so full, I would have to be the best, not just average.

Chase Von: Do you ever see yourself writing scripts, if you aren't already doing that as well? Having read your resume, I for one, would not be at all surprised. (Smile.)

Shawn: Now writing is closer to me doing in the near future than anything. (Smile.)

Chase Von: Judyth Piazza herself is going to be in a movie called *Horrorween.* I was wondering if you might be coaxed into doing a cameo appearance in that one, as well. I bet Judy will ask you about that also. (Smile.)

Shawn: *Horrorween? Bring it on!* I heard about this project a while ago. That would be fun.

Chase Von: And now a tough one for you, Shawn. I was born overseas to a military family. I have spent much of my life in different states and countries. Still, what happened on September 11th, though, really hurt me to the core. When I was in Kuwait in Operation Iraqi Freedom on a flightline, a man shook my hand, thanked me for serving our country and walked off to shake more hands. He had left a New York City Firefighter lapel pin in my hand. When I asked someone who he was, she told me he was a man that had lost both his sons on that day--one a firefighter, one a policeman. I have two suit-lapel pins. One for retiring from the Marines, and one from that man that lost two sons. I don't really feel I need anymore. Being a proud New Yorker yourself, how were you affected by that and, also, how proud are you of your New York people that have bounced back from that horrific day and made New York a place that is still as strong and popular, even after that historic nightmare?

Shawn: I still get physically ill thinking about it, Chase. New Yorkers are unique and they didn't surprise me with their reaction. I was in Los Angeles when that happened. The entire world was there for the Big Apple. *That is humanity.*

Chase Von: How important is family to you, and what is your take on the state of our current world?

Shawn: Family is whoever you choose to allow in your intimate space, not just for the sake of saying "family." The world is going through a change, and it is long overdue.

Chase Von: What would you say if you were standing in front of a microphone that could be heard by every child on the planet, and regardless of what language they

Photo by Vivien Sainz

spoke, they would understand you? What positive advice would you give the children, if that were possible?

Shawn: No excuses for mediocrity. Life is a gift, appreciate every second and make it count!

Chase Von: How can our readers find you and more about you? I know you are also the featured actress right now on the popular website for artists called www.nextcat.com. You have your different websites and movie links out there so they can learn more about lovely, incredible actress, model, spokeswoman and dancer, and so many other things it is truly hard to list, but all make up the unique and talented Shawn Richardz?

Shawn: My website is constantly being updated, and I love hearing from positive and inspiring people. It's: www.shawnrichardz.com. From there they can find all the other different links; my resume, my MySpace and videos are there, as well.

Photo by Vivien Sainz

Chase Von: On behalf of the *Student Operated Press* and myself, thank you again so much, Shawn, for finding time in your hectic schedule to share yourself with our readers. I also wish you continued success with your career, and I would be willing to share some Cool Whip with you at any time. (Smile.)

Shawn: Thank you for your consideration and your thought-provoking questions, and if I ate my *own grandmother's* Cool Whip that she had set aside for a recipe, do you think I'd share now? (Smile.)

****

"No excuses for mediocrity. Life is a gift,
appreciate every second and make it count!"
- Shawn Richardz, Actress, Model
****

Interview with Kitania Kavey

AMAZING, KAPTIVATING KITTY
By Chase Von

Chase Von: Hi, Kitty, and on behalf of myself and the *Student Operated Press*, I really thank you for doing this interview. We've been getting to know one another through e-mail, and the more I learn, the more you fascinate me. So again thanks for sharing yourself here with our readers. You've led, and continue to lead, a very interesting life by anyone's standards. To look at you one wouldn't guess...but before we get into that...I know you were adopted. Before going out on your own, what to the best of your recollection were your younger years like with your adopted mother?

Kitty: I was close to two years old when I was adopted and there were few adoptions by single parents back in those days. I came to my adopted mother with memories and history that preceded her, and I was a difficult, troubled child. I was able to retreat into the world of books and was well known as the quiet, shy loner. I felt abandoned, unloved and unlovable...not by my adopted mother, but by my birth parents/family and the foster parents I had before I was adopted. I felt as if I was the loneliest person in the world and had no idea where I came from or what my genetic background was. (I was a lovely light tan color, not quite Caucasian-looking.) As a younger child, I wasn't yet able to articulate or clearly identify the empty hole in my heart. I just simply believed that I was a bad, unwanted, unlovable person.

Chase Von: You were, admittedly, a very rebellious child. You got kicked out of school while still a teenager and then just ran away. Through communicating with you, it's easy to tell that you are more than bright, but you bounced around all over America and were literally homeless for five years. As beautiful as you are, one might assume how you may have clothed and fed yourself, but I get the feeling you were a part of some of the more notorious biker gangs. You don't have to say which ones or if that is even correct. We can all, I guess, wait until you release your biography *Homeless to Hollywood, With Stops In Between.* But what I really wanted to ask is: If you, during all that time, ever contacted your adopted mother? And are you in contact with her now? And what kind of relationship do you two now share?

Kitty: Before I give my answer, let me preface it by saying that none of my childhood troubles were because of or related to my adopted mother. She was, and is, a wonderful person who has always tried her best. Well, I would love to say that I was part of a biker gang, but unfortunately, I was so very homeless that my kind lived outside of all society, including recognized motorcycle clubs. Generally speaking, and without naming names, the larger motorcycle clubs are well organized, and do have both money and investments. Many of the members are able to ride bikes that cost more to own than I care to think about. More than likely, many of those who are members in motorcycle groups also have a place to live, a job--or at least job skills--and probably a bike that isn't held together by dreams and duct tape. And just to add my personal observation, I have noticed that women are less likely to be thought of as equal, or in some cases are not allowed to be full members of a few of the groups. Perhaps that is changing a bit with modern times, but certainly "back in the day" women were more likely to be riding on the back of a motorcycle, more of an accessory rather than a club (or gang, if you prefer) member.

Chase Von: Your wild, carefree days all came to an end in one horrible incident. A devastating motorcycle accident, and if I understand correctly you actually died and definitely had a near-death experience. You suffered a brain injury, broken bones in your face, and a loss of vision. You also went into cardiac arrest and had a stroke, which--considering you were a mere twenty years old-- also speaks of the severity of the crash. And then, sadly-- because you were without health insurance--they released you prematurely from the hospital still with serious injuries. And there you were, so permanently disabled that you yourself didn't even know to what degree, and once again homeless with nowhere to go or anyone to turn to. If I understand correctly, you weren't in the crash alone and that individual didn't make it. So you were seriously injured, grieving, and once again all by yourself in the world...Painful as I know this must be, could you share what some of your thoughts were then? And did you ever entertain any thoughts of suicide?

Kitty: The other guy *did* make it, with a lot of broken bones but no permanent injuries such as I had. The accident itself was a blessing in disguise. It, of course, changed my life and the direction of my life. I'm really not sure where I'd be right now if that hadn't happened. The being dead part--or the near-death experience--was incredible. I spoke to my grandmother and another person I had known as a child. I did not see the tunnel of light, perhaps because death was so sudden or the physical trauma so great. I was just in a place that looked very much like earth, but felt vastly different. I had no past memory of anything at all before being there in that place. At the end of our conversation, my grandmother told me I had to go back; there were still things I had to do. I had no idea what she meant, as there was no past to me. I felt very strongly, however, that going back to wherever or whatever she meant, was most certainly *not* something I wanted to do. She kept repeating herself: *You have to go back*--and everything began to fade away and grow distant. The next memory I have was waking up in intensive care. I later had a talk with a guy in the bed next to mine. He was brain-dead or in a coma, hooked up to life support. He was unable to communicate with the outside world, but gave me a message for the doctors and his family. I've seen research done on the brain and NDE; what it really means if we die. *If there is a soul.* I can't say I have any answers for anyone else, but I do know what happened to me and where I will go when I die. It was, and is, a great comfort to know that no matter what kind of person I was, or whether I followed a particular religion, it is a great place that is waiting for me with family and friends who have passed on. The flip side of that is that when I came back, what I was returning to was the hardships of life, along with new disabilities. It was very difficult. When I was twenty, I thought I was invincible. Things like the accident...well, that happened maybe to other people, but not to me. I have never been physically perfect or athletic, but I felt like I was suddenly a hundred-year-old woman. My vision was fuzzy, distorted, off color. The stroke affected the right side, so that in order to move my leg or arm I needed focused concentration and effort to do so. My broken and fractured bones ached, and my brain felt similar to when one has the flu and takes too much cold medicine. Suicidal thoughts have been part of my life both before and after the accident. Prior to the accident, I was always uncertain if I killed myself what would happen. Maybe the pain would continue in another life, or afterlife, and it would all be for nothing. And, like with physical disability, my emotional state also has its ups and downs. There are good days, and not-so-good days.

Chase Von: But you *didn't* give up! I read where you were rejected by two brain-injury rehabilitation clinics because you were unable to take care of yourself. They also wanted to put you in a state-run facility but you were determined to get better! So you actually taught yourself how to speak again, walk again, and learned skills to compensate for your brain damage and vision impairment all on your own. I once worked in a mental facility in New Jersey called New Lisbon. Things there were divided up in cottages, and each cottage held a different ability level. The ones I worked with were ambulatory but still needed help with the most basic of things, like bathing, eating...and a few were pica, meaning: if it wasn't nailed down, they would put it in their mouths, even feces. Do you think now, living a relatively normal life--with some areas of obvious difficulty and lingering effects, but as a fully functioning lady--that you would ever have reached that if you had been placed in a state-run facility?

Kitty: It is so easy, once you have lived your life as a victim, to be hit with a disability and then to continue down that same path. In my case I was cognizant enough to make choices. There are others who cannot. I completed two brain-injury rehabilitation programs and was not judged capable enough to be able to live on my own, or hold gainful employment. I did not even graduate high school, and had no job skills to begin with. So when numerous neurologists, psychologists, rehab specialists-- and other occupations that end with an "ist"--are telling you that you're not capable, it's pretty easy to agree. It was suggested that I live in a state-run facility in Florida, similar, most likely, to the one you worked in. It would have been paid for, and instead of having to work for a living, I would be able to do arts and crafts, be fed three meals and snacks each day, and my days of struggle would be over. I would be cared for. They even had a swimming pool... It would be so easy to have given in to the safe choice, the sure thing, but the same stubbornness and will to live that had gotten me to those two brain-injury rehab programs, compelled me to try for more. I didn't care what the odds were of success. Don't tell me what I *can't* do, I already know that bit. I wanted more from life, and from *my* life in particular.

Chase Von: When I was listening to one of the radio interviews you did, I couldn't help but be reminded of the extremely famous actor Gary Busey. He too also had a horrible motorcycle accident and nearly died. We know of him from the many roles he's played, from *The Buddy Holly Story* to enormously popular *Lethal Weapon* along with mega-star Mel Gibson. He wasn't wearing a helmet. He's also now a strong advocate for wearing protective equipment, but he also had a spiritual experience, as well, that has dramatically affected his outlook on life. Did you yourself go through a spiritual experience? And were you wearing the correct protective gear when this horrible thing happened to you?

Kitty: Yes, and I mentioned briefly the spiritual part. I try not to talk about what happened to me while I was dead too much, other than to say that it greatly impacted me, and that I don't know what will happen to everyone else when they die. There are a great many religions in the world, or different ways that people view God, the universe, and spirituality. The nice thing is when someone has a positive faith or belief and follows that and it brings them a sense of comfort or peace. I have my own unique perspective on what God is, and it works for me. The accident just gave me the proof I needed. And "not completely" is my answer to the second question. I was wearing a helmet, but not protective clothing. Most of the damage occurred to my face and head. The padding on the inside of the helmet disintegrated upon impact, and the helmet came off, leaving the chinstrap still around my neck. Two good things: as someone was there to get the strap off of my neck, and your head tends to swell to quite large proportions following such an injury. So it's a good thing it didn't do that inside the helmet.

Chase Von: Roughly ten years after making your remarkable recovery, you found yourself homeless yet again. Only this time you were at least receiving a disability check. So you found a place where you could live on that amount, and this time because you weren't able to work a normal job, you did some serious soul searching on concentrating on what you felt you knew you could do. *Now you're an actress, a model, and an award-winning screenwriter!* You also started your own modeling agency and have also gained back a great deal of the vision they said would be permanently lost. I do know you can no longer drive or ride a motorcycle by yourself, but you do anyway, meaning you ride passenger. (Smile.) From standing homeless yet again--and still seriously injured after a premature release for not having insurance--to riding all over Europe and living in Amsterdam! How grateful are you for where you are now, considering the many rough places and trials you have had to overcome?

Kitty: Like I mentioned, there are both good days and bad days and periods in my life where I have to remind myself of everything I have already done... and relax for a bit. Fundamentally, I am deeply grateful for having a second chance at life. A way I like to look at it is that because I have known hunger, I can absolutely relish food. Because I know what it's like to live without electricity, running water, toilets, heat/AC, a bed, etc., most of the time I am consciously aware of and thankful to have such things. I try to see the best side of whatever situation I am in, and most of the time manage to have an unending supply of hope for the future. What's true for me--though, may not apply to everyone--is that to know true joy, you must also have true sorrow. Through the greatest of suffering can come the greatest positive change. For me, death was not the end but the beginning. And still life is not all bliss and rejoicing, but it continues to be ups and downs, challenges to face, things to overcome. There's usually a moment of surprise when I wake up every day, followed by a moment of happiness that I did, and then a moment of thanks if I am in a comfortable spot, safe from the elements of nature. Then the day continues as it does for many of us: physical/mental limitations, situations to deal with, finances to assess, chores, all the more normal distractions that help one forget all the things we do have, and have survived and will continue to get through, as well.

Chase Von: You've been on *The Real Radio Show, 98.5 FM* in New York or www.TheRealRadioShow.com. You have an interview published in the February issue of *Womanly Insights* magazine. The online version: *True Story: Lonely & Broken No More.* So has my friend Kim Kline––she's on the cover––small world. (Smile.) You're a member of MENSA and you have your own production company in Los Angeles, called "Secret Visions Pictures." You're also in *Lifted Magazine, LA's The Place Magazine, Poker Pro Magazine, Brand India Magazine, Valley Scene Magazine* for Minorities in Hollywood and been recognized for *Smashing Stereo Types, Shades of Sin, The Man With The Package, East Meets Western, Sunny Springs*, and *Script Pitch.* I'm going to have to ask you later in this to list your various websites so our readers can see all the many awards you have won or been the runner-up for because you're also nominated for a few unknown scripts as well. Your acting credits are numerous: *Star Trek New Voyages* as Lt. Turkel, *Smashing Stereotypes, Cruel world, Scorched, What if.* And on top of all that, you have also done voice-over work for *Revlon, Wizard Air Fresheners, Payless Shoes* and *Jell-O,* just to name a few. And you sound lovely, and what is more amazing is you had to teach yourself how to speak again... What can our readers expect next from you; or a few things because you are apparently capable of anything you set your mind too?

Kitty: Are you sure about all those credits? Goodness, I've been at it for a long time now. I have had help along the way, of course. My first agent saw my website (Florida-Models.com) and although I lived four hours outside his market, he was not only willing to give me a chance, but made special arrangements so that I could work as both a model and an actress. I needed to be booked with someone who could help me get around the sets (my vision) or who knew of my medical conditions. Since I don't drive, it has always been a bit tricky getting picked up and dropped off from sets, and the rest is just making sure I don't do too much, or overtax myself. I'm really good at doing simple work (like background work) but tend to try and push myself too hard to do what regular people do...like learning lines/extensive dialogue. Modeling was easiest to begin with, and the working days are shorter. Acting was something that was more difficult, but I never had a problem calling my agent and telling him that I wasn't available for the next week, as I needed a rest. He understood completely if I said *No* to a job because it was outdoors in the Florida sun for twelve hours in the summer, and never held against me that I wasn't looking for lead roles that involved dialogue. I was doing what I loved to do, on time, professional, and the brain injury makes it easy to do a take over and over and over again. A simple mind likes simple instructions, and I did well. Voiceover is even easier, as you are chosen by the voice that you have, not hired and then told to create a brand new one. I'm not great at public speaking, and still have some problems with speech, but can, and have, done radio and voiceover work without noticeable difficulty. At least, I think it wasn't noticeable. Now that I'm living in

Europe, it's been harder to find the same kind of representation that I had before. I am still a member of the Screen Actors Guild, but have only recently made clear to my agent that I think I'd be better suited for commercials or roles that require little dialogue. Luckily, they also have a voiceover department, so I'll be doing a new demo tape for them soon. Modeling I still want to do, of course. I've always found it ironic that I look good in photos, while under my skin I feel like I have half of a bionic face. I have been recreated with metal, plastic and bone cement--and I love to see a photo where I look like a regular person. Oh vanity, thy name is woman! I'm still writing and doing script coverage. I've had some setbacks with my health since October `07, but the scripts that I've already done, and the ones I am working on now, have been able to progress despite that. I'm working with the US Embassy to get my disability status back. Again, I'm really lucky that I became so ill *after* I moved outside America. They don't count pre-existing conditions here for health insurance, and it's much more affordable than the US. I had surgery in February, and have been trying to manage additional conditions that have manifested-- other than things related to my existing disabilities--so my priority has been more focused on my health than work. Again, there have been people along the way that are willing to hire me, work with me, represent me or be helpful and supportive. I believe that I can still be a part of the entertainment industry, and find other creative ways to use my media/marketing skills for business, both here and for the US market.

Chase Von: How is life in Amsterdam? And do you have any intentions of coming back to the states...or is that your actual home now? Also what are some of your favorite meals? And I saw on one of your websites where you are about four feet in the air, diving for a volley ball on a beach! Are you still able to do strenuous exercises, and how do you keep you lovely shape?

Kitty: I'm about an hour outside of Amsterdam, but the city itself reminds me very much of New York City, my birthplace. NY is always my first home, in my heart. There are so many things to love about Holland too. I lived for years in Florida and Los Angeles, so it's been really cool to see the seasons. I love the rain and snow-- especially if I am looking at it through a window with a nice hot cup of coffee... such a cozy feeling. The people are very different here than what I'm used to from America. They have traditions, a culture and architecture that pre-dates the existence of the United States by centuries. In my area, it is usual for a child to have both a mother and a father. Divorce is not as common as some parts of the US. Extended families live and stay close together. Crime is less here, the economy is better, and there isn't constant mention of the price of gas. It's always been expensive, that's how it is. In many ways, it's a simpler life. Farmland everywhere, beauty, and you're never that far from Germany, Belgium/Luxembourg--or even the ocean--that you can't make a day trip of it. So *No!* No plans to return to the US just yet. I'm really happy on this side of the world. *Oh, and the food!* No, it's not American. Funny thing ...many of the things they think are American here aren't at all. And there are no Cool Ranch flavor chips. Apparently the Dutch don't know what a ranch is, so they call them "Cool American." I like that. My favorite addiction here is *patat* (French fries). If you've seen the movie *Pulp Fiction,* you know they eat them here with mayonnaise, not ketchup. But, it's not exactly like American mayonnaise, so don't knock it till you've tried it. It's the best!

Chase Von: Recently I saw the movie 50 *First Dates* with Adam Sandler, Drew Barrymore, and I remember telling you about it (Smile.) The movie itself, for a comedy, has some really touching parts in it and one of them was where Dan Akroyd who plays a doctor, says, "I have someone I want you to meet," and they call the guy Ten Second Larry or something like that. He meets them, sounds perfectly fine, is totally with them in response, and ten seconds or so later he has already completely forgotten them. I'm sure you know more about the brain than most physicians, but can you expound a bit on what you suffered and how that affected you? And how difficult it was for you to reach where you are today? I say that because I know different parts of the brain control different things. I remember when I was working with some of them, how shocked I was that an individual who I believe was also a traumatic brain injury victim could read. And as good as anyone else, it appeared. But of course he was lacking in many other areas or he wouldn't have been there. My wife's sister also, sadly, suffered a stroke a few years ago. She can't really say more than a few words now but when it comes to Karaoke, she can sing along with songs. Which still amazes people. (Smile.) So I was hoping you could give a little brief class of sorts to our readers on how we have a left side of the brain and a right side and a thing in our brain called the pineal gland or more commonly known as the third eye and just some general information that most wouldn't know.

Kitty: Brain injury is interesting because the exact same type of injury can have very different effects in different people. Quite a few people who sustain such an injury cannot be easily diagnosed and categorized by statistics and previous medical documentation on other brain injury patients. We don't always fit what's been written about in a medical book, and each case has to be assessed and treated individually. In my case, if you don't bring the visual deficits into it, the brain injury extent and consequences were difficult for me to discover. There are many little things in my case that seem unimportant, but when added to the total picture can be frustrating to live with. Memory is the easiest to explain. I remember longer-term memories of my life, or vivid bits or moments, while other pieces of my past are just not there to be recollected. You can describe a missing bit; show me a photo, and nothing, nada. *Zip.* Short-term memory is much more frightening to deal with. I have just enough awareness to know that I should know something, and yet I don't. *And not all the time...and not in all situations.* There are episodes...or just a bad day. The skills that I learned before the accident often stay in my memory, while skills I learned after the accident do not. I have run my own websites since 1996, hand coding HTML nearly every day, but if I take a break for a few days, I have to go back to the Internet or books to relearn it. I am an award-winning screenwriter, using the strict formatting that film scripts have, and if too many days pass when I am not using that skill, I start at the beginning all over again, relearning format. I can't reverse things in my head anymore. Remember aerobics tapes or classes? The instructor in front of the class, facing you, and you are supposed to do the opposite. Impossible... Mathematics, gone... You can put coins in my hand and ask me to add them up. I know three quarters, two dimes and one nickel equal one dollar. See? I can write it. But it just looks like a pile of shiny things in my hand, and it doesn't make sense. Sometimes, I am in my home neighborhood. I know it is my home; I know that I've been living there for a long time, years perhaps. I know that I have seen the buildings and landscape a zillion times, and it all looks absolutely unfamiliar, as if I have never been there before. Thank goodness that usually passes after a little bit--but I have panicked more than once over that. *Same thing with people.* I know I know them. I live with them; have lived with them for some time. And for a few minutes, they are a complete stranger, whose name I do not know. I have a lot of other disabling conditions besides the brain injury, and what makes it most difficult to deal with is that it's not a constant thing...where I can expect the exact condition I'll be in tomorrow or next week. I wake up, see how I feel, and do what I can when I am able to do so. And when I can't, I try not to be so hard on myself.

Kitty loves Fry's ELECTRONICS
sponsor of the Poppy Jasper Film Festival

KITTYSTAR.com

Chase Von: Who are some of the people you truly enjoyed working with? And who are some you would like to work with in the future? I also know you are a strong advocate of supporting those who like yourself are disabled in the film industry, but what are some of the other causes you feel truly strong about?

Kitty: I already mentioned my agent, and there's not room enough to list everyone by name who has been kind, supportive, comforting, or offered me work, opportunities, or took a chance to help me in some way. People in general are incredible, brilliant and inspirational in what they do and have done in their lives. The only people I have not enjoyed working with are those who just refuse to be anything but a victim, or as we used to say back in the old days a "Negative Nancy." It reminds me too much of the old me, and I need to surround myself with those who are willing to do more, be more and live the dream along the way. It's so worth it. Besides being a supporter of other disabled folks in all aspects of media/entertainment, I am quite passionate about working to fight negative stereotypes and discrimination. I have been discriminated against because I am disabled. I have been more often discriminated against because I am a woman. The woman who adopted me is white, her natural son (my brother) is black, and I am in between that. To this day, without a DNA test, I'm not quite sure who my birth father is/was. Anyhow, I grew up in a color-blind family. America loves to divide people into groups. There are issues with race, gender, sexual preference, age, origins, and religions. I think you should judge people by what they do, help those who need help, or are able to be helped, and find a way to do it that doesn't take away the rights of identity and self-expression. It's a challenge, but discussion brings awareness, awareness can lead to action, and action can bring about change.

Chase Von: As you know I have PTSD, and there are so many service members coming back with that as well. One thing that I think needs improvement all the way around is how we do health care here. I'm not talking about the various professionals *per se* in the health fields, but the availability of health care to those that really need it. Your case is a perfect example. You were discharged prematurely after incurring a life-threatening injury that nearly killed you and has left you with--despite all the amazing things you have accomplished--some lasting aliments you have to endure for life. I also remember hearing somewhere else that an alarming number of people on our streets are veterans both from previous wars, as well as this one. I believe it was in a speech Presidential-hopeful Cynthia McKinney gave. What do you think would be the best way for everyone in the US to receive the proper health care that they need? You may have seen the movie called *John Q* which starred Denzel Washington who as a laid-off auto assembly worker, had a son who desperately needed a heart transplant. In order to make that happen he also has to take some drastic measures to save his son. Granted, it is a movie, but...The sad truth is that people are indeed dying or not receiving proper care because they can't afford it. And, morally, I don't see how one life is more valuable than another life because one might have money and the other doesn't.

Kitty: That's one issue the US can look to other countries to help find an answer. Canada, England, The Netherlands and many other countries do have medical coverage for citizens. There are problems, of course; waiting lists for operations, substandard care, etc., but to have something is better than nothing, and I know that the US can do something better than it has done. Also, what we know about medicine and treatments is constantly changing. According to Wikipedia, the existence of PTSD has been around since at least the 6th century B.C. The term post-traumatic stress disorder was not coined until the 1970s, and effective means of treatment is currently being studied. There are ongoing debates as to what works and what does not work so well. Living life is a learning process, not just for the individual, but also for the government and society as a whole. If there was an easy way to fix the problems, it would be done, and it's just not as simple as that. Homelessness, in and of itself, is not just a matter of giving someone a place to live and the problem is solved. And your point about one life not being more valuable than another based on how much money they have (or don't) is dead on. I don't have the solution for the US healthcare woes. I'll bet there are people who do, who may work in the healthcare industry, or have a better understanding of government and finances. I have to trust that those people who choose to run for political office listen and take into consideration possible solutions to the problems, not just with medical care but with the other major issues facing us all today.

Chase Von: You have done so many things in your life, Kitty, it's amazing! I've even seen you flying, literally, in an air chamber. (Smile.) You've also been touring Europe and taking, if I might say, some fantastic pictures so you might have to add photography to your already vast resume here soon. (Smile.) Having, by all rights, been given a second chance on life, are you one of those people who is truly living each day as if it is your last?

Kitty: Since I'm not always sure how much longer I have, anyway, and have been quite ill for over a year now (plus the disabilities), I do try to live each day to the fullest that I feel up to. I do tend to do things with my life quickly and seemingly spontaneously at times, and I usually don't take long making decisions. There's a whole list of sayings I try to use in my life: It is better to try and fail than to never try at all. There's many people who have tried things and failed, and people who have succeeded at those same things. You can choose to look at the ones who have succeeded as inspiration, but maybe more importantly are the lessons you yourself learn from what you have failed at. Another one that's important to me is: Don't judge all people by the actions of one...or a few. Or even if everyone you know is a complete blithering idiot that does not mean that the next person you meet will be. To put an example to it: Rape! It is something many women and men, too, have been subjected to. Some as a one-time thing, some multiple times or ongoing. You cannot change what has happened. The only thing you do have control over is your reaction to future relationships. I have been violated in that way myself in the past, but will not allow the actions of a few to change me into a distrustful, suspicious, frightened person who is emotionally distant with future relationships. It is my choice as to who I want to be, and I seek out help with those memories when I need to. Which leads me into the thought of fear. I think that is something that stops many from living their dreams. It's easy to tell someone who doesn't like some part of their life--their job, their relationship, or whatever--to change it. It's difficult to do that, because there is fear involved. Usually it can be transferred into another issue. Finances is a big one, but in the end we are afraid. For many people our lives are filled with what we can't do. Usually, the excuses are quite legitimate. I can't begin to tell you the number of times I have been told by well-educated, well-informed people that whatever it was I wanted to do just wasn't feasible. I also, however, know people who travel the world because that is their passion. They aren't rich--they don't stay in hotels or eat in fancy restaurants, have a trust fund or an ongoing job. But they are happy, because they think outside the box and find a creative way to make things possible. They may take a flight as a courier--for free or very low cost--take a crew job on a boat going to the Caribbean, or work as an *au pair* for a family sent over to Europe. There are people who move to Los Angeles to pursue their entertainment dreams, find apartments for $350/month--yes, currently, not twenty years ago. Maybe they aren't taking meetings at big-name studios or playing the lead in the next blockbuster film, but they are happy because they are living the way they want to...right now. They come from varied backgrounds and upbringings, and you'll probably never have heard their names, and maybe never will. Each of us gets to decide what we can do, what our dreams are, and that can be something that changes as our lives change. What's important, is what we do now, not necessarily what we might accomplish ten years from now.

Chase Von: I, personally, want to thank your reconstruction doctors, though I don't know who they are. I do know you joke sometimes about being the bionic woman--with all the pins and screws--but I have to say: considering how severe your injuries were, they did a beautiful job and you are still a truly physically beautiful woman. (Smile.)

Kitty: I figured out a long time ago that I was never going to be like one of those girls in a men's magazine, the glamorous sexy ones that seem to be so beautiful to me. Nor was I ever going to have the figure of a high-fashion model. But as I grew older, I began to appreciate in myself other qualities that I do have and can continue with. I need the support of others to reach my goals, and I can also be helpful to the people around me in achieving theirs. If the lights are out and no one can see you, are you still the most beautiful person in the world to someone? Or if you suddenly find yourself to be ninety years old-- with all the ravages that time plays on the physical body-- are you not still capable of loving and being loved? Youth maybe does not give you that advantage, particularly if you are admired for the way that you appear. But if today is my last...or tomorrow...I can say that I have lived the way I wanted to live; I do the things I want to do; and I have done the best that I could. That being said, I have never lost weight, worn makeup or done my hair for anyone else but me.

****

> *"I can say that I have lived the way I wanted to live; I do the things I want to do; and I have done the best that I could."*
> *- Kitania "Kitty" Kavey,*
> *Actress, Model, Screenwriter*

****

I am responsible for my own self-image, and when it needs to be addressed, I do what I can to fix the problems that bother me. You may see the photographs, or what I look like when I go out of the house. I don't have the energy to dress up every day, so at home I just look like me. I did lose a lot of weight, changing from an American diet to a Dutch one, but a lot of physical activity had to be curtailed in the past year since I became sick. I will never be stick-thin, twenty years old with symmetrical features again. I do try to improve upon what I look like when I wake up. And I will continue to dress up to go to the supermarket-- there are people in Holland, too, who show up at the grocery in pajamas or sweats and slippers--because it makes me feel better.

Chase Von: What would you say if you were standing in front of a microphone that could be heard by every child on the planet, and regardless of what language it was they spoke, they would understand you? What positive advice would you give the children, if that were possible?

Kitty: I think I would try to get the message across that they can live their dreams, dreams can be altered to fit the individual's situation or capabilities, and that knowledge is power. Everything is possible.

Chase Von: Can you share where our readers can find your various websites?

Kitty: I can, but I haven't been able to update them recently. Just e-mailing me directly is great for work offered, support needed, or that sort of thing. I will update my various sites when I get a chance. www.KittyStar.com is my personal site, with my demo tapes, resume, photos, etc. www.StarTime.com is my media consulting business that I own here in Holland. www.SecretVisions.com is the production company back in Los Angeles, California. www.Florida-Models.com and www.Florida-Actors.com are both advice/info and jobs available to talent in Florida. I'm an expert on the modeling/acting industry on AllExpert.com for the US market; I'm on most of the other .com social and business networking sites; MySpace, Facebook, LinkedIn, Ecademy, ModelMayhem, OneModelPlace, et al; and my scripts are out on WithoutaBox, WinningScripts and, of course, available through me.

Chase Von: Kitty, on behalf of the *Student Operated Press* and myself, I truly want to thank you again for finding the time to share yourself with our readers. Your story is remarkable and I am certain will inspire many people. I also befriended a young lady on another site that is a rising and talented actress named Brittany Risner, http://www.myspace.com/Brittanyrisner24 who I think would be the perfect choice to play the younger version of you should your story-- which it should--make it to the big screen. I know from reading what I have of the *Screen Writers Bible* by David Trottier that you shouldn't pick people for certain roles, just do the screenwriting. You know far more about that than I, mind you, but I think she's a dead ringer for you. I also hope the offer still stands of having a place to stay if I ever make my way back to Amsterdam. And when you all pull off on another massive motorcycle trip around Europe, I promise to stand there and wave...Heh-heh :) I'm a four-wheel kind of spirit. (Smile.) So love and light, and thanks again for sharing you and your remarkable story with our readers.

Kitty: My home is always open to you, wherever I am. The pleasure of doing this interview has been all mine. And I *have* written roles specifically for actors I have known. Now all I need is a literary agent, and we're all good to go. (Smile.)

****
"I think I would try to get the message across that they can live their dreams, dreams can be altered to fit the individual's situation or capabilities, and that knowledge is power. Everything is possible."
- Kitania "Kitty" Kavey,
Actress, Model, Screenwriter
****

Interview with Dozie

SENSATIONAL SOUL/R&B SINGER
by Chase Von

Photo by Nana Kofi Nti

Chase Von: Dozie, I really want to thank you for taking out the time to do this interview. I first learned of you on My Space and I have to tell you, I fell in love instantly with the song "Gabriel's Lounge." I love the way everything is so perfectly orchestrated in that song. Each instrument completely complements the others and your voice is one to be reckoned with. I ordered your CD, and to my surprise, every song on it is fantastic. In the past--like many others--I've bought CDs because I liked a particular song, only to find out that I wished they would just make a CD of that song by itself because the rest was...well, I think you know where I'm going with this. How much time do you devote to the creation of each of your songs? People are certainly getting more than their money's worth!

Dozie: Thanks, Chase. It actually takes me a long time to write songs...usually months. I have several songs in the works at a time because I try to perfect them, if there is such a thing. I just think it's important to be creative and different. Plus I do a lot of the production/playing/singing by myself, so it takes time. I'm starting to change that though--bringing other people early into the creative process.

Chase Von: You've lived in England, as well as Nigeria, I myself used to live in England. I also know you're a huge fan of football. Although here we call it soccer. Although you're obviously a world-class musician, how far along did you get in the game? And is it true what I hear? Do you still play football, against the wishes of those that want you to be healthy and unhurt so you can perform? Also, when we lived in England, we used to do what we called "knee-ers," meaning you bounced the ball with head, knees, feet and any part of the body other than the hands. Each time the ball made contact, it was counted. What's the most knee-ers--or whatever you use to refer to it--

have you done? One time my brother went over a thousand. *Me?...*I'm asking the questions here! (Smile.)

Dozie: LOL...I love football. I just played a couple of days ago. I've had five knee surgeries from it and I still play. *It's better than sex!* LOL...just kidding. But I really love football. I'm a pretty good player, though not premiership level, obviously, but decent. But I've been slowed down by injuries...Maybe I'll think about retiring soon. As far as *juggling*, I make past a hundred, but I never really count... ;-). *You?*

Chase Von: Changing the subject...(Smile.) Your debut CD "Redemption" is, quite frankly, off the charts! I can already say now: If people are reading this and they know that person that has everything and they don't know what to get them for Christmas, if that individual doesn't have your CD, they couldn't go wrong giving it as a gift. You are being compared for you intricate music and smooth vocals to the likes of Sade, Seal and Maxwell, all verifiable legends in music. For you to be rated in that class of singers with your very first release must be amazing, even to yourself. Who are some of the people you most admire in the industry and how long before you're sharing the stage with the people I've just mentioned? And in the song *"Uwa Ke,"* is that you speaking African?

Dozie: Thank you. Obviously, Sade and Seal are big influences. They are also Nigerian/British, so there's an intrinsic link. But I like lots of people; Fela, Isley Brothers, Tori Amos, and the Cure are some of my favorites. And I'm really into Mindy Smith and Raheem Devaughn right now. As far as comparisons go, I'm flattered that people would mention me in the same breath as other great artists. I really just try to be myself, though, which is why I speak a little Igbo or Pidgin in my songs every now and then. I grew up in Nigeria, after all, and it is who I am.

Photo by Nana Kofi Nti

Chase Von: I read somewhere that you began singing at first in church, and, also, that you taught yourself how to play the guitar and the piano, and that you used to sneak into the church after hours to hone your skills. Are you still sneaking in churches to play and keep on top of your game? (Smile.)

Dozie: LOL...The church doesn't see much of me these days, unfortunately. Probably should go more. But yeah...I started singing in church when I was in Class 1 (7th grade), and then sang in gospel choirs when I came stateside. I started playing piano when I was nineteen or twenty. Because I started late, I figured I needed to practice more, so I would go and play at night in the local church when nobody was around.

Chase Von: Anyone that has heard you sing knows that you are incredibly gifted, but your band is also made up of top-notch performers. You call the sound you produce "AfriSoul," or soul with an African twist. How did you go about gathering members for your band that would be able to bring into the real world the vision and music you feel in your soul? And what are some of the actual African instruments that are part of your music?

Dozie: Hmmm...I've been lucky to have some great musicians who like my music and want to play with me. I found them through word of mouth, and we just all clicked. For instance Joel Jaffe--who worked with everyone from Aretha to Santana to Bonnie Raitt--plays guitar with me. He's fantastic. And Jamie Brewer, who is currently on tour with the Whispers, plays bass. It's just a cool group of people. Old-soul folks, if you will. I also try to mix in some African instruments to give my music a little down-home feeling. I'm not sure what the English names are but *udu, igba, shekere,* stuff like that.

Chase Von: Not trying to reveal my age, but when I lived in England, one of the things I really loved was the "fish and chips," and back then they would wrap them in newspaper. Did you like them, as well, and have you found any places here in the states that are comparable? Because I sure haven't!

Dozie: No, it's really hard to find a good chippy here in the States. It's a little easier in San Francisco because we are right next to the ocean and there are quite a few British ex-pats out here. But still, there's nothing like the real thing.

Chase Von: You write all the lyrics for your music, as well as arrange it, and all the lyrics are very deep and thought-provoking. A while ago someone by the name of Maxwell released a CD called "Urban Suite," and the music that was on it had a feeling to it; if it had of been released in the 70s, it would have fit perfectly with that time. But it was also a blockbuster hit in more recent times because every song on it was truly worth listening to. I know you're a relatively young man, but I think if there is a CD that is out right now that is comparable in quality to Maxwell's "Urban Suite," it is yours. Every song on your CD is fantastic, as well, but what I want to know is: Do you sometimes get asked if you are in possession of a very *old* soul?

Dozie: LOL...Yes! Well, I grew up in the 70s and 80s, and as you know, music was a little different then. I wouldn't say that I focus on music from that era, but I think it's natural that one is influenced by the music one hears growing up, and I think it's evident in my music that I grew up in that era.

Chase Von: Needless to say, your music is fantastic. You're obviously a rising star and also becoming--because of your sensual sound--a sex symbol of sorts. :) How difficult is it dealing with your rising popularity and all the fans that are becoming enamored with the man that goes by simply Dozie?

Dozie: Thank you so much. Well, it's still early stages but I'm touched that people like my music. After all, that's what it's really about at the end of the day.

Chase Von: How important is family to you, and what is your take on the state of our current world?

Photo by Tyler Thornton

Dozie: Family is extremely important. I do everything for my family. And mine is a fairly large and extended one. As far as the state of the world...LOL...I don't know that I can talk about my political views in public. ;-) Let's just say that the world would be different if I had my way.

Chase Von: What would you say if you were standing in front of a microphone that could be heard by every child on the planet, and regardless of what language it was they spoke, they would understand you? What positive advice would you give the children, if that were possible?

Dozie: Never be afraid to dream. Doesn't matter how hard it is or how old you are. You can be whatever you want to be. Just look at me as an example. There is *always* a way forward. *Always!* It's up to you to seize the opportunity.

Chase Von: How can our readers find you and your music and more about you? And are there any future projects you are working on you care to share with our readers? Or any shows that you will be doing in the near future?

Dozie: Just visit www.dozie.com. I'm playing in Oakland next week and then I'm off to Africa for a couple of months. But starting in January I should be playing a lot more. I've got lots of new material and I'll be hitting the studio in January, too, so expect more music from me in 2008.

Chase Von: On behalf of the *Student Operated Press* and myself, Dozie, it's been a pleasure to interview a truly multi-talented individual and a veritable rising star. Thank you so much for finding the time to do this. It's greatly appreciated.

Dozie: Much appreciated, bro. One love.

****

"Never be afraid to dream. Doesn't matter how hard it is or how old you are. You can be whatever you want to be. Just look at me as an example. There is always a way forward. Always! It's up to you to seize the opportunity."
- Dozie, Singer, Musician, Songwriter
****

Photo by Nana Kofi Nti

Interview with Alina Smith

RISING SINGER AND BEAUTY
By Chase Von

Photo by David Graubert

Chase Von: Alina, thank you so much for finding the time to do this interview. I know you are incredibly busy. I do want you to know, though, the more I learn about you, the more amazed I am. Anyone looking at your pictures can easily see you could be a world-class model if you chose to be. In a way, you *are* a model since your face is so well known. You're beautiful. But there's this saying that everyone here is familiar with that basically goes: "I'm more than just a pretty face." In your case, that is like one of the biggest understatements one could possibly make. *You're a prodigy!* As I was doing my research I was thinking, *When are they going to make a movie of her life?* You could read and write at two. You were singing at age three... Began painting and speaking English at four, even though your native language is Russian... Writing poetry and stories at five... I know, also, that your mother was a teacher and an actress, as well as an opera singer, and all that is truly remarkable. But most remarkable is that--at the tender age of six--you were being faced with choosing between a scholarship to a music academy or going to the famed Vaganovsky Ballet School. *Six?* I think I was still wetting the bed! (Smile.) Not really...busy failing the first grade, though. :) No, really though, I heard that someone else had problems in school. I think his name was Einstein. (Smile.) How was your childhood? And did you truly choose to do all those things at that young age, or were you driven to? I only ask because sometimes parents can be extremely demanding on some occasions with their children, although I am certainly not trying to cast yours in a bad light. You have turned out nothing short of spectacular.

Alina: Hey, Chase, thank you very much for all of your compliments. Also, thank you for arranging this interview with me-- it's one of my very first ones, so I'm really excited. You know, whenever a child is actively involved in art, music or sports, it is questionable whether the decision to do all of those things is really theirs. In many instances, parents really do push a little too much. I think that my case was pretty much a mix of both. I have pictures of the two-year-old me painting, and I remember my favorite pastime at five was writing short stories and poems about my teddy bears. Playing piano and singing, for me, was like playing with toys is for most kids. I was always creative and really did love doing all those things. My mom was never aggressive in driving me to develop my artistic side, but she really did try to take advantage of every interest of mine. At one time she had me simultaneously going to ballet, music, dancing, art and gymnastics schools. Having to get straight A's in regular school too...I did cope with it all well for a while, but as the time went on, the classes started getting more challenging, the teachers more demanding...I had to make a choice.

Chase Von: You were raised in Russia. I've been there once and wasn't prepared at all for how friendly the people there would be. Many of them had never seen someone of my complexion, so they wanted to take pictures with me. Felt a bit like Michael Jordan. (Smile.) I was in Vladivostok, and so many of them also spoke English. But from what I understand, perhaps the part where you grew

Photo by David Graubert

Photo by David Graubert
Alina, featured performer with' Songs From Shenzhen out of China'

up wasn't quite as friendly. How bad was it really? Also, do you ever miss Russia and have you returned? And I guess the big question is: Do you have as many fans there supporting you and your dreams as you have in the United States? Although, I am also sure you have fans worldwide, but with your being one of their own, I would think they are immensely proud of you.

Alina: Growing up in Russia in the 90s was definitely a unique kind of experience. From what I know, the kids born in the late 90s-early 2000s are being raised in a much safer, pro-Western environment. I would even go so far as to say that it is very comparable to the U.S. now. Of course, everyone born before me had gotten a taste of the communist Russia. I can't imagine what that was like. The 90s were difficult for many people. The country was just barely bouncing back from perestroika, there weren't a lot of good clothes or food and most people didn't make much money. The Russian currency (ruble) wasn't stable either. The prices had tripled around '98. St. Petersburg (my hometown) looked drab and run-down with its dusty yards, littered sidewalks and gray rainy sky. *Were the people friendly?* Why would they be friendly? *They were miserable!* I have never been to Vladivostok, but I'm sure that the culture there is very different. It's like East Coast and West Coast here. I miss Russia a little bit, but I miss my family a lot more. I have been back once for my grandma's 80th birthday. I felt kind of like a tourist – so many things have changed. Though the majority of my fan base is Americans, I do have quite a few Russian fans. R&B is a very new genre there, so I'm not sure if the older people would like my music. Young Russians dig it, though.

Chase Von: Although you sing so very soulfully, you're also classically trained, as well. You also can sing in Russian, German, Spanish, French and Latin. How many languages do you speak? And do you ever plan on doing a purely classical piano CD, since you play so beautifully?

Alina: It would be really cool to do something with classical piano and/or orchestration. I would probably mix it with some funky drumbeats and soulful vocals. It would also be great to use a gospel choir with that. Hmm...As far as the languages go, I'm only fluent in English and Russian. I know a little Spanish; I even wrote a few songs in it, but I would have to study more to be able to converse freely. I can sing in pretty much any language---I have really good sonic memory. I once had to do a tune in Japanese for a concert at my school. *That was pretty funny!* I wrote out all of the words in Slavic letters to help me learn faster. I had no clue what I was singing about.

Photo by Brad Smith
Alina, performing in support of Student Olympics ("Universiade").

Chase Von: Your new CD *Piano and Sax* is incredible. Your voice is truly amazing. You have what appears to be a pretty direct message for men and women alike in your song, "Pull Your Pants Up," and "I Wanna Live" is the kind of slow song that really tugs at the heart. You, however, didn't grow up listening to R&B in Russia, but you have so much soul in you. I know since learning of R&B, you have a great respect for the legendary Aretha Franklin and Isaac Hayes, but do you care to tell our readers more about your fascination with Michael Jackson? And have you met him in person yet? Also, this is going to break a lot of male hearts, but I want you to share if you will, how Michael, in a way, is sort of the reason you met your husband. (Smile.)

Alina: When I was fifteen, I had picked up a *Michael Jackson Greatest Hits* album in a record store––I'm really dating myself now––and once I popped it into my boombox, I just couldn't stop listening. After that, I started buying every MJ item I could get my hands on. I had this tape with his videos, and I learned the dance moves of every single one of them. I got myself a man's suit, a pair of white shoes and a black hat. I would start the tape every day after school, throw my suit on and dance for hours. My mom still has those white shoes; they've got almost no soles now–– it's all one big hole. I was obsessed with MJ for the longest time, and I even made up a website where I fanatically ranted about him. I'm so glad that I did, because it was that silly site that connected me up with my husband, Brad. He was making travel plans and researched Russia. My website came up. My husband collects autographs of musicians and he had a sheet-music book signed by Michael Jackson. Seeing how crazy I was about the King of Pop, he figured that he'd give me the book when he was going to be in my city on my birthday. I was kind of excited to meet an American and practice my English, but I never expected anything beyond making a new pen pal. It does really sound like a fiction love story, but, once I met Brad, I knew that he was *The One*. He felt the same way about me. Two weeks later we were engaged. I haven't met MJ yet, but I really hope that I will. I don't know how I'm going to react when it happens. I'll probably be so startled...I'll just stand there and go, "Um...uh...huh."

Chase Von: You were the youngest singer ever invited into the prestigious choir "Aurora" and the only one honored with solo performances. What was it like touring all of Europe at such a young age and performing in so many different languages?

Photo by David Graubert
Alina with 'Songs of Shenzhen China Singer'

Alina: *It was awesome! I absolutely loved it!* We toured all around Europe in a bus and sometimes we'd go days without stopping in a hotel. We slept in the bus and everything. I think the older girls found it pretty uncomfortable, but I couldn't have cared less. It was so much fun, looking out the window, seeing all the different buildings, the people, the landscapes. Performing was great too. The choir participated in many contests, so a lot of times we would sing in front of huge crowds. I remember being nine and having to sing in front of 5,000 people, *acapella*.

Chase Von: If I had to try and tell someone who had never heard you sing, I would begin by saying, "If you like Mariah Carey, Christina Aguilera, Kelly Clarkson, Norah Jones, Sara McLaughlin, Alicia Keys, Whitney Houston, Chaka Khan and...I could go on, but anyone born with a gold mine in their throat you will love Alina." I know of your admiration for Michael Jackson and Aretha Franklin, but who are some of the other people you truly admire?

Alina: I'm probably not going to sound very original on this question, but I love pretty much all of the great R&B/Soul artists of the 50s, 60s, 70s and 80s. I'm a huge fan of Stevie Wonder; I love Marvin Gaye, James Brown, Prince, Etta James, Ray Charles, Sam Cooke, Curtis Mayfield, Ashford & Simpson, Otis Redding...I really could go on and on.

Chase Von: Ok, I happened to see on your page where you said you missed your mom's cabbage-and-carrot omelets. *Boy, did I suddenly feel hungry!* (Smile.) But I've never heard of any omelet in my life with cabbage in it. Is that a Russian dish? And strange as it might sound, I wouldn't be surprised at all if people, particularly women, started eating that religiously, so they could look and sing like Alina. (Smile.) And do you also ever plan on pursuing acting in your future?

Alina: Hahaha...No, there's no such thing as a Russian cabbage omelet. I don't particularly love vegetables (c'mon, who does?), and I especially hate raw cabbage. I always have an omelet after a workout, so my mom started sneaking all of these veggies into it to make me eat better. I didn't even know it was in it until she told me. The whole thing tastes delicious. I would say that acting is pretty much required now for anyone wanting to really make a living in the music business. It's all about the expansion of your brand. The more people see you, the better your concert tickets and albums are going to sell. I would certainly be interested in doing commercials and small TV/film roles. I have never acted on television before, so I would want to start out slowly and see how good I am at it before trying out for bigger roles. I wouldn't want to star in a movie and be horrible. I've seen singers do that, and I don't think that's at all helpful to their careers.

Chase Von: How important is family to you, and what is your take on the state of our current world?

Alina: Family is my #1 priority. I work ten to fourteen hours every day, but I always try to find time to spend with my husband and to call my parents. I have a very small family, so luckily there are not too many people to keep up with. I don't want to sound like a downer, but I definitely think that our world could use some major improvement. Aside from the obvious tragedies like war, hunger and disease, I feel like there is enormous degradation of the human mind. There are really a lot of people who are just mindlessly consuming the products of mass media and are completely unconcerned with having an opinion of their own. Just look at some of the profiles on Myspace. I see so many teenagers that have their profiles swarmed with curse words and offensive images.

Photo by Brad Smith
Alina performing "Love Is The Answer." 'Songs From Shenzhen China' supporting
'Student Olympics' ("Universaide"), Pasadena Civic Center.

Some of the most popular music videos on YouTube are promoting sexism, racism and disrespect to anyone who doesn't have a "pimpin' ride." Half the songs on the radio are about "hooking up." What happened to being kind, generous and intelligent? Are those qualities going the way of the dinosaurs?

Chase Von: What would you say if you were standing in front of a microphone and be heard by every child on the planet and, regardless of what language they spoke, they would understand you? What positive advice would you give the children, if that were possible?

Alina: I would say: Find your dream and follow it. So many people are dissatisfied because they never really take time to figure out what they're all about and what makes them happy. They're just doing what their parents, teachers or friends expect from them. Find out what your dream is and go for it. It is so incredibly rewarding to be doing something you actually enjoy.

Chase Von: How can our readers find your music and more about you? Can you share your links and web pages? And are there any future projects you are working on you care to share with our readers? Or is the novel you're working on a secret? Oops... (Smile.) Also, will you be performing any time soon in the near future?

Alina: Myspace is probably the best way to check me out online: www.myspace.com/alinamusic. To watch my videos, please visit my YouTube channel... that link is: www.youtube.com/alinamusix. There is a lot going on with me these days. I have a Christmas album that I was commissioned to record by a German company. I am shooting a music video for one of my songs early next year. I will also be consistently performing in New York and Los Angeles. I have been really busy with writing and recording this year, so I have been selective about doing shows. My next live performance is in NYC in a club called "Sugar Bar," owned by my musical idols Ashford & Simpson. Your readers can check my Myspace page for more info on it, if they're in the area and would like to come. My novel is kind of a secret. It is still far from being finished, so I haven't shared the contents of it with anyone but my family. It is my first English-language novel––I have written a couple in Russian––and I'm actually really psyched about it. It's about a high-school romance in a very strict, upper-class academy in Russia. I will reveal more when it's time.

Chase Von: I have a special request, Alina. I know you put up videos on YouTube of yourself playing and singing. I've seen you singing Carole King and even Marvin Gaye songs, and beautifully, I might add. If time permits, can you do one song I truly love? I think you would do just as lovely as you do with all the songs you approach: "I Can't Make You Love Me," originally, I believe, by the great Bonnie Raitt?

Alina: Sure, I like that song too, I would love to learn it. OK, I'm putting it down on my to-do list right now. #254. LOL

Chase Von: On behalf of the *Student Operated Press* and myself, Alina, I really want to thank you for taking the time to do this. With all you're doing it is really truly appreciated that you managed to find time for this. I would wish you luck, but you have so many natural gifts that you're surely going to simply keep rising, based on your God-given talents. Thanks so much, again, and best wishes to you, your husband and your entire family.

Alina: Thanks a lot Chase. I had fun answering all the questions.

Photo by David Graubert
Alina and 'Songs from Shenzhen China.'
"Unifying The World Through Music!"

****

"Find out what your dream is and go for it.
It is so incredibly rewarding to be
doing something you actually enjoy."
- Alina, Singer, Pianist, Songwriter

****

Photo by David Graubert

Interview with Bazhe

POET, ARTIST, AUTHOR
by Chase Von

Photo property of B.K. Bazhe

Chase Von: Bazhe, I am so blown away by your book. Being someone who is (quote and unquote) "straight," I have to tell you that I never would have imagined, going in, that I would be unable to stop turning the pages. I reached a point early in life, not to label people or to consider anyone--who isn't trying to impose whatever their beliefs might be on my life--as an enemy.

I'm a live-and-let-live kind of guy, but that took some living to reach that point. I know that there are many people who don't conform to the norm, and to me, they are simply people who are written about throughout the history of the world. Many times, I might add. I don't profess to know everything, which is why although I have my lines––which no one should cross or they face the consequences––as all people do. I am always open to learning new things. But, I have to tell you, though, that your autobiography is the most unabashed and honest "don't-care-if-you-like-me-or-not" book I have ever read. And in that honesty, things that I myself don't personally see me wanting in my own life *per se,* still made me feel a respect for you, because of your blatant truth and honest delivery. I was also touched by how much you cared for your mother; one of the most important parts of your story. I will definitely ask you about that, to be sure, but what I want to know first is why you wrote this book to begin with? Was it to capture your love for your mother in print for all time, as well as describe your own life?

Bazhe: Dear Chase Von, I am glad that you invited me for this interview. The fact that you love my book makes me very happy. I do love your writings as well. Your words are like beautiful colors. Thanks for introducing them to me. Well, I'll start talking about my book *Damages* by saying this: It doesn't matter what one's race or sexual orientation is to identify with many of the things that have happened to me. I had a strange and very unusual first twenty-four years of life. However, anyone can find things that are identical to my upbringing, especially in our dealings with parents...that is, in so many ways, universal. But besides the unique and crazy experiences of my young adult life, *Damages* is about my mother who adopted me. People say you have only one mother, but I had two. Telling what happened is a very important part of my story because one mother continues to stay in my heart, while one mother is completely out of it. *Damages* is also about my dealing with the political turmoil of the Balkans between the Muslims and the Christians and that makes it very timely for all of us. And now to answer your question directly: I wrote this book to tell the truth about a human who endures everything to get to the truth. You are right, *Damages* is, as you've said, a don't-care-if-you-like-me-or-not book. I needed to tell the truth in this work and educate those who search for independence and freedom from suppressive families and societies. Here is the short synopsis: *Damages* is a saga of a young man caught in the political crossfire of a country torn apart by Communism, Christian nationalism and Islamic fundamentalism. It is one man's fight to find his true identity and freedom, as he awakens to his own sexuality in an oppressive society and comes to realize that he can no longer consider his own home a safe haven. Thus, he eventually flees to America where he builds a new life in the land of freedom.

Chase Von: You are, in my opinion, not only a prodigy but also a warrior. I can think of few people who would have lived to tell, had they been in your situation. And, I am not talking about a single event. You went through, literally, years of violent abuse, being ostracized and being an outcast; and perhaps––although they didn't think so at the time––all because of your parents, and in particular, your father. Your ability to write, and I told you this before, is on the level of the masters. You remind me, on occasions, of the incredibly gifted writer Anne Rice. And English is not even your first language. You speak how many languages? And how did you master the English language to the point you can write works comparable to the likes I've mentioned just now...Anne Rice?

Bazhe: I am very touched by your comparison of me with such a big American writer as Anne Rice, so thank you. I speak seven languages. I did not speak English when I came here in the beginning, but instantly I began to learn it. I have a weakness for languages. I also consider English one of the most beautiful languages of all. Conrad and Nabokov wrote in English as a second language, as well. These two are some of my super idols and it is natural for me to relate to them, as I, too, am an immigrant. I also learned English by reading my favorite American writers and by talking to anyone, regardless if I would make mistakes or not. I would make people laugh, and I didn't mind. I didn't mind even their put-downs when I would make mistakes, since I had a secret. And that secret was that while they were ridiculing me, I was gaining knowledge. That was all that mattered to me. My motto is to win the war, and losing battles is not important. *So I won it and learned English.*

Chase Von: I don't want to give your book away too much, but there was a part in your book that took me completely by surprise. Well, many parts, really, that knocked me senseless. I was first blown away, however, when you were someone who didn't want to finish your "greasy" meat. I only mention this because I want to know whether you feel--and I know you can elaborate eloquently--whether homosexuality is something people learn or are born being?

Bazhe: The sexual orientation is in us when we are an embryo. That is for sure. I knew I was gay ever since I was born. It is not something one learns. An individual can suppress it because of the prejudice of their family or the society, but it is there. *One is born with it.* I am so glad that young people here don't seem to care about it. I am also so happy they are getting more free and liberated, and *that* is priceless. That is the main motive of my book *Damages.* Freedom and liberation are so universal, so essential and most important for all of us.

Chase Von: Who are some of the writers you yourself admire?

Bazhe: Mostly I love the classic writers. I love Proust, Faulkner, Capote, Marquez, Nabokov, Voltaire, Pasolini, Balzac, Salinger, Baldwin, Williams, Conrad, Selby and Vidal because of their exquisite style of writing. Their writings are real art. From the poets, I adore the love poetry of Rimbaud and Plath and the bold poetry of Neruda and Lorca. I consider Kushner, Waller and Ondaatje as exceptional modern writers. I find them fresh and innovative. But no one is like Orwell. He is truly my number one.

Chase Von: I know they are making a movie of your life story. When can we expect to see it?

Bazhe: Soon, I hope. I am working and talking often to an important movie connection who is assisting me in finishing the film script for my book. It will be a collaboration, which I prefer. It will also enable me to learn a new area of writing, and I am very excited about this. And I will invite you, for sure, as my special guest for the film's premiere.

Chase Von: Thank you, and I have to tell you, Bazhe, I am, as I said, a live-and-let-live kind of person. But I wasn't always that way and not because of me, *per se*, but because of what society wanted me to think. Because of that, I used to look sideways at people who lived alternative lifestyles. You know, I am blatantly honest-- perhaps to a fault--but having read your book, I see things a bit differently now. Do you think if more people read your work, it would lessen the hostilities we both know exist?

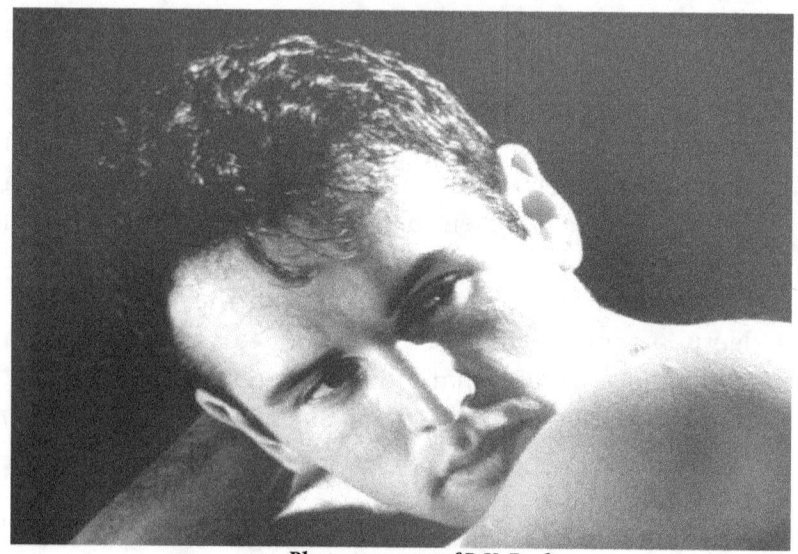

Photo property of B.K. Bazhe

Bazhe: I love your honesty. I admire that in anyone and, let me be frank, what is there to hate? Families and societies are, by default, oppressive and hateful. They are the most oppressive and hateful circles of humanity. Big Brother wants that so he can control you, your family and your friends. Freeing yourself from this oppressiveness and hate will help you to be true humans, not just another creature in your circle of clones. All people who hate and are oppressive are crooks, hypocrites and criminals. Being hateful and oppressing yourself turns you into being a religious fanatic, homophobe, racist and/or nationalist--which, all together, makes you just like a Nazi, a fascist. And we all should know what fascists do, and have done, throughout recorded human history. My book *Damages* describes this. It makes anyone rethink his or her oppressiveness and hate. Hopefully, it makes you understand different people, races and cultures; and, it makes one grow free from being a hateful and oppressive human being, into kind and understanding people.

Chase Von: People tend to think, or a lot of them, that people who are attracted to the same sex are inferior or shallow, misguided or sick, wrong or...well, *you* name it. I was, however, struck again--as I was struck many times throughout your book--by how--if I removed the fact that you were speaking of another man and replaced that character with a woman--that it mirrored the feelings that I have had for women in my life. In your mind is love genderless? And if so, what about the natural order of things as in: Only men and women together can produce children for future generations?

Bazhe: I strongly recommend for anyone to put on the opposite sex role for one day. Then one would learn a lot--truly a lot. It is a very useful thing to do. It is especially helpful for the straight folks out there. I was into that role out of my need to survive and escape the tough situation, and I never regretted it. It was a precious lesson. It was amazing being...I mean acting, 24/7 for six months, as a woman. On top of it, being in the arms of a very good-looking man and in the exotic city of Istanbul didn't hurt at all, either. LOL...My female readers love that part. Women are less intimidated by what I did, and they also understand easier my purpose for doing it. Many tell me they envied me. LOL...I have told women I wouldn't mind giving them Genghis for some romance.

The question of reproduction is also easy. I know many who reproduce and they are gay or lesbian... not counting the closeted ones. Trust me, we won't run out of babies even if 99% of the population is homosexual. LOL *The real problem is that we are running out of parents. That is the tragedy.* We should really open our eyes and see what humans have done as parents. They have produced, and keep producing, many orphans and abandoned children. Very sad...and, this mess affects me very much because I am an orphan. I wrote about this a great deal in *Damages.*

Chase Von: Now to the question I really wanted to ask you: Your love for your adoptive mother pours from the pages of your book. And how you took care of her and-- people will have to read that themselves--made me think of you not as a man, but as an angel. I am curious, out of concern mind you, that you are content that you did what had to be done. My other question is this: Are you OK knowing you did what I can't imagine any one I know doing so carefully or lovingly. Or do you--who did what so few of us have had to do--still wonder if you could have provided better care in her last days? Because I certainly don't think anyone who reads your book would think that possible.

Bazhe: Thank you for your respect for what I did. I had to care for my true mother, my adopter, immaculately. It was my physical and emotional duty. *She was my savior!* Just imagine what kind of life I would have had without parents. Many sane orphans and adoptees, fortunately, feel this way. We see and respect these women like my mother as if they are saints. Unfortunately, many true children don't provide such care for their real parents. Sometimes, they can't, and we should understand those circumstances. But many times they can, yet they just throw the parents in the terrible nursing homes. I did not, and I am glad I went back to Europe and took care of her until the end. And I did it with all my love and respect for her dignity. She told me when she was dying, "If I could have bore 100 children, I would have traded all of them, just to have you." Those words gave me the feeling of being the most happiest and accomplished as a son. It was the best thing I did, and in the process, I learned a lot about life. Very precious knowledge! This knowledge of life, I will be writing in my next book...coming soon.

Photo property of B.K. Bazhe

Chase Von: How important is family to you, and what is your take on the state of our current world?

Bazhe: Family and friends are most important. Since I came here, I have been involved with one partner only, in a stable and long-time relationship. He is an American guy, very smart and reliable. Also, he is one handsome scientist. Scientists and artists are tough yet powerful combinations, I think. I was lucky. But I work on building my continuing relationship. Being alone here, I needed a family more than you can imagine. Building long-time and steady relationships is hard work. Hard work is the recipe to building a stable relationship. It is not to just throw in the towel easily, as some of my fellow Americans would say. I took that proverb seriously and did it. Besides, I am a very loyal creature to anyone who respects me—which is just natural to be.

Chase Von: What would you say if you were standing in front of a microphone that could be heard by every child on the planet, and regardless of what language it was they spoke, they would understand you? What positive advice would you give the children, if that were possible?

Bazhe: Cherish your parents. Respect anyone. And to those who are unfortunate, the orphans, I would say: It is hard to be in your shoes, but you must fight to survive— and never give up. *Never!*

Chase Von: Let our readers know how they can find out more about you, and more importantly, where they can get your book. I can tell all reading this: If you are straight gay or breathing, you will still love this book, because it is packed with so many things that life is about. But you will have to read it to understand why I feel that way.

Bazhe: Thank you, Chase, I am flattered. And I truly enjoyed your book *Your Chance to Hear the Last Panther Speak*, as well! My book can be found on most online and offline stores, like on Amazon.com, Barnes and Noble, Borders, and independent bookstores. Just provide to the booksellers this info: *Damages* by Bazhe, ISBN: 0-595-29714-5. Also, it's available as an e-book. And you can order it by calling a toll-free number: 1-877-823-9235. Or you can get *Damages* directly from me as an autographed copy from my website: www.Bazhe.com

Chase Von: I want to thank you, Bazhe, busy as you are, for finding the time to do this. I am wishing you continued future success, and on behalf of myself and the *Student Operated Press,* thank you so much for sharing and giving us some of your time.

Bazhe: It was a pleasure to be interviewed by you and the *Student Operated Press*—wonderful organization. Thank you very much. Keep up the good work and stay well. Love and peace to all.

****

"Cherish your parents. Respect anyone.
And to those who are unfortunate, the orphans, I
would say: It is hard to be in your shoes, but you
must fight to survive—and never give up. Never!"
- Bazhe, Poet, Artist, Author
****

DAMAGES

by

Bazhe

Interview with Betty Dravis

LOVELY, TALENTED, WISE
by Chase Von

Photo by John Manha of JM Holdings LLC

Chase Von: Betty, you know this is truly an honor. So on behalf of the *Student Operated Press* and myself I thank you so much for finding the time to share with our readers. Jumping right into the fray, I want to say as a seasoned veteran reporter and long-time journalist, you know far more than I. But when I am reading up on people to present them with, hopefully, great questions--that will provide the reading audience with something they will enjoy--I can't help but get a feeling for them. Sometimes I'm primarily business, sometimes I joke a bit. Well honestly, I always joke, but again I get a feeling from researching and it kind of feels like questions I might ask one individual, wouldn't go over so well if I asked the same ones of another individual. Having said that, I will be serious, but I also have my silly hat in close reach, as well, because you're a riot! Have you always had this sense of humor, and how important do you think humor is to just life in general?

Betty Dravis: Well, Chase, you're pretty funny yourself, and I, for one, enjoy your brand of humor too. (Grin!) Seriously, I think a sense of humor is vital to everyone's happiness. And since humans are the only creatures that God granted the ability to laugh, I plan to use my gift and use it often. I find that when I'm laughing and joking around with my friends, all my irritations and resentments vanish and a sunny spirit takes hold.

Chase Von: You've lived a life most people could only imagine! We'll get to you interviewing Clint Eastwood and Jane Russell a bit later. *Both huge, major stars!* But the truth of the matter is, you yourself are considered a star in the literary world as well. You've authored three books so far: *Millennium Babe: The Prophecy*, a supernatural mystery adventure; *The Toonies Invade Silicon Valley*, a young adult sci-fi fantasy adventure; and *1106 Grand Boulevard*, an epic romantic thriller--plus too many short stories to list here. I understand you're presently working on a horror novel! Is humor something that you include in all your stories? Because about the only thing I have seen you being genuinely serious with when it comes to writing is when you do reviews on Amazon. (Smile.)

Betty Dravis: Let me speak of my current WIPs (works in progress) first, and then I'll get back to the question about humor. Chase, as I informed you earlier, second printings of my Toonies and Grand novels will be out in mid-2009 under a bright, new independent publisher. (This is hush-hush, of course. Grin!) Besides that, I have already completed two children's picture books--*The Love Alphabet* and *The Dog Who Likes Cat Food*--and am preparing them for submission ASAP. I've completed the third draft of a horror novel and a serial-killer thriller novel, also. Both of those need fine-tuning before I submit them, so I'm juggling a lot of storylines at the same time. I'm also on the second chapter of a Toonies sequel: *The Toonies Invade New York*. My problem at present is deciding which of the projects should take high priority: getting a new novel out there or getting two current ones back in print. It's like a Catch-22. (Grin!) As for humor in my works, there's a zany weatherman in "Millennium Babe: The Prophecy" who's a lot like Jim Carrey, so readers can expect tons of humor in that novel. Here's what author Chad Thompson had to say about "Babe": "Ms. Dravis's breezy style sometimes threatens to undercut the seriousness of her theme (a prophecy fulfilled during modern days), but in the end it serves as a kind of innocence reminiscent of Vonnegut, though not as acerbic." Isn't that cool, Chase?... My Toonies has a lot of humor, too, but Grand is more serious. I always manage some humor, though, because I feel that any good book needs both drama and comedy mimicking life in all ways. And I love satire, so I write a lot of my short stories with my tongue planted firmly in my cheek.

Chase Von: I want to make something clear to those unfamiliar with your writing right now: I always find myself laughing when I read anything you write--other than your reviews on Amazon, and you even have a lot of humor in some of those. You take things that are serious and paint a picture around it or weave within it this

incredible humor that you have been blessed with. But it is all extremely intelligently written. Can you share a short portion with our readers so they can get a brief taste, if they aren't already familiar with your writing?

Betty Dravis: I'd be glad to, Chase. One example is how I turned my humor on myself (self-deprecation) when writing a short memoir of my interview with actor Clint Eastwood in the late 60s. I titled it "A Bad Hair Day," and you can tell by the title not all went as well as I would have liked....lol... Not to tease your readers or anything, but for the sake of brevity of your interview space, I'd like to refer them to the "Celebrities Section" of my website. There they can read about the "Bad Hair Day" I had when I interviewed Clint Eastwood. The link: http://bettydravisauthor.googlepages.com/celebrities

Chase Von: lol...*Of all days to have a bad hair day!* But I've seen that picture of Clint Eastwood looking at you all googly-eyed, so is there something else to this story you aren't sharing? (Smile.)

Betty Dravis: Truthfully, Chase, it all happened so fast that I didn't realize how Clint was looking at me (and I at him... Grin!) until I saw the photo. Later when I thought of his fingers embracing my throat that way... well, that's when I had the delayed "goose bumps"--and believe you me, those bumps were as huge as those golden eggs in that old nursery rhyme. *What a thrill!* If I hadn't been mesmerized at the time, I might have taken advantage of him... LOL... I'm only human, after all.

Chase Von: And how come you didn't show up late for Clint Eastwood? Hmm? And how come you were late with Jane Russell, but didn't have a bad hair day? *Inquisitive minds want to know!* (Smile.) And on the serious tip, what was it like interviewing *her?* She's another huge star and legend!

Betty Dravis: Well, Chase, you got me there...LOL... Seriously, I ran into a "road spill" en route to San Francisco where I was to sit in on the press conference with Jane Russell, so ended up late. If anyone cares to read that story, it's posted on my website under the celebrities section, also. The link: http://bettydravisauthor.googlepages.com/ And you're right, Jane Russell was a huge star and another living legend. I found her to be charming, gracious and very kind. Did you know that for over thirty years now, she's turned the extraordinary publicity of her acting career to focus on the plight of homeless children? She devotes her heart and soul to the placement of children in loving homes through her WAIF organization. *She's my kind of woman!* I felt so fortunate to have interviewed her and Clint Eastwood. I also interviewed other celebrities; a few of the stories are on my website too. Those interviews were delightful highlights of my life. I plan to add more of the stories behind the interviews as I work on the website in the future. As for my hair on the day I interviewed Jane Russell, I was wearing a wig. They were in vogue then, and since the one I wore was too "bushy," you could say that was another bad hair day... Oh, well, she's a woman so I wasn't too concerned. No points to be made with her... hehehe

Chase Von: Your book *1106 Grand Boulevard* has the picture of the actual house you lived in as the cover. What was your childhood like? And since you have been around a bit longer than some of us here, what do you think is the biggest thing that is most different now with kids coming up today, as opposed to when you were growing up?

Betty Dravis: You're right, Chase, the photo on the cover of Grand is my childhood home in Hamilton, Ohio and the address is the title of my third book. I took that photo when the heroine of my book, my sister Billie, and I were visiting our father in the early 80s. For old times' sake, he drove us past the home, and I shot that photo from the passenger side of his auto. My father's silhouette frames the house, which made the perfect cover when later I wrote a book about my sister's dramatic life with seven marriages. At that time, I had no plans to write the book, so it just goes to show you how all things work together in the long run... You ask about growing up in a small Midwestern town. Well, Chase, *I count my blessings!* My parents were good, hard-working Christians who took good care of us seven children and "loved us to pieces." Adding to the family cast were my grandparents and numerous aunts, uncles and cousins. I'm sure my parents had their share of problems, but they never bothered the children with "adult matters." *Life was good!* Hamilton had a good educational system, which was an added blessing.

Life was simpler in those days, despite my parents' strict Baptist principles. (We kids had a way of getting around those...lol...) The biggest difference I can see for children growing up in today's world is the openness of the media regarding everything from sex to crime and warfare. The children are exposed to too much too young. It's everywhere: in books, magazines, on TV and in the movies.

Best-selling Amazon short story

Chase Von: Also Grand and your Toonies book have both gotten many rave reviews. And I've heard from our mutual friend, Chrissy K. McVay, author of *Souls Of The North Wind,* that there was talk of making *The Toonies Invade Silicon Valley* into a movie. Can you tell us a little about that?

Betty Dravis: Ohmigosh, Chase, when my publisher phoned to tell me that a famous movie production company had called for copies of the "Toonies," I thought I was going to faint. I'm not at liberty to give the company name, but I held my breath for about six weeks while they considered it for an animated film. Sadly, the timing wasn't right and they ultimately returned it. They said it had great "visuals" and would make a great animated movie, but some other project with more urgency came up and... well, that was that! But, I remain optimistic. It's my dream for Toonies--or any of my books--to become a movie.

Chase Von: I read some of your rave reviews. Author J. Buchanan called Toonies "the next movie toon phenomenon," and said Hollywood should recognize it as a "guaranteed motion picture gold-mine" for its marketing potential. And one of Amazon's top reviewers, Todd Burger, said the unique description of your characters was "reminiscent of some of Baum`s magnificent creations in his classic Oz series." How does it feel to be compared to the mighty Baum?

Betty talks "Toonies" with kids at BN/Westgate/San Jose

Betty Dravis: Wow, Chase, you've really done your homework! I'm impressed! Thanks for mentioning those two fabulous compliments. I'm in awe of Burger's comparison, of course, but I feel undeserving of that praise. "The Wizard of Oz" is a true classic. It's humbling that anyone would mention my Toonies in the same sentence as Oz. I love my Toonies characters, but ... Whoaaaaaaa... *That review blew me away!* As for what Author Jerome Buchanan said about marketing ops, he started my imagination soaring. I could picture my Toonies characters as marketing products. Actually, I can see Uncle Wom, Doog Toonie and the ape-bird Mischief Makers as toys to be sold in Toys 'R Us and as giveaways by Jack-in-the-Box and Mickey Dee's. I hold that "dream bubble" still firmly in my mind. Perhaps some fine day...? hmmmmmm... Dream on, Betty...

Chase Von: I've always advised my friends and family to "Dream Big," Betty.

Betty Dravis: Yes, "*Dare* to Dream Big," as author Cheryl Kaye Tardif advised me.

Chase Von: Is a movie also something you are considering for *1106 Grand Boulevard,* as well? And although, when it comes to screenplays and things, they prefer you don't say who you think should play whom, if you had your way, who do you think would best portray your sister, on whom the novel is actually based?

Betty Dravis: Chase, that's every author's dream to have his or her book made into a movie, so the answer is a definite *yes!* So if any of your fans are directors or producers (or know anyone who is), my e-mail address is: BettyDravis@gmail.com. Send them my way--*fast!* When one of my books becomes a film, I'll buy you a fast sports car... (Grin!) Oh, and if Grand is made into a movie, I would love to have Sandra Bullock play the role of Billie Jean. She's wholesome and beautiful, yet sexy, too... She would make a perfect Billie Jean.

Chase Von: Who are some of the authors you yourself most admire?

****

"Writing a book is like sliding down a rainbow; marketing it is like trudging through a field of chewed bubblegum on a hot, sticky day."
- Betty Dravis, Author, Journalist

****

Betty Dravis: I love everything from juvenile fiction (I also adore children's picture books and Young Adult) to horrors, thrillers and general audience books. I'm not big on romances, but I still have my faves in that category, too, including a few author friends who are up-and-coming in that genre. I'm not big on poetry either, but I find your book *Your Chance To Hear The Last Panther Speak* fascinating. It's different, and so-ooo from your heart. It's *the real you*, Chase. I wrote a review on Amazon.com that I hope your fans will enjoy... My very favorite all-time author, living or dead, is the great Pat Conroy. His stories are so thrilling and real, and I love his similes. He has a poetic, rhythmical style of writing that enthralls me. *This Good Ol' Southern Boy is a genius.* I also love Dean Koontz, Stephen King, John Saul, James Patterson and Maxine Paetro, the usual beloved "biggies." Of up-and-coming authors, I adore Chris Platt's young adult novels; Christy Tillery-French's "Bodyguard" series; Chrissy McVay's Indian cultural books; Cheryl Kaye

Tardif's novels, especially *Whale Song*; Mary Lou Cheatham's cookbooks; Laurel-Rain Snow's "women friendship" books; and David Rehak's more "daring" fare. This list could go on and on because I'm partial to helping new authors achieve their goals. If I missed anyone, I'm sorry... Oops—almost forgot David Michael Slater who has written so many children's books that I adore: *Cheese Louise, The Ring Bear, The Flour Girl*...and now has a longer YA novel that's destined for glory: *The Book of Nonsense*. It was just released in October 2008 and is already winning awards. *Go, David!*

Chase Von: And because you're not only an acclaimed author, an honorary Kentucky Colonel, a former member of Romance Writers of America and Sigma Delta Chi, a top Amazon Reviewer, but also a former newspaper publisher and long-time California journalist, who has also hosted a Cable TV talk show...what do you think about the news of today? Not to guide your answer, but I find myself seeking alternative sources instead of listening to the major stations, because it just feels like it is News Entertainment to me.

Betty Dravis: Thanks, Chase, for your confidence in me. I agree with you wholeheartedly: in order to get unbiased news in today's world one has to be more selective where one gets the news. I still enjoy watching the prime-time evening news programs because they summarize the day's events quite well, but my alternate choices are panel discussions such as Barbara Walters's *The View*, CNN and educational channels. In this way, I receive various viewpoints and more detailed analysis about world events. And there's nothing I enjoy more than reading local news in the small daily paper...over a nice cup of morning tea. That gets my day off to a fine start.

Chase Von: Also, excluding the Great Depression, have you ever seen this country in a worse condition all the way around, from the mortgage crisis to the bail out to the over-extended troops and so on? And do you think that a change in Washington's leadership is going to really change anything?

Betty Dravis: Well, I may be getting older, Chase, but I'm not exactly a horse-and-buggy girl, you know. (Grin!) I was an infant during the Depression and my parents struggled through it just as other working-class Americans did. But seriously, *no*, I've never seen our great country in worse condition all around. *It's terrible...frightening...what's going on!* But I like to remain optimistic and hope that our President-elect Barack Obama will be able to make a difference. I think he's an honest, sincere man--fully dedicated to the citizens of our country--and that he'll try mightily to make a difference. I further feel that in order to accomplish anything, both political parties must learn to work together in better harmony for the good of all. I pray that God continues to bless our great country and "sheds His light on thee," as it says in the patriotic song "America the Beautiful."

Chase Von: On a lighter note, I saw photos on your Amazon Profile blog of you and your best friend Linda Bulger dressed up like "Gangster Girls" when she visited you in California. (Smile.) If you had said to me, "Go get me a Cabana Cigar, the *best*... and right now, *see*, and you hurry up about it, *see?*"... Well, I'd of jumped to do your bidding! You looked *that* authentic. *But your friend?* Sorry, she just looked huggable. (Smile.) She also needs a little more coaching on her Gangster "lean," if you know what I mean. (Smile.)

Betty Dravis: Aw-www, Chase, quit picking on Linny. She was visiting all the way from Maine, you know, and didn't bring her full Mafia gear. Whereas, my closet was right here and I had access to the proper clothing for the role. And are you saying I'm *not* huggable? Better be careful, buddy, my Don has a long reach--and Linda`s even longer. (Haven't you ever heard of "Whitey" Bulger?) If not, you should Google him... LOL

Chase Von: Uh-oh, I better change the subject. (Smile.) How do you stay so fit and healthy, and what are some of your favorite meals? Because I also saw where y'all fired up the grill, as well. Heh-heh :)

Betty Dravis: Don't let my photos fool you. I just happen to come from a very photogenic family, Chase. It's the high cheekbones, y'know. (Chuckles.) As for food, my favorite is lobster, of course, but I love salads, most Mexican food, and just about anything.

Chase Von: I recently got a manuscript that was written by my grandfather. I haven't finished reading it, but I am digging what I have read so far. It's like a snapshot of history. In one part he speaks of a boy getting his first pair of real pants when he is fourteen... In another, he talks about if a person didn't smoke or chew tobacco, at the end of the year they could buy themselves a brand new pair of shoes. (Smile.) How well do you think a book like that-- written with down-home country wisdom by a man who farmed all his life--would sell in today's market? Because I am going to be publishing it for my Mom, even though he is now deceased.

Betty Dravis: If you write it as a memoir with care, precision and clarity, then present it in dramatic fashion, it could sell well, but most of selling is in the marketing, as

Betty receives California State Award

you know. My favorite self-quote is: "Writing a book is like sliding down a rainbow; marketing it is like trudging through a field of chewed bubblegum on a hot, sticky day." In other words, writing a book is fun; marketing it is hard work. Nonetheless, I find it admirable that you wish to honor your grandfather in that way; that will make your mother happy too. Best of luck with that project. I'd love to read it one day.

Chase Von: What are some of the causes you feel most strongly about?

Betty Dravis: I have a dear, dear grandson who suffered a spinal injury in an accident. He and his family are active in the Christopher and Dana Reeve Foundation for Stem Cell Research. In fact, a portion of the proceeds of *1106 Grand Boulevard* has been ear-marked for SCR. To learn more about my grandson Seth James, go to this link:

http://bridges2hope.unite2fightparalysis.org/home/story/
52 SCR and Diabetes, Cancer, and Breast Cancer causes
are my pet charities. I also have a soft spot for Veterans
and support them whenever I can.

Chase Von: How important is family to you?

Betty's children: Debra Pangborn, Denyce "NeeCee" Dravis,
Mary Lee Francis, Robert Dravis, Mindy James, Allison Rodriguez

Betty Dravis: God, family and friends are the most
important things in my life. My children, grandchildren
and friends keep me happy, and grounded in reality. They
motivate me and keep me moving ever onward, ever
upward. But before anything or anyone comes God
because He's the one who has blessed me with loving
children and wonderful friends. I also love to read, write
and review books, as you might know. I'm an Amazon Top
1000 Reviewer (Top 37 in Amazon Canada), and am
branching out into reviewing for Midwest Book Reviews,
TeensReadToo and GoodReads, three of my favorite

websites for authors. I would be lost without my writing, and I know you will relate to that. (Big grin!)

Chase Von: What would you say if you were standing in front of a microphone that could be heard by every child on the planet––and regardless of what language it was they spoke, they would understand you? What positive advice would you give the children, if that were possible?

Betty Dravis book signing at Borders in Los Gatos, California

Betty Dravis: You know, Chase, this is a very hard-to-answer question because there are so many things children need to know in order to make it in today's world. But considering that these children speak many individual languages, the most universal thing to say would be "LOVE." I think everyone knows the meaning of that word, and when you get right down to the nitty-gritty, love is the primary moving force for good in the entire world...always has been, always will be! If I had access to TV to reach the world's children, to get my point across, I would have children, dogs and cats with me, and I'd demonstrate love by hugging and kissing the children and stroking and nuzzling the pets with great affection. But you know, Chase, *talking* love is easy. What we need to do is to *follow our words with action* by endeavoring to see that everyone in the world has food in their bellies and roofs over their heads. That not only *tells* them about love, it *shows* them love.

Chase Von: Where can our readers find out more about you? Your various websites and links to your books and other information?

Betty Dravis: First, Chase, thanks for this welcome opportunity to reach your vast audience with news of my writing. I appreciate it. I'm impressed by the caliber of your guests, and wish you continued success with this interesting, entertaining format. After speaking with you, I can see why you're so popular! Keep up the awesome work. My primary website is:
http://bettydravisauthor.googlepages.com/
My Amazon Profile website is:
http://www.amazon.com/gp/pdp/profile/A3MFUoGVZUV
H3K/104-5637778-6149507
My other cool sites that may interest your readers are:
http://yaynot.ning.com/profile/BettyDravis
http://coolbookoftheday.com/toonies/
http://www.coolbookoftheday.com/2008/09/02/1106-
grandboulevard/

Chase Von: On behalf of the *Student Operated Press* and myself, Betty, this has truly been an honor. I'm also looking forward to your audio interview with Judy because you are such a joy! May God continue to bless you, and you know I'll be in touch. Love and light always to you and yours.

Betty Dravis: Thanks for the kind words of inspiration, Chase. It has been my pleasure to speak with you. I'll let everyone know about your program––via my Amazon blog and other avenues. *You rock!*

Linda Bulger, President of Betty Dravis Fan Club

****

*"Seriously, I think a sense of humor is vital to everyone's happiness. And since humans are the only creatures that God granted the ability to laugh, I plan to use my gift and use it often.
I find that when I'm laughing and joking around with my friends, all my irritations and resentments vanish and a sunny spirit takes hold."*
- Betty Dravis, Author, Journalist
****

Interview with Vanessa Jay

TALENTED SINGER, DANCER, RAPPER
by Chase Von

Photo by Luca Rosseti

Chase Von: Hey, Vanessa... I'm really honored to do this interview with you, so on behalf of myself and the *Student Operated Press*, thanks so much for finding the time to tell our readers more about you!

Vanessa Jay: I am really honored to do this interview. So thank *you* for having me.

Chase Von: You're busy doing so many things it's hard to pick a place to start with you. But can you tell us what your younger years were like? I know you were born in Suriname and raised in Amsterdam. Also you were what we refer to here in the United States as a "child star." You even appeared at a very young age with the likes of Time Bandits and DeBarge as a dancer and back-up singer. How old were you when you went to the prestigious Amsterdam Ballet Academy and studied all the various forms of dancing? Is this something you truly desired as a child or were you placed there by your parents? And my main question, were you able to have a relatively normal childhood, being famous at such a young age?

Vanessa Jay: Well, my younger years were very happy. Like you said, I was born in a beautiful country and raised in a great place like Amsterdam. I've always had a huge passion for music and dancing, so for me it was only natural to start dancing at an early age. I started when I was twelve years old and was one of the lucky kids to be admitted to the prestigious Amsterdam Ballet Academy, so I felt really blessed to be given the chance to make my dreams come true. I was also surrounded by girls like me, so we really had a down-to-earth up bringing. The Dutch mentality is also very different than the one in the states; they tend to keep your feet firmly planted on the ground. *No big heads tolerated!* (Smile.)

Chase Von: The reason I ask is because sometimes kids do show--at a very young age--what they truly want to pursue in life. And other times they are forced into it by parents who want to live their own dreams through the lives of their children. Alina--an amazing singer and friend of mine who has a CD out now called *Piano and Sax* and quite a few others--did show very young what her calling was, and because you have turned out so sweet, well-rounded and kind-hearted, I felt that was an important question to ask. I don't have to tell you about some of the child stars that have had a difficult time adjusting to the adult life. So, VJ, I know you speak English and Italian, but just how many languages do you speak fluently?

Vanessa Jay: By traveling as much as I do, I was able to

Photo by Luca Rosseti

pick up some different languages on my way. I speak Dutch, English, French and Italian all fluently and I can safely get "about" myself in Germany.

Chase Von: While researching a bit on you, VJ, I saw you in pictures with Bono, Tears For Fears, Tommy Vee, Simon

Le Bon, the lead singer for Duran, Duran, internationally known supermodel Randi Ingerman, as well as with Michael Bolton and even Zucchero, whose 1988 album *Blue* was the highest-selling album in Italian history. And he's worked with everyone from Eric Clapton, to Shelia E, B.B. King, Luciano Pavarotti, Andrea Bocelli, Italian rapping sensation Jovanotti, Miles Davis Jeff Beck Cheryl Crow and even Elton John... You're also pictured with Savion Glover who starred in TAP with two legends: Sammy Davis Jr. and Gregory Hines! Not to mention, like yourself, he was a child prodigy and spent many years on *Sesame Street* and later--among his other many achievements--starred in the video by Stevie Wonder, *A Ribbon In The Sky,* and more recently as Mumble in the smash children's movie *Happy Feet* which also included Brittany Murphy. You're no stranger to stars, having so many of them as friends, but are you going to pursue a few more things here in the United States so more here can learn about your considerable talents?

Vanessa Jay: I had the opportunity through my work to meet a lot of great artists and people, so I always consider myself blessed. I'm always looking to expand my career and really don't put any limitations to the possibilities life will, or can, send my way. I just keep working hard and *who knows...?*

Chase Von: Not only do you know all forms of dance, rap and song, but like supermodel Randi Ingerman, you also model as well. I've seen some of your pictures and they are truly lovely. What are some of the magazines and articles you have appeared in, and also, since you are so multi-talented, do you ever see yourself tackling the big screen as an actress? Also, what are some of your favorite meals and how do you stay so lovely and in shape? Or in other

words, in addition to dance, which is a workout in itself, do you also have an exercise regime?

Vanessa Jay: Well thank you very much, indeed! But I've never been a professional model, even though I did some photo spreads and cover shoots for magazines. Some names for a few of them, off the top of my head, were *Trend Magazine, Hip Hop Magazine* and *Fashion Mag.* (Smile.) Regarding acting, it's not something I have given serious thought to, since I really respect every art form and think that to consider such a serious step, you really need the right preparation. Plus, there are so many talented actors out there. As for staying in shape.... well, I know it sounds cliché but, believe me I'm one of those people who can eat everything and not gain any weight. *Really!* Of course, I keep dancing and exercising three times a week, but I can't say *no* to my daily dose of chocolate! I also love Chinese, Thai, Italian and, of course, the food of my country—Surinamese!

Chase Von: One of my more recent interviews was with the lovely singing sensation Leah DeVon. She is also one of the new faces for Zale's Jewelry, as well. I know you have modeled for products in Amsterdam, but do you see yourself doing that in the future here in the United States?

Vanessa Jay: I'm definitely looking forward to breaking into the American market, so we'll see...

Chase Von: In 1990 you moved from Amsterdam to Italy and you have been busy ever since. You've done commercials, live TV and appeared in *Pavarotti & Friends, Festivalbar* and *Buona Domencia.* You've also done a live tour with Delmar Brown and worked with the talented and exceptionally well-known DJ Massimo Padovani on the track *Nasty Rhythm.* You've also collaborated with DJ

Enzo, Master Freez, R. Fame, Hit Aliens and Francesco Farfa. You've also hosted your own television show on *Match Music* called *City Day* and teamed up with Veronica Hit Radio where you co-hosted *We Can Dance Live*. Not to mention you have been the opening act for Rita Marley and Lauryn Hill in Pisa at *A Tribute To Bob Marley*. You're also widely known as one of the most successful MCs in all the best clubs throughout Italy. You're on "Tutti x Uno" and "Life Stories" with DJ Enzo, "Acidazzo" with Francesca Farfa, "La Colegiala" with Hit Aliens, "Back To The Track" with Ricky T, "I Can't Love Anymore" with Soul Division-ElectroBoogaloo, "Wildchild" with Abletone, and many, many more. You also have two CDs out now: *Abletone* featuring Vanessa Jay, Wild Child and Channel Balance, and *The Biggest Club Anthems Of All Time, Vol I*. How soon will you be releasing your solo project to all your fans? And where can readers purchase the two CDs just mentioned?

Vanessa Jay: My solo project should be ready by the end of the year and I'm very excited since I'm working with some very talented people. I can't reveal anything just yet! As for the two other CDs, those were collaborations with two well-known Italian DJs (DJ Castello and Ivan Iacobucci) and those tracks are available on websites like Beatport.

Chase Von: Who are some rappers, singers and just people in general that you yourself admire, and who are some of your mentors or role models?

Vanessa Jay: Well, I really admire those who obtain their goals and are positive role models at the same time...those who have the courage to change the world through their actions, even if that means risking their lives. So I'm really inspired by people like Gandhi, Malcolm X, Bruce Lee, and most recently by Obama. And of course, a little closer to home, my Mom and my Grandmother have been real inspirations. They've always taught me to be proud of my heritage. Seeing them raise a family with so much pride and dignity has been a great example for me. I also really respect strong woman like Rita Marley, Betty Shabazz and Mrs. Coretta Scott King...just to name a few.

Photo by Luca Rosseti

Chase Von: Where can our readers find out more about the lovely and multi-talented woman who calls herself Vanessa Jay? You know, like your websites and your links on YouTube?

Vanessa Jay: Basically, I keep my MySpace page really updated so by clicking; www.myspace.com/jayvanessa they can pick up on my latest releases, news and gigs.

Chase Von: What are some of the causes you truly feel strong about, VJ?

Vanessa Jay: I feel very strongly about causes like fighting AIDS, violence against women and children, poverty, cruelty against animals and child abuse, Chase. More really needs to be done in all of those areas!

Chase Von: How important is family to you, and what is your take on the state of our current world?

Vanessa Jay: Family is fundamental to me. I have a fantastic family and I am so proud to be part of them. Being a very spiritual person, I really believe in Karma, and looking at the state of the world it makes me realize that we human beings are in serious need to re-evaluate what's really important. Being successful is not the main thing in life. It's so much more important to be loved and to spread love as much as you can. I'm a serious believer in "what you sow is what you reap." *So you better sow roses!*

Chase Von: What would you say if you were standing in front of a microphone that could be heard by every child on the planet, and regardless of what language it was they spoke, they would understand you? What positive advice would you give the children, if that were possible?

Vanessa Jay: I would love to be able to tell every child that they have everything they need already in them. That each of them is beautiful and precious. That they deserve the best of life; to never underestimate their worth; and respect themselves and others. To stand united 'cause that's the only way that we human beings will get somewhere.

Chase Von: Are there any other projects you have in the works you can share with our readers and your fans? Maybe a little heads up so they can be on the lookout for them?

Vanessa Jay: Well, I'm busy expanding the project I've founded together with the well-known Italian DJ/Producer Castello named Electro Boogaloo. We've just done a successful club tour for Redbull in Europe and have different house-music projects that will be released by the end of this year. We're talking about another tour that will take us all around Europe, and *who knows*—we might even hit the states? And we're branching out with two sister companies called Electro Boogalounge—which has produced the successful single "Saxy" for widespread magazine *Acid Jazz*—and Electro Boogabeat, which will produce some of the material for my solo project. I've also got my own radio show in the works, so I'm really excited about that, and of course, my album! So that's what's keeping me busy.

Chase Von: On behalf of the Student Operated Press and myself, VJ, I really want to thank you for still finding the time to share yourself with our readers, especially with all you're doing. Wishing you the very best life has to offer and continued success always. And don't be a stranger. OK? (Smile.)

Vanessa Jay: I have to thank you once again for giving me the opportunity to share some of myself with you and your readers! I definitely hope you'll have me back in the future!

Photo by Luca Rosseti

****

"I would love to be able to tell every child that they have everything they need already in them. That each of them is beautiful and precious. That they deserve the best of life; to never underestimate their worth; and respect themselves and others.
To stand united 'cause that's the only way that we human beings will get somewhere."
- Vanessa Jay, Rapper, Singer, Dancer

****

Interview with Al Cole

AMAZING, TALENTED, ROMANTIC
by Chase Von

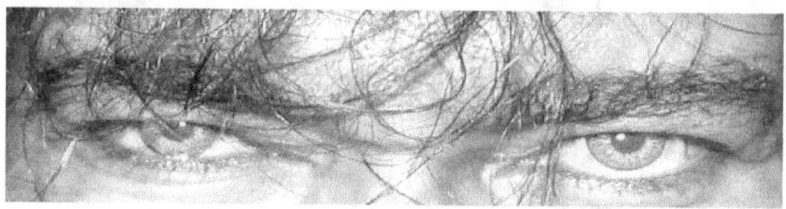

Chase Von: Al, on behalf of the Student Operated Press and myself, thanks for all that you do to squeeze this in. You are one busy man! I can think of a multitude of questions I want to ask you, but since you're one of those people who has done so very much, I figure I better start at the beginning. (Smile.) What was your childhood like? Where did you grow up? And did you have any idea all the things you are involved with now would be taking place in your adult life? And also, I know you have your own fan base all over, but I do want to truly thank you for sharing yourself with our readers.

Al Cole: Thank you, Chase. I've been asked the question many times: "Al, what was your upbringing like, how did you come to be so ardent in the area of 'Romanticism?'" I always love the question because it helps to define who I am. It's such a strong part of me, it's *real!* I can answer this question in a number of ways: The first and most direct answer is that I was truly born a romantic. I'm a product of a very loving, very special mother and father. I was blessed to have been born into a family where "the man of the house" was not only unafraid and unashamed to be loving, thoughtful, caring--even at times tearful toward his wife and his children--but knew that, in fact, this made him even more *the man!* As for my mother, she's the one who should really be talkin' to y'all 'bout romance, Baby... (Smile.) *What a great, loving and wise woman!* Another answer is all of the fantastic, innumerable influences I've had in people that I've met nationwide. I've had the good fortune to have traveled extensively across the U.S. Sometimes I feel as if I've met half of the American population first hand. So many of the marvelous people that I've met have left in me a part of their Individual greatness and brilliance. The flame lives on long after the acquaintance has ended. I know for a fact that all men carry in them the hope and the capability to be romantic... However, in so many cases, they just haven't really sought it out in themselves. And I know that all women carry within them the hope and acceptance of that romantic capability in a man...even if they are sometimes the ones who have to be the catalysts in a man's own yearning to seek it. I've learned, too, that we all sometimes make mistakes in our relationships. And that a relationship need not last forever in order for the truth of love to have been revealed in it. I've been most dearly blessed to have learned love from many of life's most wonderful, intelligent and deep-feeling women, and I know in my heart that without this factor, the other two factors that I have named--no matter how influential, no matter how endearing--would simply not have been quite as potent.

Chase Von: You interviewed a friend of mine recently, Donna Solitario, poet and author of *Embrace The Light.* A truly sweet soul... And when I was listening to the interview I have to admit, when I heard the intro, I was like: *I know Donna, and this doesn't sound quite like the show she should be on.* But I kept listening and I was amazed at the depth of your questions, and how you brought out all the things I am sure she wanted to share with the audience. In short, it was an amazing interview! And it made me think more on the intro and the things you had in the beginning by your adoring fans. It's like it began, and one thought it was going to be really about an adult conversation or theme. But then, when the actual interview kicked in, you were asking questions––and I mean deep questions––and giving deep feed-back as well as getting deep answers. What one might have thought was going to be a superficial thing, was really a very deep philosophical discussion. I know you have a lot of women that adore you and your show for obvious reasons, but how often do you get compliments on the actual serious things you address? And the truly in-depth things you bring out of your guest to share with your listeners?

Al Cole: Excellent set of questions, Chase. Yes, I do understand about the group of intros that I often use on my Radio Show "It`s All About Romance!" (Smile.) One uses standard intros to establish images of one's general show theme, regardless of the particular guests involved. In Donna's case, I already knew that I was going to make the shift to accommodate the real woman and her unique set of circumstances. The good TV- or radio-talk-show host should always have the knack of making himself a "blank slate" during the interview process. A blank slate that is written upon by––and expresses the true character of––his guest. After this is done, the host himself can address the particulars of his own experiences and character and re-direct them to the particular interests of his guest. The good host must always respect the dignity and life-direction of his guest. To address the second part of your question: Yes, I've been very lucky with women in my life; lucky with my radio show in Boston; lucky with my MySpace site; and now lucky with my HotMix106. com show. I do have many women who "adore me"(Smile), because I adore them. *It's a Mutual Adoration Society, Brother!* (Smile.) With guests who come on my show and compliment my eyes, voice, music and poetry, I go through the same sort of process that I've already described. However, we may joke, talk about sexuality; we may even get flirty with each other, but I always make it my business to turn the corner to the more serious, deeper side of them too. I love to explore all facets of where a person is coming from because I identify all of those facets within myself: the light-hearted, the flirtatious, the deep (sometimes the despairing), the philosophical and the spiritual. *That's real life! And I adore it all!*

Chase Von: I'm sure you're aware of this, as well: legendary actor Paul Newman went to be home. He was known for so many things, but his blue eyes were certainly one of them. I wasn't aware until watching a tribute that all the profits made on his salad dressing went to charities. I already admired him as an actor, but that was another side of him I wasn't, quite frankly, aware of. He didn't just entertain people, he really cared about making lives better for so many others on the planet. You, too, are known for your eyes, which might be even bluer–er---is that a word?– –than his were. (Smile.) I know they melt many of your female listeners, but you yourself are also not only a writer, a musician, a singer, and a radio host, but you also are very caring about the needs of others, as well. What are some of the causes you feel strongly about? And does having a platform like being a radio show aid you in being able to help those who really need it?

Al Cole: I'm glad you brought up Paul Newman. He's always been one of my favorite actors. I love his blending of cool and sensitivity in *The Hustler, The Long Hot*

Summer, Cool Hand Luke, and all of his other great movies. He has always been a creative inspiration to me, and I'm so impressed and moved by his long-term marriage to actress Joanne Woodward. I've always believed that one of the "measures of a man" is the woman in his life. With Paul Newman, that measure was indeed magnificent, having so elegant, intelligent, and captivating a wife as Joanne Woodward.... And regarding your other observation, *Yes, I do receive my share of compliments on my blue, blue eyes, man.* (Hah Hah!) And of course, I love and appreciate the compliments, but there is a very serious side of my life devoted to social and political involvement too. I am a member of a number of organizations that are directed toward fair housing, the severe problem of homelessness and education. These are topics that I would feel very comfortable to discuss on my show *It's All About Romance,* too, because when I use the term "romance," I know inwardly that I'm talking not only about my deep regard for men-women relationships, but for my ongoing love affair with the human race, as well. And to the second part of your question, being a radio show host can often aid in one's getting on some of the right committees, but after that, it still comes down to "de ole elbow grease" and sticking it out even when frustration tells you that you wanna quit.

Chase Von: I'm married, but I still adore women. (Smile.) I know you do, as well. For me, I was raised in a house where I had a father who was very strict, and it was a speak-only-if-spoken-to kind of thing. The only parent I could really relate with and share my thoughts with was my mother. He's passed on, but I still share everything with my Mom today. She's certainly not only my mother but a friend, as well, and the first friend I have ever had. Because of our relationship, I am one that, quite frankly, loves women. And about the only woman I have no liking for is what might be commonly called a gold-digger.

Attractive? Not necessarily pretty, large or small, tall or thin, black, white or whatever race... It doesn't matter to me. There is something--if you are willing to look--in them all that is beautiful. And I think that the most beautiful thing, regardless of how they might be appearance-wise, is they *carry* life. And no male, like it or not, would be on the planet had not one decided to do that for them. What are your feelings regarding the fairer sex? And do you think the world, or more precisely the US, is one day going to have a female president?

Al Cole: I truly believe that there is nothing more beautiful in the entire universe than a woman. And I am not speaking from simply the physical perspective. A woman generally has a more determined, tireless mentality than a man. It is not a question of intelligence here, but a stance of commitment. Women stand for greater compassion, dedication to feeling, and to more of an effort to inner values of honesty.... I guess I'm making us guys seem awful small in the comparison, aren't I, Brother? (Hah Hah!) But the truth is, we men could really "help our ownselves out" by listening a little bit more to the heart of a woman.... I believe that one day the US will have a woman president, very much in the same way that the US is currently on the verge of having its first black president. But whether any future president of the US is a woman or a black, the country certainly couldn't lose by electing a person with not only a tireless sense of determination, coupled with an effort toward honesty... but also a person with a woman's compassion.

Chase Von: Can you share one of you poetry pieces with

our readers, Al? One that deals with women and one that you think they would love to read.

Al Cole: This is a long one, Chase, but it's one of the most popular poems from my book *Romance for Women.* It's called "The Good Family."

The GOOD FAMILY!

In the beginning the Word was Mother kind.
The gift of earth lay enclosed beneath her captive hands -
That one certain Rush veiled in uncertainty.
Melt in her Innocence the warm, blue heavens,
Meld in her Wisdom the wild and flaming earth!

Here the fires of doubt and disbelief unchained
in a moment's call -
The call of Shadow extending its Light-tipped Bow
through the arrow of Creation!
Circling the Cool entrail,
Center-directed ...
Her Vision the foundation of all Existence!

...Mother kind now suddenly lost in the stillness
of Father time,
And Father time himself but a ghost-trimmed fume-
Created less from purpose than of need.

...At the moment this Gift was breathed,
the Wind ceased to be,
The Heavens shook at the dust of their own departure
And Sun echoed out a narrow heat-stained exit,
As all Hands joined Force in the whirl of its
Energetic stream -
Smile and Concept winced in the Throes of Darkness,
Shadow suddenly reveled in Light-trimmed Depth!

Two Bodies Sighed in a Power mix so complete
that they shed in an Instant all illusion of skin,
...Then forcefully twisted upward to become
the vast Entrail from which Skin is carved!

And there!
The First Miracle lied unearthed
in the warm recesses of its streaming black Shadow,
Through Cool strands of unearthly White Light-
Heaven-stunned, streaking,

Till...
In the wake of this Miracle,
Fatherhood rose to Heights he had never known Existed!
The Angel of himself Climaxed in Amazement!
...And all for the Love of Miraculous Mother Nature!

...For the Love of this Woman, Father time stood still ...
Then stood on his head!
Walked on air!
...For a riveted second of Motherhood's Time
he played the Court Jester
mindlessly mimicking the character and craft
of that Wonder-Lady now locked Deep inside him!

Look!---he Captured the moment with mimed Perfection,
Seized her fascination in his playful hip-swiveling strut!
...Oh, let the knees buckle, the calves dip,
Stand on tippy-toes and make the ankles pray to high
Heaven
for the solid and steady support of the feet!

...For the precious and lasting Acclaim of a Lady ...
This Miracle gave Birth to Reality!
...And beamed with the pleasures
of Innocence and Baby Talk!

Yes, that came too---the Baby Talk!
Man's kind Tribute
to this honey-bunny, wide-eyed, passion-poodle, love-dove!
To his dream-dipped, sugar-charmed, honey-dumpling
Sweetheart
named Womankind!,
this Angel! this Darling!---
...A Vision of Mother kind as our Nurturing, Adorable
Baby!---
a Baby who needed a baby . . .
A Baby needing Now,
to become also Mother!!

No, you can't fool the Mother in a Woman,
She will respond.
She can sense the good Father in the appetites of her womb,
The pangs of her breasts;
In her thirst and hunger to nourish him,
Nurture him, to Reproduce with him;
In her yearning to become his Baby -
Special, darling and precious...
And for him to become Hers!

Motherhood can sense the good Father in the truth-
revealing testimonies of her very own "Male Ideation",
In her prime Intuitive Savvy to Produce with Fatherhood
the Pride & Joy of everything we have as Humans,
The integrity and wonder of <u>our Nature & Time</u>---
In her Delicate, Time-Honored Wisdom to produce with
Fatherhood
the endearing and ongoing Reality
of the GOOD FAMILY!!!

Chase Von: Thank you, I'm sure the women reading this are going to be like: *Where can I find more?* I myself like to think that regardless of color, humanity is really just one big family, wish more saw it that way. (Smile.) You're a professional musician who has performed throughout the nation, you also play R and B, Jazz, Rock and even Country! You're also a poet, an author, a radio host, and... well, is there anything else you do we aren't aware of? I imagine just from listening to your interviews you must be an avid reader, as well. Because your questions are always informed and intelligent and also coming from a place where, you know, you actually care when you ask them. But my friend Willard Barth has made it clear to me that the people who are generally the most successful are those who expand their comfort zones. Meaning you do something you haven't done. What you haven't done is beyond me, but I'm wondering if you perhaps see acting in your future... or the Olympics? (Smile.) Which could happen, mind you, but something more that I could see for you with your genuine concern and communications skills is your own talk show––like a TV talk show. Has that been anything you have considered? And what are some things you might not be doing now that you think you can see yourself pursuing in the future?

Al Cole: It's notable that you bring up acting. I admire the art form, even though I have never myself been involved in it. Something must have been passed on here, though, because my son is studying acting and is committed to doing that as a career. He's such a talented and compassionate individual, and truly relates to the inner feelings of the characters that he plays. I'd love to try my hand at the world of being a TV talk-show host too. I think it's important to have hosts out there who not only talk about "the heat of the moment" but can also get down into "the heart of the matter too... the human heart. Another thing I want to pursue is the tragedy of human starvation, especially when it affects children. *There's no damn excuse for it!* People have a right to the basics––no matter whose special interest it might shake up!

Chase Von: Recently I saw a video by Wayman Tisdale. He's a former NBA star, gold-medal Olympian, and world-class musician. He also recently lost his leg above the knee due to bone cancer. He has this video where he is talking to his fans and saying he can't wait to get back out there! He's so motivated and happy and positive and it's like he knows his amputation is big, but he is not letting that stop him. I was so blown away by how he could take such a huge thing and refuse to let it stop him. I can't watch it without crying tears of respect. Who are some of your mentors? And some of the people you admire and that you feel helped guide you to where you are today? And who are some of the people you have worked with you would love to work with again, and people you haven't yet, but aspire to?

Al Cole: Good question about mentors. The truth is, my mentors have typically come from family! Family, in the broad sense of the word. Of course, starting with my mother and father, whom I've already mentioned. Also, my sisters, elegant women married to great men; my Aunts, Uncles, many of my cousins; my closest friends. Also the very special and beautiful "Romances" in my life––the many fascinating and astounding women that I've been blessed to have shared love with. But perhaps the greatest mentor of all has been my son. *He's a fantastic human being!* When he was born I was right there as he entered the world. That night I spent the entire night right in the hospital bed with his mother and him (of course it was breaking the rules, lol), and it struck me that there was a natural magnificence about him that indeed made him "the Father of the Father!" *He is that Wonderful!* He is a born romantic, a sparkling talent, and the best combination of both his mother and his father.

Chase Von: Your fans can catch pieces of you already in so many ways (Smile) from listening to your popular radio broadcast on Boston's 100.7 WZLX to reading your popular poetry book *Romance For Women* or your CD *Captivation*, which is an absorbing blend of your music and your many poetry readings. But being a popular radio-show host in a huge city like Boston, and having acquired fans in Los Angeles and New York and all over the country and the world for that matter, how difficult is it for you to handle the "being famous" part? Which, incidentally, is not something I have any issues with yet. Heh-heh :) You have to be famous to have famous-like issues. (Smile.)

Al Cole: I always try to keep things in perspective in the area of "fame." I'm famous in certain sectors, but not yet in others. I'm well-known and admired by certain people, but relatively un-known by others. When my abilities are exposed world-wide, and when a large sector of humanity is privy to what I do, then I believe that humility and responsibility will be the two most significant aspects of fame that I'll have to come to terms with. I would expect myself to be as humble and responsible with fame as I have, generally, been forced to be with oblivion!

Chase Von: Judyth Piazza is my boss here and what an incredible soul she is. You're going to be doing an audio with her in the future and that's something I really don't want to miss. She started the *Student Operated Press* herself and it has grown incredibly since its inception. Students all around the world not only read the news here, but they contribute as well. She's also gathered together mentors like John Basedow; world-famous fitness expert Djelloul (Del) Marbrook, an intellectual with few equals and the former chief editor for a few of this countries top-notch newspapers; Deremiah *CPE mentor/columnist, and inspirational speaker and motivator; Simon T. Bailey, mentor/columnist; Dr. Christina Bautista, MD (MA) who contributes; Glenn Brandon Burke mentor/speaker who also speaks at prisons to motivate people throughout the country; and a host of others who are some of the finest individuals you could come across. She was in her thirties when she began, from what I remember, and she has created a vast empire, and as the host of *The American Perspective*, she has interviewed so many famous people, I can't keep up with all of them! When did you, yourself, pursue the radio-host thing, and more importantly, do you think that it is ever too late for someone, anyone, to pursue their dreams?

Al Cole: I have been doing full-time radio in Boston for the last seven years. It was only a month-and-a-half ago that I was offered the chance to be a regular host on the very popular Internet Station HotMix106.com! For me, it's never too late to pursue my dreams. For others, the question would be: *How much do I want it compared to all of the pressures that are telling me to drop the hell out?* It is possible to prevail against the torrents, especially if you have that inner voice telling you that this is your particular "calling," that the message you carry is of benefit to all of humanity. In short, if your inner voice coupled with outer response is telling you that you were *born* for this! When you're truly born to deliver the message, only the throes of death can stop the procession...and if you're a believer in reincarnation, even death ain't a big enough foe, Brother!

Chase Von: Earlier this week I dropped my kid off at

school, one to the babysitter, and then I went to a store to try and find a computer program. Maybe it's just here, or this state, but it hit me: I didn't see any bumper stickers on *any* cars for any political candidates. *This close to an election for the future ruler of this nation?* I just thought: *How strange?* If it is just here, so be it, but is it like that where you're at in Boston? And if so, is that, perhaps, a silent statement being said nationwide as to what people really think about the whole process these days? If I had my druthers, Cynthia McKinney would be our next POTUS, but since you are a respected radio-show host in a large major city, I would like to know what you think about our political situation here, and especially what you think about this bail-out thing. I see dark days ahead for this country, and I don't know if the masses are even aware that might be the case. What are your thoughts, and do you think we will be able to get back on track here or what?

Al Cole: I'm with you—I don't see the bumper stickers, either. Not to mention the gut enthusiasm. It's easy to get worked up over a media extravaganza like a convention... but when it comes down to individual heart-to-heart talks in the quiet of one's living room, I think that a lot of people are seriously questioning whether either candidate would really impact a sizable dent into the mass of the average American's dwindling pocketbook. As to this bail-out thing, the general method to "big-business madness" seems to be that the public is expected to suffer through their successes (with no individual profit) and to subsidize their failures. Is there really anyone with an ounce of sense that would honestly hold to such a poor business standard?

Chase Von: I started asking this question a while ago,

from politics to food! (Smile.) But I think readers really do like to know what some of the celebrities like to grub on. So what are some of your favorite meals?

Al Cole: I try to eat healthy, while not sacrificing taste. Is this the sort of thing that can still be done? (Smile.) Yogurt with blueberries, peaches, flax meal and tofu! *Awright!!* ...countered by Campbell's Chicken Noodle Soup! (Hah Hah!) This is true! Sometimes I make my own chicken soup by throwing a whole bunch of chicken legs into a great big kettle with a few ounces of rice, some mushrooms, and a few bouillon cubes on the side. I let it all boil up for an hour, and––*voila!* Well, what can I say?... I'm a bachelor!

Chase Von: How important is family to you, and what is your take on the state of our current world?

Al Cole: Family, of course, as most people would answer, is extremely important. My son is the shining star of my accomplishments. My involvements in education matters have led me to believe that some of the essential problems in our educational system could be greatly remedied by a little bit more "hands on" involvement by parents. I believe the over-riding factor contributing to less than optimum parental involvement is overworked schedules. We've become a society of people enslaved to work in order to subsidize our exorbitant mortgages and rents. Everyone knows that this is hell on the family, on education, the economy, and on our quality of life, in general, but it might take the tragedy of a bail-out to finally bring us to our senses. Either a bailout or a sincere opting on the part of individual families to take the bull by the horns and slow down the pace. Essentially, to settle for a lower standard of living for the sake of doing justice to the overall quality of life of the family itself... But of course, this sort of justice is not really justice at all, and it's a damn shame that the average family would even have to put themselves through the process of opting for this alternative, when it seems more and more obvious to us all that the brunt of the problem is really embedded in our top "leadership" in the first place.

Chase Von: What would you say if you were standing in front of a microphone that could be heard by every child on the planet and regardless of what language it was they spoke, they would understand you? What positive advice would you give the children, if that were possible?

Al Cole: Children hold the experience of their future adulthood in their here-and-now present. Adults hold the experience of their past childhood, also in their here-and-now present. Many have come to understand that the real key to lasting communication lies in connecting with the power that is inherent in the *now!* The fact that both a child and I are living *now,* indicates that I actually have more in common with that child than I would have with an adult my own age who was living 3,000 years ago. We must, as human beings, strive to identify with each other's problems, accomplishments and exultations as though they were our very own. I know that in my own situation as a father, I have never sought to diminish the importance of my son's problems, accomplishments and exultations simply because he is "a kid" and as a result he has generally been able to allow the "future adult in him" to relate positively to my own problems, accomplishments and exultations as if they were his own. I would encourage more adults to presently connect to the past child in themselves when dealing with children, and thereby encourage the children of our planet to tap into all of the present delights and challenges that life could hold for them in their coming adulthoods.

Chase Von: Can our readers find your music and book and more information on you and your radio show at MySpace? And can you give them your other different websites and links where they can also buy it and learn more about you and your multiple talents?

Al Cole: Sure, My three main links are:
www.alcoleradioandromance.com
www.myspace.com/alcolemusic.com
hotmix106.com
My book *Romance for Women...and for All Mankind* and my CD *Captivation* (Music & Poetry Reads for the Inspired!) can be both purchased at my main website www. alcoleradioandromance.com ––just Click on the book cover or the CD cover and it will take you directly into my PayPal purchasing site!

Chase Von: Al, on behalf of the *Student Operated Press* and myself, I really appreciate you finding the time to share yourself with our readers. Now they can learn more about what Al Cole Holics and check out your broadcast and see what I am talking about when I say your shows are very deep and thought-provoking. I'm wishing you continued success, and how long do I have to prepare before I go on your show? (Smile.)

Al Cole: A lifetime, Brother! (Smile.) Actually, Chase, I'm pretty easy as an interviewer. I've come to know, in my life, that we all share certain basics as human beings. When I tap into the basics with one person, I find that, barring the specifics, it generally strikes the right chord with other individuals. It's kind of like the same Interview with different and fascinating individual twists. A little bit of a variation on the same sort of human adventure!

Chase Von: I think you should have Judyth Piazza on first, then me. That way, I can prepare myself more, and since you two are veterans at it, it would be a great learning curve for me. (Smile.) Again wishing you all the success in the world, and thanks again for finding the time for this. One love, Brother!

Al Cole: My pleasure, Chase. I look forward to having you and Judyth on my show *It's All About Romance* on HotMix106.com real soon.

Romance For Women

Al Cole

****

"When you're truly born to deliver the message, only the throes of death can stop the procession...and if you're a believer in reincarnation, even death ain't a big enough foe, Brother!"
- Al Cole, Radio Host, Poet, Musician

****

Interview with Barbara Evans

BEAUTIFUL MODEL, SINGER, ACTRESS
by Chase Von

Chase Von: Barbara, on behalf of myself and the *Student Operated Press*, I thank you for doing this interview. I know from speaking to you, you have various things on your plate, so thanks so much for squeezing this in.

Barbara: Thank you and the *Student Operated Press* for taking time out of *your* schedule to give me this opportunity!

Chase Von: Just from speaking with you on the phone, it's obvious you've led what some would call a fairytale life. Going to model in Europe and living there all those years and even becoming fluent in various languages... How many languages do you speak? And what was it like for you, initially, going to a foreign country and not only having to deal with the very demanding profession of modeling, but at the very same time, adjusting to what must have, at least at first, been an entirely new world, literally?

Barbara: Initially, it was quite a challenge. It was all so new. *Everything!* From traveling to a foreign country, professional modeling, dieting, getting by in a brand new language... whewww... I was lucky, because at the time I had an Italian boyfriend who possessively stood by my side. Thanks to him and my ability to adapt, I was able to stay focused. I spoke Spanish before I left the states. Spanish helped me with the basis of the romantic languages--which include Italian, French, Spanish and Portuguese. Now I can communicate in each of those languages. I particularly embraced Italy's culture and became fluent in Italian. The modeling profession has changed drastically in just the last ten years. Back then they still wanted models with "meat on their bones." Thank goodness for that because I was not what they call "slim." The average size was an eight. I measured in at a whopping size ten and still worked. I was accepted because they said my "pretty face" and "features" saved me. Whatever the case may have been, I was happy. Now the designers demand an average of a size zero, no matter what your face looks like!

Chase Von: What were your younger years like? I know from interviewing Shawn Richardz, who is also a model as well as actress, she knew very early in life what she would eventually be doing. Did you know you would enter into the entertainment field at a very young age? Or were you drawn to it later... or "discovered" by someone with an eye for talent? Also, how supportive have family members and friends been of you pursuing your dreams?

Photo by Alex Garcia

Barbara: I've always been a clown and always loved to make everybody laugh. Being the youngest of eleven kids, I guess that was my way of getting attention. I love to see people laugh and be happy. Even today I feel that laughs cause an abyss of positive energy and a spiritual connection that spreads throughout the atmosphere. When I was five I knew that I wanted to be in the entertainment business. My siblings always thought that if anybody in the family would "make it," it would probably be the kid sister since I always was a clown. If I hadn't become a model and singer I probably would have become a comedian. But wait...! Maybe it's not too late...

Barbara Evans and Richard Gere

Chase Von: Being an American and in a foreign land now, regardless where it might be--I've heard from some--is not smiled upon. Did you run into any of that or was it something you didn't experience at all? Friends of mine who travel pretty regularly have told me that, generally, wherever they go, there isn't any hostility directed at them, *per se.* But people are curious as to what they, themselves, think because the genuine consensus seems to be more anger towards our government rather than individual Americans... because there are plenty of Americans that aren't pleased, as well.

Barbara: I spent most of my time in Italy, so I can tell you about my experience living there. I ran into some people in small Italian villages who had never seen black folks before in their entire lives; maybe on TV, but never in person. Some were receptive and open and some were narrow-minded and ignorant. In Italy you get a mix. However, I must say that Italians have issues amongst themselves. Many northern Italians are racist towards the southern Italians. Be it because southerners are darker skinned or they talk differently, etc... Does that ring a bell? Many of the northerners have it out for the southerners because they say the southerners are lazy and don't like to work. Consequently, the northerners have to pick up all the taxes. But, hey, that's totally political. In several occasions I was looked at differently than a brother or sister straight from Africa. Even some of the Africans in Italy looked at me differently. I accept our cultural differences, but we are still one. Ever since the 1950s or so, the Italians looked upon America as the "American dream"... Hollywood... the "land of opportunity." I explained to my friends that although America was the land of opportunity for many of their Italian ex-patriots, opportunity was not equal for all. Many Europeans see

America as "The Land of Oz"... a kind of utopia composed of exaggeratedly large buildings, highways, etc. Some of them find it fascinating, but many others like to come here on vacation and head back home. What America lacks in culture and history it makes up for in diverse opportunity.

Chase Von: One of the reasons I asked that was you were a very public person overseas, not only modeling but also appearing on television there, as well as performing music for live audiences. In Milan alone, you appeared in *Scherzi a Parte, You've Been Punked, Come Thelma & Louise,* a reality series *Diretta Stadio,* a sports TV program, *TG Rosa - Italian Celebrity News,* as well as *Re x Una Notte,* a look-alike talent show, just to name a few. All this, while also performing back-up singing for the likes of Mariah Carey, and various other engagements with the San Remo National Italian Music Festival. You've also worked with Timbaland and music sensation Wyclef's videos, as well as a celebrity psychic! Are you really psychic or was that just acting, and who are some of the people you truly enjoyed working with and performing with...and ones you hope to work with in the future?

Barbara: I was called in for the Celebrity Psychic commercial to speak to another person who had a reading done. I believe everyone has the ability to tap into their right brain hemisphere and develop the so called "psychic abilities." I did some research and found out that, apparently, the human race communicated telepathically long before we had the ability to speak. The San Remo National Music Festival was a blast. I was fortunate to perform there three times. It is *"the"* music event of the year. It's kind of like the Grammys, Oscars and American Idol all rolled up into one! In San Remo I sang backing vocals for different artists, and it helped take my career to another level. Mariah came to Milan for a show on her European tour, and at the very last minute she requested a gospel group to back her on her hit "Make it Happen." I was called in with a number of other performers. We did rehearsals and all and didn't get to see the girl until she set foot on the stage. *Can you believe that?* I saw Mariah for the first time on the same stage... singing together with her! It was exciting. I spoke to her at the "meet-and-greet" and she was social. That was the year she was receiving bad publicity, had a breakdown, her movie plummeted and people were dissin` her. I remember telling her, "No matter what people say about you, you keep doing what you're doing in your music career because you are making a difference––even for your brothers and sisters overseas!" She then smiled and asked where I was from... Many artists come to Miami to record and to film their videos because of the low production costs in the calm, laid-back atmosphere of Miami. I was an extra in Flo-Rida`s (feat Timbaland) *Elevator* video plus the Wyclef`s *The Sweetest Girl* video. It was cool being on the set chatting with those guys, but it only fed the fire in me. I then started taking my songwriting more seriously and decided to become a recording artist in my own right.

Chase Von: There's no doubt that your stunning good looks will continue to carry you far in the modeling world but singing and acting are too different animals, so to speak. Yet you're excelling in both of those, also, and even produce and publish your own music. In the future will you be producing others with your company? Or are you doing that now? And who is this famous relative of yours that won Star Search? My mind's drawing a blank. (Smile.)

Barbara: The Italians have an old saying: "*L`occhio vuole* *la sua parte,"* which basically translates: "it's nice to see beauty/beautiful things." This may be true, but just like those old church people used to say: "It's not the outside but the inside that counts." I feel that modeling, singing and acting go hand in hand. They complement each other and have the same basis... the projection of emotion, whether it be a beautiful fashion shoot where you have to project a certain emotion to get the right shot, or projecting your emotion to interpret a certain song, or even projecting an emotion to portray a certain character. As of 2006 I became an official ASCAP publisher. I collaborate with some of Italy's top house music DJs and co-produce house music for Europe, featuring the likes of soulful international vocalists from around the globe. Together with my partner Roberto Livesu, we produce some of Europe's hottest club tracks. The website is www.cool-live.com The 2 latest tracks Roberto and I produced were signed with the German record label Kingdom Come. And... that famous relative of mine who you mentioned who won Star Search is Tiffany Evans. She's my big brother's daughter and is signed with Sony/Columbia Urban Records. She's collaborating with Ciara and Bow Wow. *Shout out to Tiffany! Props to you!*

Chase Von: I know you just released four songs and they're all hot: *Angel, Some 1's Talking, It's Your World Now and Rare Sensitivity.* Was there anything that is taking place in your own life that is being reflected in your lyrics? Also, what are some future projects you are going to be working on you can share with our readers?

Barbara: Right now I'm spinning twelve plates on long sticks... Chicago's Radio Station V103 together with Clear Channel provided my first national platform:

Photo by Alex Garcia

400 national Internet radio stations to play my songs, the ones you mentioned above.

"SOME1'S TALKIN":
http://www.v103.com/cc-common/artist_submission/player.html?art=185808&gateway=exiting

"ANGEL":
http://www.v103.com/cc-common/artist_submission/gatewayplayeroas.html?art=186328

"IT'S UR WORLD":
http://www.v103.com/cc-common/artist_submission/player.html?art=186310&gateway=exiting

"RARE SENSITIVITY":
http://www.v103.com/cc-common/artist_submission/player.html?art=186307&gateway=exiting

Anthony Mac (aka Trac-a-Minute) of Sikol Entertainment, N. J. and Daniele Manca (Nutkee Productions, Sicily, Italy) recently produced those brand-new songs that were released in August 2008. We're actually looking for a record label, so if any of you major and/or independent labels are reading this... Holla at me and check out those beats at:
WWW.MYSPACE.COM/THEREALBARBARAEVANS
Some of the lyrics reflect situations I, personally, went through, but all in all, I keep positive and prevail. When I first started writing songs I'd shut a part of myself off. Now I write with my heart on my sleeve, which can be

somewhat disconcerting, but I'm at peace with myself when I do. I'm also collaborating with Theos Eaton. He's an international songwriter and performer. We've formed a group with some of the *meanest* musicians ever. The group is called Master Classe. We perform a review of the 40's Cotton Club, 50's & 60's Motown, 70's Funk, 80's old school...up to today's hits. We'll soon tour south Florida and hit major cities in the US and Europe.

Chase Von: How do you stay in such fantastic shape and what are some of your favorite European Meals? And were there any American meals you call favorites you had to miss out on while there? And are you filling that void now that you're back? (Smile.)

Barbara: On a good week I'll go to the gym three, maybe four times. I love the Italian Mediterranean cuisine and all the local specialties you find in the different regions. There's much more to Italian cuisine than just pasta. At first it was new and different. They don't put mayonnaise on their sandwiches. I remember eating those dry *panini*. You'd almost choke on that dry bread if you didn't quickly wash it down with some cappuccino or something. I quickly got used to it because "models didn't need to eat that stuff anyway," they used to tell me. Whew... Ironically, today I don't use mayo or any condiments at all except for olive oil. By embracing the Italian culture, I adapted quickly. Even now whatever I cook, I prepare it *Ala Italian,* I must confess. I have a sweet tooth, but my diet mainly consists of no meats, no pork, etc. I eat only organic whole foods and drink lots of water. However, I still eat fish. Can't take *everything* out all at once, now can we?

Chase Von: Normally, I would just say, "Who are some of the people you truly admire?" and an actress would name normally other actresses. But in your case, who are some of the actresses and actors, singers and models you truly admire and look up too?

Barbara: I admire people who are in the entertainment field and some who are not in this field, but as far as actors, I feel many have mastered their craft. There are too many to mention, but to name a few, I really admire the work of Morgan Freeman, Jack Nicholson, Angela Bassett...and I can't forget my fellow Italian-Americans like Robert DeNiro and Al Pacino (by the way, their ancestors come from the south of Italy). Those guys are phenomenal. I'd really love to work with them in the near future. *I'm ready to pay my dues!* In the music world, if I could just *meet* Michael Jackson. If I could *sing* with Michael just once, I'd do cartwheels and backward flips across the stage. Michael can sleep in a tank, be Peter Pan, or dangle his baby... I don't care. *I love him!* I'd also absolutely love to do at least one song with Prince. Come on Prince...let's coronate just once! Patti La Belle (my idol), Madonna, Ne-Yo, Timbaland, Missy Elliot, Pharell Williams (I met Pharell in Rome) and many others I'd like to work with.

Chase Von: How important is family to you, and what is your take on the state of our current world?

Barbara: Coming from a family of eleven kids, just the mere existence of my brothers and sisters is sacred to me. We don't see each other as often as we'd like, but we share an unconditional love and respect for each other. Our mother passed away when I was a little girl. I, naturally, counted on the older ones for the support, comfort, friendship and the love that our mother gave me. Our father passed away twelve years ago, but throughout the years he was able to instill his values upon us. Just like many other families we've been through trials and tribulations, but love saved us in many occasions and that's what I feel the world needs now. I agree with all those treehuggers and hippies from the 60s. All the "Woodstockers" out there that spread the love that exceeded racial and cultural diversities and transcended geographical boundaries. Who knows...maybe the enlightening effects of Woodstock helped to curb the Vietnam War? Who's to say? But after that, something else happened in society, and up until this day I look around and see how many people still need love. It may sound corny, but I feel love conquers all.

Chase Von: What would you say if you were standing in front of a microphone that could be heard by every child on the planet and regardless of what language it was they spoke, they would understand you? What positive advice would you give the children, if that were possible?

Barbara: I would prefer to give a message to the adults because we are the ones guiding, molding and teaching those children. I'd tell the adults to wake up *at once!* Take charge of your own mind, efforts and decisions. Develop self-esteem, self-respect, seek evolution and create values--and most importantly: spread love.

Chase Von: Where are the best places our readers can find out more about you and all the various projects you have worked on and are you working on?

Barbara: Everybody can check me out at:
www.myspace.com/therealbarbaraevans
www.impnow.com/Profiles/BarbaraEvans and www.cool-live.com

Chase Von: On behalf of the *Student Operated Press* and myself, Barbara, thanks again for fitting us in so our readers could learn more about you and all the various things you are doing. It was a true pleasure, personally, to speak with you on the phone, and I hope we do that again some time soon. Love and light to you and continued success in all you do!

Barbara: I thank the *Student Operated Press*, and thank you, Chase Von, for taking time out of your schedule to talk to me. Peace, love, light and music.

****

"In the music world, if I could just meet Michael Jackson. If I could sing with Michael just once, I'd do cartwheels and backward flips across the stage!"
- Barbara Evans, Singer, Actress, Model, Songwriter
****

****

"It may sound corny, but I feel love conquers all."
- Barbara Evans, Singer, Actress, Model, Songwriter

****

Italian fashion photographer Maurizio Montani

Interview with Dawn Huffaker

GIFTED POET, VOICE OF NATURE
by Chase Von

Chase Von: Hey, Dawn, and on behalf of the *Student Operated Press* and myself, I really want to thank you for taking the time to give us this interview. I've read your book *Flights of Fancy Vol. 1* and you truly write beautifully. I felt as if I was transported back to another world that used to exist, one where things were a lot more peaceful than they currently are in this world of ours. But before we discuss your writings, I would like for our audience to learn more about you, the author. Can you tell us what some of your first memories were--when you realized due to the mysterious illness you suffered while you were only eight months old? How you might have felt differently than perhaps other children?

Dawn: Thank *you*, Chase. I'm happy to be here. My first memories weren't all that different from other kids. I knew

I couldn't run and play like my younger sister, and yet it didn't make me feel left out. My family just found a way for me to participate, even if I was just the scorekeeper at times. I do remember trying to learn to stand by myself, and attempting to walk with crutches. Neither was very successful. I fell a lot. Mom worked with me every day for several years. By the age of ten, I had to give up on the idea of using crutches. I needed surgery on my back to fix the scoliosis curve that I had. Spent a year in a cast from my neck to hips. I was sad at first that I couldn't keep trying. However, Mom had told me from the start that I was no different from anybody else. This philosophy gave me a basis to grow from—that the inability to walk would not hold me back.

Chase Von: You've spent a great deal of your time living in New Mexico, and your love of the beauty that the state has to offer is truly evident in your writings. Also, you've shared with me that some of the teachers weren't apparently all that pleased to have to deal with a student in a wheelchair. I also know from first-hand experience that children, themselves, can be quite cruel when it comes to people that they perceive are a bit different than themselves. How was it going to school for you, and do you think that overall it was a rewarding experience and that people, in general, are becoming more accepting of those who have different challenges bestowed upon them by life?

Dawn: Yes, New Mexico is a very beautiful place. Mom was wise to start me in first grade. I was with the same kids for twelve years. We learned to rely on each other like one extended family. When I was in first through third grade, my friends thought it was neat that I had wheels. During school time, I used either a wheelchair or walker.

At recess, we'd play that I was a train and they'd take turns pushing me. It was fun. In fourth grade, I was teased by a couple of bullies for a few weeks, but they were cruel to several kids. It stopped when I told on them. School was great. I loved to learn new things and found it very rewarding. The problems with certain teachers were difficult and upsetting, but other staff members would step in and offer their help. I was very blessed to know these caring people. I think people are more accepting of people with challenges now. It helps that they see us out and about, and living our lives.

Chase Von: It became evident to me while reading your life synopsis, that you have done some incredible things in your time. You'd managed to fit in with your classmates, and despite having to deal with a world that wasn't quite made for your particular situation--i.e. just getting access to the buildings because they weren't always accessible by wheelchairs--surely you managed somehow despite that. However, something else deeply disturbed me, and that was that you went on to make straight A's in every class from seventh through twelfth grade, still some of the teachers thought you might be slow or retarded. And you continued on to do that in college, as well for a total period of ten years. You graduated co-Valedictorian in your class, and then went on to major in Computer Science with minors in English and Biology and again graduated at the head of your class with a 3.975 GPA from Western New Mexico University. So the first question I wanted to ask is: Do you think if you hadn't have been the one who was forced, because of fate, to be in a wheelchair, that you would have applied yourself that hard in your studies? And the second one is: Do you think that you, who were the student, ended up teaching the ones that were the teachers far more than they perhaps taught you?

Because it's clear that they had already reached some inaccurate judgments and preconceived notions concerning you...and who knows how many others?

Dawn: I don't know how hard I would have studied under normal circumstances. I am a go-getter, though, so I think I'd have still done my best. Besides, my parents were both teachers and they valued education. *Yes, I did!* I believe I changed their minds about associating academic ability with physical limitations. They do not go hand-in-hand. In fact, in my computer business I met up with some of my former teachers. They told me that they were very proud of me. I even trained a few on how to use their computers.

Chase Von: How long do you believe it will be before the state of New Mexico recognizes you as one of their state treasures? Because you have certainly made it evident in your writings how beautiful a place it can truly be. (Smile.) I would think travel brochures would be hitting you up constantly to get the go-aheads to use pieces of your work, and that's a serious statement as well.

Dawn: (Smile.) I honestly don't know. It takes time to get noticed and develop a readership. It would be a great honor, though.

Chase Von: You ran your own computer business for sixteen years. *That's a feat for any one of us!* And I'm especially awed because I--who manage somehow to jack them up on a regular basis--love them, but often end up with crashed ones. (Copyrighted, by Chase Von on this date, May 6, 2008, Chase Von and Dawn Huffaker have sole rights on the disposal computer.) I like to copyright ideas, and it would sure be nice to have computers you could do all the various things I do on, and when they crash, just take out a small piece that saves everything, go to that "disposable computer" box of ten disposables and grab another one, and put it in and keep rolling. I know you're supposed to back up and save things to disk, but I certainly can't be the only one that is instant-messaging, checking emails, writing another piece and downloading another program and posting messages on blogs and then looking at a frozen screen and saying. "You've got to be *blank-blank-blankety-blank* kidding me!" (Smile) I think we've all spent a great deal of our lives in this present world wondering how in the "blank" we can get what was lost back—or am I the only one? We'll have to go more in-depth on that one later. (Smile.)... You also created your entire book yourself, including the cover image, which is beautiful. Do you operate from a belief that there is really nothing any of us can't do if we put our minds to it? You are already working on Vol. 2. How soon before that is shared with this world of ours? And do you ever plan to do more than write poetry? You know, like branching out into writing stories or other things as well?

Dawn: LOL...Yes, I believe that talents are meant to be explored and honed. You never know, until you follow your heart and try. Volume 2 is being composed as we speak. I want to include a lot of new poems. It will probably be out in twelve to eighteen months. I plan to branch out into short stories, magazine articles, and, perhaps, novels.

Chase Von: Who are some of the writers you, yourself, admire?

Dawn: Hmmm...let's see. I admire Chase Von, Tony Prewit, Robert Frost, T. S. Eliot, Andre Norton, Mercedes Lackey, Anne McCaffrey, Christopher Paolini, and JK Rowling.

Chase Von: Well, thank you so much, Dawn. (Smile.) I went to my first poetry reading in years, about two weeks ago. I also want to publicly thank the Camp Pendleton Main Library for having me. Unfortunately, I also had to abbreviate my stay there because my son had taken ill, and you were aware of that also. I truly appreciate your prayers and support. He's back to his old young self again, but one of the things that I was asked to recite by the head librarian really struck a nerve with one of the ones present. They actually left the room in tears, which really made me feel bad until another one of the ones present said she was glad I had said what I shared. It gave her a better view of things, so to speak. Do you ever find that some of the things you have penned are well accepted by some and not accepted by others? And how do people reach you if they would like for you to come and share some of your poetry? And how can learning institutions, like elementary schools and high schools and colleges, order your book in bulk for usage in their curriculums, and will they get a discounted price, if they do so?

Dawn: *Congratulations, Chase!* A reading is a great honor. Yes, I was sorry to hear about your son's illness. I'm glad that he is better now... I've had people react differently to a poem. Most will love it. Some will not understand my use of anthropomorphism. There's always one who wants me to expand a poem. Others say they want it to be shorter. I've learned to listen to their suggestions, but ultimately I have to trust my inner voice and go with what feels right. For now, I can do readings via webcam. My current health situation does not allow me to travel far. I can be reached at flightsoffancypoetry@gmail.com. Institutions can purchase multiple copies for 40% off of the retail price of $11.95 at https://www.createspace.com/3334396. They can e-mail me at the above address for a discount coupon code. Single copies can be purchased through my website at http://flightsoffancypoetry.googlepages.com/index.htm.

Chase Von: Can you share one of your shorter pieces? I know I told you I was going to give my daughter, who is seven, your book to read for her "reading log." I'm also going to share it with her teacher because I really think that so many things in it will touch her and be things she can use to teach her students, both present and future, about the wonder of nature. I think your writing is really, in so many ways, a reminder of what it is that we as children seem to know instinctively: that nature is, in fact, full of wonder, beauty and mystery. And unfortunately, the older we get, we seem to lose interest––in many cases because of a "rush-and-it was-supposed-to-be-done-yesterday world"––in that appreciation for the beauty that is ever present and around us, or the time to give it its just due.

Dawn: Yes. Here's one:

Summer Storm

Rich, blue skies greet the rising, summer sun.

Clouds soon begin to puff higher and higher,

As the heat reflects skyward.

Black, they become, when the sun is shut out.

Lightning suddenly dances to the ground,

And thunder returns to the clouds.

Rain slowly drips in patterns

Like a sprinkler on a hose. Expectation is a hush all around.

Drops fall faster and faster.

The air is sliced with their descent.

Thirsty ground drinks gulps

Of cold, sacred water. Thunder chants an ancient song.

The rain lessens with time.

What remains of the clouds move on.

The ground sighs with happiness.

Trees soak their dusty roots.

Balance is restored. The sun returns.

2008 © Flights of Fancy – Volume 1

by Dawn Huffaker

Chase Von: How important is family to you, and what is your take on the state of our current world? And who are some of the people you consider your heroes?

Dawn: Family is very important to me. Children need good role models in their lives. My parents and grandparents were mine. The world is like a top that is spinning way too fast, and out-of-control. Few find the time or energy to remember that life is about the journey and the people in their lives. We are to reach out and care for others. The majority of the world's problems occur when people forget this. My heroes have been my parents, sister, grandparents, friends, teachers, doctors, and nurses. I've been blessed with heroes that were always there in the nick-of-time. I feel that God sent them to look after me.

Chase Von: What would you say if you were in front of a microphone and could be heard by every child on the planet and, regardless of what language they spoke, they would understand you? What positive advice would you give the children, if that were possible?

Dawn: I would say to them, "Believe in yourself! Have a dream and see it through. But most important of all, care for those around you. They may not be perfect, but you can learn from them, and they from you."

Chase Von: How can our readers find your book? I know it is available on Amazon but are there other places, as well? And do you have any websites where they can learn more about you and your writings, because we certainly can't cover your life––which has been a truly remarkable one and an inspiration on many levels to all? *Certainly to myself!*

Dawn: (Smile.) I'm looking for other booksellers besides Amazon, but nothing is firm yet. My website makes it easy to order a copy, though. The address is:
http://flightsoffancypoetry.googlepages.com/index.htm
More information can be found at the Authors Den, including several new poems. Once you log in, go to:
http://www.authorsden.com/dawnhuffaker

Chase Von: On behalf of the *Student Operated Press* and myself, Dawn, I want to thank you again for taking the time to do this interview with us. A lot of our readers are college students, and I really think the sharing of your story and all the obstacles you have had to overcome is something that will inspire so many. So once again, thanks for not only sharing your poetic talents with the world, but a portion of your story in this journey we call life!

Dawn: It's been a real pleasure, Chase. *Thank you!*

****

"I would say to them, 'Believe in yourself!
Have a dream and see it through. But most
important of all, care for those around you.
They may not be perfect, but you can learn
from them, and they from you.'"
- Dawn Huffaker, Poet
****

Flights of Fancy
Volume 1

Poetry of
Dawn Huffaker

Interview with Crystal Myrick

RISING REPORTER
by Chase Von

Chase Von: Hi, Crystal, and thanks for doing this interview. I haven't really been doing these very long, so I am sure you're going to teach me a thing or two. (Smile) You have been writing, it appears, almost all of your life. I read where you published your first piece when you were in the third grade, and another story you wrote by yourself was published the following year. Also, you started the first ever newspaper in your school at the young age of ten and held the title of editor. What was your first story about when you were in third grade and where was it published?

Crystal: My first story was published in the school literary magazine. It was about a homeless boy and girl who lived in an old abandoned car. I remember the librarian who was in charge of the project kept badgering me to change the story because the two children died in the end. She said the story was too depressing. I just thought it was realistic and I wanted to be different from everyone else. The next year, I was inspired by the game Clue and I wrote a story called "Who Killed Mr. and Mrs. Jenkins." One of the teachers who read the story thought something was seriously wrong with me because the couple committed suicide and left a note.

Chase Von: What was the name of your newspaper and how popular was it in your school?

Crystal: I don't remember the name of the newspaper, but I think it had something to do with a bulldog because that was our school mascot. It was pretty popular because each class had its own reporter. They, much like myself, would get excited about seeing their name in print.

Chase Von: I understand you also sang in the church choir and in your school's choir as well. And also that you play the piano. Do you have any songs of your own you're working on? And if so, does talking to so many celebrities give you an opportunity to share your love of music with them? And also, I read you also wrote for your local newspaper as well. Are you somewhat of a celebrity yourself in your own community?

Crystal: I remember when I started learning about chords, I tried to put a song together, but it just wasn't happening. I do tend to mention music one way or another in an interview, whether it's about what artists they like to listen to or who inspired them to sing or rap. I used to write for my local newspaper, but I have since moved on. I'm from a small town, so everybody knows everybody. A lot of people know I write, so I have some repeat readers.

Chase Von: I was on my high-school newspaper staff, as well. For the life of me, I can't remember anything I wrote. That was (clearing throat) a few years ago though. (Smile.) Well...*many* years ago. Do you still have copies of your school newspaper and do you sometimes look back at them to see just how far you've come? You also pursued writing and a degree in Mass Communication at Saint Augustine's College. Did you always know that interviewing celebrities like Adina Howard was in your future? I didn't see it mentioned in that interview, but did she... well, you know, ask about me? (Smile.)

Crystal: *My bad...* Adina and I were talking and your name must have slipped her mind. (Laughs.) Actually, I threw away all of my newspapers and I deeply regret it now. I won't name names, but there was a teacher who told me that I would never have a future in writing and that I should find something else. Because she was a teacher, I figured that she knew what she was talking about. Shortly after she made that comment, another teacher praised my work and told me that I should seriously consider a writing career and to not let anyone say anything different. I haven't dropped my pen since. As far as interviewing celebrities, I knew I wanted to, but I didn't know how to get in contact with anyone. I just happened to luck up one day and find a website that had the names of celebrities and their publicists.

Chase Von: My boss here, Judyth Piazza, happens to sound a lot like you. (Smile.) She got the bug early, as well, when it came to writing. I can't remember it verbatim, but apparently when everyone else was interested in Clark

Kent as Superman, she was interested in Clark Kent, the reporter. (Smile.) Actually, I wrote my first poem at twelve or thirteen. I've done various other things in my life, but I have to admit my first love is writing. You seem to have known exactly what it was you were placed here to be. Is there anything else you do or have done aside from writing? And, where do you ultimately want your reporting to take you?

Crystal: That's funny you mentioned Superman because I was a Lois Lane fan. I was a Peter Parker fan too. I remember that I was one of the few students who enjoyed learning how to write. Doing writing exercises was my favorite part of the school day. When I knew I was writing sentences without the help of others and that they made sense, I was so proud of myself. I can't see myself doing anything besides writing. I've worked as a pharmacy technician, a photographer, a sales representative and a barista but nothing has been more satisfying and fulfilling than being a writer... I hope that through my writing career I will achieve fame, but not for the reasons that some may think. I have a two-and a-half-month-old son and I want him to be able to look at me and say, "Wow! That's my mom. She has done so much. I want to be like her when I grow up." This will sound very cheesy, but I want him to see through me that anything is possible if you put your mind to it. And I want to jump on Oprah's couch. Tom did it and got away with it, so why can't I? (laughs)

Chase Von: You have done articles on R. Kelly, Boyz II Men's new CD, interviews with Adina Howard, who is huge, and Tiffany "New York" Pollard, who is quickly making a name for herself. My interviews are written, but were yours--with just the two I just mentioned above-- over the phone? Or in person? And are there certain guidelines you follow, or rules that you've learned to ensure that the subject is comfortable? Also, are there certain questions that are just off limits? I know that I prefer doing written interviews, at least for now, because it allows for the one interviewed to be comfortable. It gives them time to ponder the answers they give, and also to simply not answer if they don't like the question or feel as if it is probing into an area they would rather not entertain. Some journalists seem to get a kick out of catching someone off guard. How do you feel about that kind of journalistic reporting?

Crystal: Most of my interviews are over the phone, but I have done some in person and through e-mail. Questions that I feel are off-limits are the ones where I wouldn't feel comfortable answering myself. The point is to make the person you are interviewing comfortable. Just because they make larger deposits in their bank accounts, they are still real people, just like you and me. If I want to catch someone off guard, it won't be in a negative way. For instance, I wouldn't bring up the Superbowl Halftime show to Janet Jackson. I would rather ask her a question about how do the friends of her nieces and nephews perceive her, being that she is Janet... Miss Jackson if you're nasty. She may possibly laugh, and humor is always a good thing in an interview. I want the person I am interviewing to know that I truly care. Otherwise, I wouldn't have interviewed him or her. Once you make them feel uncomfortable, they close up, and you won't get the type of responses you want. One of my favorite people to listen to when she interviews someone is Wendy Williams. Sometimes you can actually tell the celeb is nervous because you never know what will come out of her mouth. With Wendy, expect the unexpected, and with Oprah, expect to cry. (Smile.)

Chase Von: I have many people who I admire, and that list grows daily. Often I am asked, because I write poetry and song lyrics, who I look up to in those regards. I often say Kahlil Gibran, Javan, Sade, Smokey Robinson, Maya Angelou, Bryant McGill, Aberjhani, Ed Roberts, Langston Hughes and Taalam Acey; but, the list is so long I would spend the rest of this interview naming names. (Smile.) Are there any reporters or journalist besides myself--just kidding (smile)--who you truly admire and look up to? And is there anyone out there who you feel has blazed a trail that others can follow? Or are you making your own path? I think of Barbara Walters, initially, when I think of female journalists, but are there people you admire who, perhaps, are not quite as well known as she is?

Crystal: Right now, I don't have anyone in particular. I will read anything and anybody because I still feel like I'm a beginner, and compared to a lot of people, I am. I'm still learning. I enjoy reading mainly female journalists because I feel I can relate a little more to them. Oprah has definitely blazed a trail for black female journalists like myself. To make it on her show, you have to be somebody. Besides my parents, she was definitely a role model for me when I was younger. I wrote her a fan letter "back in the day" and I got an autographed photo of her. I am working hard to make my own path. That way, I will feel a sense of accomplishment once I've gotten to a certain point.

Chase Von: Do you have anyone in particular you can't wait to interview? Or a few of them? And how does it feel to be on this side of the fence? Being the interviewed, and not the one doing it?

Crystal: I would love to interview Jamie Foxx! (Smile.) I believe he is so multi-talented. There's a letter to the editor that I wrote to Sister2Sister Magazine years ago, that now appears online, where I talk about him. I already have my questions together. Being the one interviewed feels...different. It feels like a job interview. One wrong word can make me or break me.

Chase Von: I read a very informative article written by you called, "Achieving Beauty Under The Knife." Sadly, Kanye West lost his mother to this. For my part, I think that people born with abnormalities should, of course, if they can, get corrective surgery and have those things taken care of. Years ago, most people would just have to suffer with their conditions for the durations of their lives. But modern medicine has made huge leaps in that area. A friend of mine has a granddaughter who was born with a giant nevus on her face. And this child has already undergone, I believe, nine operations to correct her face. There is also a book about it, which I am blessed to have two poems in, as well, called *The Anthology Of Candace*. But in those situations, I totally understand. There is also another book by this same friend called *My Name Is Not Monkey Girl*. I bring that up because I think there are legitimate reasons to have corrective surgery done, and there are some that just don't seem worthy of the risk at all. Burn victims, people that have been born with defects, accidents and the like, but do you think our culture has gone off the deep end when it comes to physical appearances?

Crystal: I think society is too consumed with beauty. Who is to say what is beautiful and what is not? For example, Dr. Donda West was a beautiful woman, but not because of her appearance. I listened to an interview that she did and she had an incredibly beautiful spirit. Every time I saw a picture of her, she was smiling. A smile can make anyone gorgeous, even if they don't have a single tooth in their mouth. If there is something actually wrong with a person health-wise, then get the surgery necessary to fix it, if you can afford it. But if you think your breasts are too small, then get a push-up bra and some padding. It is so much cheaper and nowhere near as painful. When I look at *before* pictures of some celebs and look at them now, I can only think: What was going on in their minds that made them feel that a nose-job or a boob-job would make them look better. There are some who have gone from being beautiful to looking cartoonish. Going under the knife has crossed my mind before, but then I said to myself *no way*, because I don't believe in going through unnecessary pain.

Chase Von: How important is family to you, and what is your take on the state of our current world?

Crystal: Family is very important to me because if it were not for them, no telling where I would be today. The state of the world today is a scary thought. Discriminating against someone because of his or her race or beliefs is just outright ridiculous. It is truly sad.

Chase Von: What would you say if you were standing in front of a microphone through which you could be heard by every child on the planet and, regardless of what language it was they spoke, they would understand you? What positive advice would you give the children, if that were possible?

Crystal: No matter what, *believe in yourself and pursue your dreams*. There will be so many people who will try to shake the ladder from under you, but just keep going.

Chase Von: I know you have a MySpace page where people can find you and your works, but what are some of the other places our readers can locate you and discover more of your articles and interviews?

Crystal: The majority of my articles can be found at Associatedcontent.com/cmmyrick, but definitely hit me up at myspace.com/kyriamichele. Kyria Michele was my pen name for about six months.

Chase Von: When I grow up and become a famous author, will you want to interview me? (Smile.)

Crystal: Sure, but I'm the type who wants to interview people *before* they become famous. That way, I might get a shout-out in the thanks section of a CD or in a book.

Chase Von: On behalf of the *Student Operated Press* and myself, Crystal, thank you for taking the time to be interviewed. I also am willing to bet that if you wanted to also be a Mentor here, because of all your past accomplishments, many of the student writers would gain immeasurably from your expertise and encouragement. I can tell you that the rewards of being a Mentor here and contributing work and just being a part of the *Student Operated Press* is something that can't be measured, monetarily anyway. Would you be interested in being a Mentor for *the Student Operated Press?* And do know that your answer is going to be seen publicly. (Smile.)

Crystal: If someone needs my advice in any way, then I'm just like the Jackson 5 and I'll be there. (Smile.)

Chase Von: Again, thank you, Crystal, and wishing you and yours a very Happy Thanksgiving and mountains of success to you in your career!

Crystal: Thank *you* so much for wanting to interview me. Have a great holiday as well.

****

"No matter what, believe in yourself and pursue your dreams. There will be so many people who will try to shake the ladder from under you, but just keep going."
- Crystal Myrick, Reporter, Journalist, Writer

****

Interview with Kashy Keegan

UP-AND-COMING SINGER
by Chase Von

Chase Von: Kashy, on behalf of the *Student Operated Press* and myself, I really want to say we appreciate your taking the time to do this. In learning about you, I found a few similarities with myself. As a child I too often felt like a loner. Although I don't think the term really fits, so many people still use it; that being "military brat." The truth of the matter, however, is that we moved so many times it was hard to really develop lasting friendships. I, myself, turned to books. You turned initially to poetry, which eventually led to music. I guess whether it's facing so many new faces or just feeling like an outsider, in general, often people that are drawn to something end up making different choices in life than many other people. I went from reading to writing. You went from writing poetry to reporting, to teaching yourself how to play the piano and developing your own heartfelt inspirational music. You, also, don't like the rigid structure of playing from a notebook. I, myself, after learning only a few chords, immediately wanted to make up my own tunes and song lyrics on the guitar. Do you also think that it's possible that your name Kashy, which actually means "soul" in Persian, led to your choosing a career path where you touch so many of them?

Kashy: I do have an unusual name, and maybe that has played its part in shaping my destiny to some extent. In any case, I tend to walk to the sound of my own drum, and always have. Growing up, I wasn't your stereotypical, boisterous little boy who was into rough and tumble, etc. I was more of a sensitive, artistic soul, and it took me a long time to realize that being different doesn't make you inferior or inadequate. I have always had a strong sense of self and was also a very strong-willed, tenacious child. Although there have been occasions in my life whereby I have experienced alienation and long periods of loneliness, I was never prepared to conform or compromise on who I truly was in order to fit in and feel more accepted. However, I think being an outsider made me more driven and determined to prove to myself and others that––despite being different––I still had something of value to offer as an individual. In essence, that means that I had to find some other vehicle in my life in order to avoid being pushed to the sidelines. My writing and music were my way of letting people know that I existed, and it enabled me to gain some recognition. Without that, I would have felt more like I was invisible. The thing was, I went to an all-boys' school and––due largely in part to the fact that I wasn't the biggest sports fan––I found myself being excluded a lot of the time. However, in particular, the success that I was having with my writing at that age, gave me a sense of self-worth that kept me afloat. These days though, I can honestly say that I no longer feel as though I have to prove myself anymore. I no longer have to be a success in other people's eyes before I can feel proud of myself. I have learnt that all that truly matters is what you think of yourself. Nature made me the way that I am for a reason. I believe that we should all be entitled to feel good about ourselves in our own skin--for no one but God has the right to judge us.

Chase Von: I seem to be seeing a recurring trend in many of the people I have had the opportunity to interview. Perhaps in my case--because I was so indoctrinated with the military lifestyle--it was a natural choice for me to pursue it. I think over all, if anything, it has in fact helped me as a writer because of the variety of experiences that I have had. But as a child, I always knew no matter what I was, I would always consider myself first a writer. You-- like Alina, Kimberly Prendez, like myself, like Crystal Myrick and even Judyth Piazza and so many others--it seems, were pretty much the "A typical" child that was destined to become a musician, and I say that because your interests led you down that road at a very young age. It also helps that you have a fantastic voice and from the female following you have, great looks. (Smile.) As a man, I just thought I would mention that so that our female readers can check that out for themselves. But for me, writing is when I feel like I am in my element. Are you also--now that you are producing moving inspirational music--in the place, so to speak, that you feel you are in your natural element for your soul's calling?

Kashy: I feel that my relationship with music will always be my closest and most enduring. I do absolutely feel as though I am totally in my element whenever I am listening to or composing music. Through the good times and the bad, I can always rely on music to be there for me. I definitely feel as though I was destined to find a keyboard and start composing melodies. The piano is just one of those things in life that I instantly connected with. It just made sense to me, and it has been like my best friend ever since. I think empathy drives me, most of the time, to want to try and uplift and empower people through my songwriting. I feel as though I just want to try and share the inner strength that I have gained through listening to certain artists and the impact that their inspirational songs have had on me. I am in awe of the power of music and its ability to touch and move people in the most profound way. Certain songs can be life altering and, if it is my calling to be a songwriter, then I just hope that--in my own small way--I can give back to others what music has given me, and touch people's lives in a positive way.

Chase Von: *Your music is remarkable!* But that isn't the only thing that you have done that is truly incredible. This is the second time I am interviewing someone that is quite used to being on the other side of this. (Smile.) Can you tell our readers more about how you started pitching your ideas to magazines, entering competitions and being recognized for your talents and eventually--all by the time you were 15--interviewing some of the biggest Pop stars of the time? And can you drop some of those names here? (smile) You also were named the ITN/Sightsavers Young Journalist of the year in 1999. And you got to interview the incredibly famous film director Steven Spielberg? What was that like speaking with a verifiable legend in our own time?

Kashy: Initially, I did intend to pursue a career in journalism. I was very precocious as a child and I showed some early promise with regard to creative writing. I much preferred writing as a means of communication because it was less direct and I had more time to consider what I wanted to express. It also comes down to being an introvert and fairly shy that made writing my preferred choice of communication. I was driven by the allure of celebrity to try and interview a lot of the pop stars that were big in the UK charts when I was growing up. I used to submit feature ideas to magazine editors, offering to write from a young person's perspective. I grew to be quite successful at this and had a series of interviews published in a lot of the teen publications. I ended up interviewing a fair few of the pop acts that were around at the time like NSYNC, The Spice Girls, Ricky Martin. I also did work placements with MTV UK a couple of times. It was so much fun being able to interview these people at an age when I was still totally sucked in by all of the hype surrounding them, etc. I also flew to Orlando, Florida to review the opening of the then-new theme park "Island's of Adventure" at Universal Studios for a children's news show here in the UK called "Newsround." Steven Spielberg was the creative director for *Jurassic Park Island* and I was given a five-minute slot to interview him about his first impressions of the new park. It was a surreal moment, but I was still young and ignorant enough at the time not to be made too nervous and intimidated by him. It's a memory that will stay with me for a lifetime.

Chase Von: Also, by the time you were just fifteen, you attended a twelve-week singing workshop run by The London Community Gospel Choir. You've been quoted as saying that "The human voice is the most powerful instrument there is." *And I wasn't even aware you had* *heard me sing!* Just kidding. (Smile.) Would you say that the time spent there was what sealed your direction in life? And also, you--like a few others--have mentioned the "Queen Of Soul" Aretha Franklin. Who are some of the other singers you truly admire?

Kashy: Never heard you sing, Chase, so can't comment. (Smile.) But I still feel that there is no greater instrument than the human voice by which to communicate emotion and stir emotion in others. I was always drawn to singers who delivered lyrics with a palpable sense of emotion. I was blown away by the power of gospel singers and just how emotionally raw a style of singing it could be. My experience of attending the workshop choir run by The London Community Gospel Choir was a seminal influence on my life. The technique and ability of some of the singers that I heard there simply blew my mind. It was so uplifting and so awe-inspiring, I just knew from that moment on that singing was becoming my release, my one avenue to be heard and to give voice to all of the emotion inside me that I had always been too shy to express or share. I admire singers like Aretha, Whitney, Stevie Wonder, Donny Hathaway, Luther Vandross, Eva Cassidy, Mariah Carey. The main thing for me is honesty. Technique and vocal acrobats are all very well, but personally, the main thing that I listen out for in a vocal delivery is sincerity.

Chase Von: You, who have done so many things in your life to date, are truly a champion of the underdog. Your music is all about hope, inspiration and following dreams. Your song "Unsung Heroes" is particularly moving, as are all your songs, but what was your inspiration for writing it? You also have a part in it where you sing:

"They'll tell you you're not worthy
They'll shatter all your dreams
Make you feel like you're invisible
And crush your self belief
Oh it's a cruel world
With little justice at all
And the ones on top won't make it stop
So convinced that they might fall."

The whole song is very emotionally moving, but when I heard that I couldn't help but think of something that happened to me early on. I showed a teacher a poem I had written that she had actually inspired, and she didn't believe I had written it. She thought that I had copied it from someone older in my own handwriting and forced me to write another poem while everyone in the class was doing something else. For many years after, because of that, I didn't share what I had written with adults. Similarly, Crystal Myrick was told by one teacher that she would never be a writer, and because of that gave it up completely for a very long time. She even threw away all that she had written previously because of this teacher's negative comments. Later, another teacher told her she did have talent and encouraged her to pursue her dreams. Now she is an entertainment reporter. You have an amazing CD out now simply called *Kashy Keegan CD*, but was there a similar time in your life when someone tried to discourage you--perhaps someone you viewed as an authoritative figure—from pursuing your dreams? And what do you think others who find themselves dealing with what I call "dream vampires" should do, besides purchase your CD? (Smile.)

Kashy: "Dream vampires." I really like that analogy. I think I learnt the hard way never to let anybody discourage me or crush my enthusiasm for what it is I love to do most. I have experienced my fair share of knock-backs and rejections... I have honestly lost count of the number of times that people have fed me false hope and built me up, only to knock me back down again. As my mother always said to me, "It's the grit in the oyster shell that ultimately forms the pearl." The hard times definitely shape us and define our integrity. Whilst I have developed a thicker skin, I have learnt that the people that we most want to believe in us, aren't God, at the end of the day. Although their opinion may carry weight, it doesn't necessarily mean that they are always right. These people aren't God and they don't know everything. What matters most is what you think of yourself. You can't spend your life people-pleasing; otherwise, you will just end up losing who you are altogether. As long as you are satisfied in your own heart with the person that you are and what you are setting out to achieve, then that is all that truly matters. We all want to feel valued and appreciated, but sometimes we have to validate ourselves and find strength through living out our own truth. I think that life is too short to afford the luxury of a negative thought. It's so easy to become a victim of things that have happened in the past and allow those experiences to dictate our future. We don't have to become stuck in victim mode. I believe that our thoughts ultimately shape our reality, and by shifting our thoughts and feelings towards truly believing that our dreams are attainable, then we stand every chance of realizing our full potential. There are a tremendous amount of hard-working and talented people out there who are never given the recognition or praise that they deserve. We see celebrities basking in the limelight all the time. Often it seems that there is no end to their quest for attention and adoration. I wrote 'Unsung Heroes' for all of the people who work behind the scenes, all the people that we never hear about who make a positive difference in their communities: People who, throughout history, have been paid a pittance for their stellar contribution to this world. People who are insanely talented and skilled but are never given the lucky break that they deserve. Currently, I work in a hospital and I see first-hand all the nurses, doctors, cleaners, etc. who surely deserve more in the way of recognition and value. I really dislike avarice and greedy, mercenary people whose egos know no shame.

Chase Von: How important is family to you, and what is your take on the state of our current world?

Kashy: Family and friendships mean everything to me. I believe that love is the only legacy that is truly worth anything. At the end of the day, as I see it, you enter this world with nothing and you leave this world the same. Material assets and possessions, in that respect, are highly insignificant. At the very most, people will remember you for the way that you made them feel. I am very fortunate to have been blessed with two outstanding parents whose love and support for me has always been unconditional. I consider my parents to be my closest friends in the world. In this corrupt world--where the emphasis is too often put on money, power and status--it's very easy to become caught up in all that's superficial and lose track of what truly holds real value. I know what I am living for, and that keeps me sane. Finding, knowing and giving love is the best feeling in the world. The times when I am most happy are the times when I am around my friends and family... All the anxieties, pressures and fears that I keep tend to just dissolve away in those precious moments.

Chase Von: What would you say if you were standing in front of a microphone that could be heard by every child on the planet, and regardless of what language it was they spoke, they would understand you? What positive advice would you give the children, if that were possible?

Kashy: I would say: Hold onto what makes you unique and never let anyone put you down. Just because you are different in some way doesn't make you inferior. I would say: Be yourself, because no matter who you are there will always be someone who disapproves. You can't please all of the people all of the time. If you have love, honor and respect for yourself, then it will be mirrored back.

Chase Von: Will you share with our readers how they can find your music and more about you? Your links and web pages? Also, are there any projects you are working on you care to share? Or any scheduled performances coming up, you can let our readers know about?

Kashy: My first EP *Kashy Keegan* is available for purchase through my MySpace page, *www.myspace.com/kashykeegan*, it is also available for download at itunes and several other digital download stores.

Chase Von: On behalf of the *Student Operated Press* and myself, Kashy, truly thank you for taking the time out from your busy schedule to do this. I want to also wish you continued success, and I do hope more and more people get the opportunity to enjoy the inspirational messages of hope you so consistently sing about. And a Happy Thanksgiving to you and yours, as well, Brother.

Kashy: I have really, really enjoyed answering your questions. There is real depth and thought behind the questions that you have asked. Thank *you* for this honor.

****

"Be yourself, because no matter who you are there will always be someone who disapproves. You can't please all of the people all of the time. If you have love, honor and respect for yourself, then it will be mirrored back."
- Kashy Keegan, Singer, Songwriter, Pianist

****

Interview with Kimberly Prendez

ACTRESS, WRITER, FILMMAKER
by Chase Von

Chase Von: Hey, Kimberly! On behalf of the *Student Operated Press*, I know I am going to enjoy this interview because you are such a lovely down-to-earth lady. I often get the feeling you were born out of time so to speak. I know of your love for romance, your love of black-and-white photography and the classic older movies. I also love how when you made your movie *Until Next Time*. It has everyone in it dressed as if they were "back in the day." *Such class and elegance!* And I must say, you look so beautiful decked out in the same kind of clothing that Marilyn Monroe, Elizabeth Taylor, and Dorothy Dandridge once wore. Are you comfortable in this present world of ours, or do you sometimes wish you were alive back then...when men opened doors, and women took such care in their dress that they looked like movie stars, even while doing dishes?

Kimberly Prendez: Thank you for the kind words about my film *Until Next Time.* Yes, I sometimes wish I were living my life as the women did in the 30s and 40s. I love the class of that era. I love that women dressed like ladies even when around the house. I suppose a lot of women back then didn't have the busy lives of women today. So many women today are holding down jobs, taking care of the kids and the house, school etc., all at the same time. To touch on the whole "gentleman" of that time, as well...well I believe that women have made it so much "easier" on men these days. We don't command respect. I suppose I shouldn't say all women, but there are a lot of women that are more concerned with showing men "we don't need you." In other words, a lot of women are taking on the role of the man, instead of allowing men to "own" that. There is nothing wrong with being a strong woman, but don't forget there are men and women for a reason. We are different, and quite frankly I love being the lady...thus being treated as one.

Chase Von: You've been really making a mark with your acting career. You've been in *Valerie and Sid, Waves, 3 Paces To The Closet Door, No Justice,* and are also slated to be in *Tales From the Other Side*--which is going to be a modern day version of the Twilight Zone--numerous commercials and also appeared along with singing R and B sensation Jaheim. You also were chosen by Artist Interviews Magazine as one of their featured "Up-and-Coming Hollywood Actresses" and were a nominee for "Actress of the Month" for the very prestigious Independent Film Alliance. With all that going on, how did you find the time to not only write your own movie, but also star in it, film it, and--with your first film out the gate--be selected for the Indiefest USA International Film Festival?

****

"Keep yourself educated, be kind and others
will follow. Believe in yourself and
help others believe. Love yourself!"
- Kimberly Prendez, Actress, Writer, Filmmaker

****

Kimberly Prendez: *Wow, you've done your homework, Chase!* Well, I had a story in mind for quite some time, and with the help of very close friend and filmmaker Angelo Bell, I sat down on New Years weekend going into 2007 and wrote my first draft for *Until Next Time.* I had many rewrites through the month of March. I honestly don't know how I found the time to do it...lol. It was a dream and I was actually going through a very hard time in my "love life," so making the film was the best thing I did for myself during that time. I went into pre-production by the end of February and we were filming by mid-April. I had an amazing director that helped so much, along with a brilliant cinematographer. Without them, I would have been lost. My dear friend Angelo Bell also helped me along the way by answering my many questions! (lol) So, here we are nine months since I sat down that weekend and began writing, and we have been accepted into our first film festival. I have also submitted to Sundance and Slamdance, and will be notified if we got "in" the first week of December. It is a very exciting time.

Chase Von: Can you, without giving too much away, tell us a bit about *Until Next Time* and, also, what the inspiration was for you to write it?

Kimberly Prendez: The film is about a woman whose lover has passed away and she makes a very "provocative" choice on how to replace him. In the end, she must decide if she is going to continue on her journey, choose to truly live or join her lover Anthony in his world. I think we have all been through a time in our life where we may have made a rash decision when it comes to love, especially after losing a special love. Sometimes we just want that "feeling" again, and we may try too hard or try to get that feeling with the wrong person; then comes the time where we need to get ourselves out of the situation. Heartbreak is always hard; there is no easy way to get through it. I suppose time--yes, time--is the way to get through. This film was inspired by love, true love...a love that is so connected no one else can even begin to understand.

Chase Von: Alas, I too, am a hopeless romantic at heart. Who are some of the writers that you like to read the most and some of the films that you find most touching in that regard?

Kimberly Prendez: Oh, goodness...well, my favorite poem of all time is Poe's "Romance." It is such beauty, the words I could read over and over. I read *The Notebook* about six years ago. Way before there was any talk of a movie--*and oh, how I loved it!* As far as films, I could, seriously, go on and on. I love films that maybe aren't the typical romance. I mean *The Notebook* was lovely and very touching, but some of my favorite films that I consider romantic are *Buffalo 66, True Romance, Malena, The Lover* and *Great Expectations.*

Chase Von: Are we going to be seeing a star on Hollywood Boulevard for you as an actress, a filmmaker, or both? And will you be adding "singer" anytime soon in the near future to your vast resume?

Kimberly Prendez: LOL! Singer? Oh goodness *no!* I wish I could sing. I have always wanted to be a singer. When I was little, I would perform for the family...poor things. I don't know if I will ever have a star on Hollywood Boulevard, but if I do, it would be for acting. That is my first love. I also love writing and I am working on my first feature-length script, as we speak. I am actually collaborating with one of the actors from my film Jeff Torres. He is an amazing talent.

Chase Von: If I was interviewing someone else, this probably wouldn't be such an integral question to the interview, but with you, it's very important: Are there actors and actresses of old that you really look up to and admire, and is there any particular actress you think has truly influenced you and how you approach your many different roles? Additionally, are there any current actors and actresses that you also admire and feel are truly living masters of your profession?

Kimberly Prendez: Again, I could go on and on here. Some of the old-time actors and actresses I love are Gloria Swanson, Marilyn Monroe, Lauren Bacall, Gregory Peck and Marlon Brando. There are a handful of actresses that I am inspired by, either by their talent, their story...or both. I have always been fascinated with Marilyn Monroe, her life, what she went through. She was so much more than the soft-spoken blonde. She was extremely serious about acting. She wanted to be great, she wanted to be respected. She battled with insecurity and depression, and I can relate to her. I have my own battles with both. I definitely have never been one to self-medicate as she did, though, so I guess I am lucky that my coping skills are truly present and strong. I, too, want to be taken seriously; I want to be great; and I want to learn more. As far as actresses of today, I love Monica Bellucci, Meryl Streep, Jennifer Connelly and Halle Berry. I am inspired by all of these women. I don't know if there is one actress in particular that influences me on how I prepare for a role. However, I do read a lot, watch a lot of Actors Studio on the Bravo channel and still study with an acting coach, so all of those things combined help me to prepare.

Chase Von: How important is family to you, and what is your take on the state of our current world?

Kimberly Prendez: Family is very important. Those are the people that will, hopefully, always support you in whatever it is you want to do in life. I also have friends that are like my family. How they say: "Friends are the family we choose." My girlfriends are extremely supportive, they are all so happy for me. I also think my mom, my sister and my girlfriends are my biggest fans, as it should be. Oh, the world today...well, I don't want to get all political, so I am going to stay within the realm of family and address it that way. I firmly believe that we don't have the family values we should. Too many people are worried about getting a bigger house, fancier car and impressing the boss, instead of spending time with the family. Children don't go to the park anymore. They are on computers and playing games that are extremely violent, and listening to music that degrades women, glorifies gangs, drugs and violence. I am so tired of hearing parents say things like, "Well, that's just what kids do these days." *That, to me, is complete BS and lazy parenting!* I would rather my son or daughter watch a beautiful film that may have some adult content, than play those violent games or listen to certain music. I think it is so funny that a parent will freak out if their child sees a topless woman in a good film, but then turn around and buy him or her a disgusting video game. Why do Americans freak out over sex/nudity, like it's dirty? It is a natural thing, a beautiful thing. Do I think young people should be sexually active? *Absolutely not!* I just think we need to focus on the games they are playing, the time spent on the computer, the music they are listening to, the shows they watch and whom they hang out with. After all, these children really are our future.

Chase Von: I know from reading up on you, that you love doing laundry, housework...and keep Starbucks in business. (Smile.) I bet every single man reading this stopped to do a double take! Are you one of those people that, although in the acting community, hasn't lost touch with your roots and don't see yourself--regardless of how visible you are to the public--above any of the rest of us?

Kimberly Prendez: Oh gosh, I am above no one and never will be. I am just one person on this earth. I am just trying to live the best life possible, a life that creates happiness for me. If I am happy, well then everyone around me will be happy. In the last year or so, I truly have been learning so much about me, others and life. It is a wonderful thing. I feel like I am becoming the woman that I have always dreamed of being. I have a long way to go yet, but I am enjoying the journey. I just want to be spiritually connected, act, write, travel, visit museums, read good books, watch great films, sip some merlot, discover new things and be happy. (Smile.) I guess getting older is a good thing...

Chase Von: Not saying this because I have to and this is an interview, but you are beautiful and very shapely. I just have to ask, though, is that simply natural and blessings from your parents, or do you have to work out to keep your figure? More importantly, how do you find the time with all the things you have on your plate, if that is the case?

Kimberly Prendez: (Laughing...) I am naturally blessed, but I do have to exercise now to keep what I have. I am almost thirty-seven years old, so it takes some work to keep that body I had in my twenties. (Smile.) I just eat healthy, mostly organic foods, walk/run my dog and do some working out at the gym.

Chase Von: What would you say if you were standing in front of a microphone that could be heard by every child on the planet, and regardless of what language it was they spoke, they would understand you? What positive advice would you give the children, if that were possible?

Kimberly Prendez: *Oh, I love this question!* I would speak softly, I would speak with such emotion... And I love children. I would tell them to think with their hearts, follow their hearts. Look at others through their hearts.

Respect themselves, always. Respect their mind, body and spirit... and be leaders. When things get tough, always remember it will not be like this forever. No matter what you're going through. Keep yourself educated, be kind and others will follow. Believe in yourself and help others believe. *Love yourself!* Speak up and always look people in the eye. Be honest; be giving. I would say all of these things over and over, until I felt that they had really heard me.

Chase Von: How can our readers find you and more about you? What websites and movie links are out there so they can learn more about the writer, actress and filmmaker Kimberly Prendez?

Kimberly Prendez: My website will always have the most current news and link you to many other sites. www.kimberlyprendez.com my myspace, IMDB, and many other links are there on the website.

Chase Von: On behalf of the *Student Operated Press* and myself, I thank you so much, Kimberly, for taking the time out to do this. I also wish you much success with your movie *Until Next Time,* and continued success with your acting career as well.

Kimberly Prendez: I would like to thank *you*, Chase, for giving me this opportunity. It was a wonderful interview, full of great questions.

****

*"Look at others through their hearts.
Respect themselves, always. Respect their mind,
body and spirit... and be leaders. When things get
tough, always remember it will not be like this
forever. No matter what you're going through."
- Kimberly Prendez, Actress, Writer, Filmmaker*

****

Interview with Chrissy K. McVay

GIFTED AUTHOR, SCREENWRITER
by Chase Von

Chase Von: Hi, Chrissy, on behalf of the *Student Operated Press* and myself, thanks for taking the time out to do this. I know you are extremely busy getting your screenplay written for *Souls of the North Wind*. It's a fantastic story that when I read it, made me think of other stories that affected me the same way. The classic *Old Yeller, Bridge to Terabithia* by Katherine Paterson, and to be frank, I think your story ranks right there with them and other classics such as *Black Beauty* and *Charlotte's Web*. I could go on, but *Souls of The North Wind* truly rates to be right beside them all. What inspired you to write it?

Chrissy K. McVay: I had a similar dream a couple times in one year where I was lost in a wilderness in winter at night, clinging to the back of a sled. I could hear wolves howling in the distance and my sled dogs panic. I felt I was being followed. Later, I came across a book by Farley Mowat called *People of the Deer* and decided to combine the dream with the Ihalmiut, Inuit culture that Farley wrote about.

Chase Von: This story is great for young adults, but I am a little past that phase and I still enjoyed it immensely. I'm not exaggerating when I say it is one of the best books I've ever read. What struck me was the intense amount of detail that you go into, involving the life, beliefs and rituals of the Inuit, as well as your gifted form of storytelling. As a writer myself, I knew a little about the subject, but you must have spent a lifetime researching this culture. Can you explain how you came to know so much that is really true in reality of these people?

Chrissy K. McVay: I researched the Canadian Inuit and the terrain for three years, but I truly have to give credit to Farley Mowat's vast research. The wonderful thing about Farley's nonfiction books is the way they're never bland or boring. He writes from his heart, incorporating facts with a hint of suspense that adds real flavor to his research.

Chase Von: You truly have your own style, but it is a style that is universal in its appeal. How long have you been writing and--normally I do this in the beginning--but what were your younger years like? Where did you grow up? How long has writing been a part of your life? And can you also share with our audience some of the other things you have written? I recall a short you wrote that did, indeed, have some adult content, although, like everything you do, it was fantastically written.

Chrissy K. McVay: I grew up in a small farming community in Michigan. My father was born in Michigan and my mother grew up in Tennessee. After living in

Indiana for about ten years, I talked my husband into moving closer to my mother's southern relatives (he's such a good sport). Having Dyslexia almost threw me a curve ball as far as learning to read and write, but we had a great school system with small classes and several tutors in the room. I remember a specific student teacher from the local college that came up with the idea of having the students write and color their own storybooks in our first grade class. *We loved it!* The teachers invited the parents to a "book party" and they made such a big deal about our books that writing became worth the huge challenge to me. I wish I'd found out this student-teacher's name. He has no idea how much this inspired me. I also have several short stories that are posted on Amazon Shorts (www.amazon.com/shorts) ranging from humor, horror, YA and even a Western. Other short stories have appeared in *Wild Violet Magazine* and *Aim Magazine*, as well as a variety of other publications. My short story "Soloist" will be in the December 2007 issue of *Rosebud Magazine*. I'm a multi-genre reader, so I don't like to limit myself to a single genre with my writing. I don't think any writer or other artist should have to if their passions extend to other genres.

Chase Von: I know you're currently working on your screenplay for the *Souls of North Wind.* How soon before we see it on screen? And will you also be a consultant on the film itself...to make sure the movie adaptation stays true to the story and how you wrote it originally?

Chrissy K. McVay: Though nothing has been optioned yet, *Souls of the North Wind* is currently being considered by a producer at Cine LA. *Reaching Hollywood with a screenplay is like climbing Mt. Everest!* With *Souls of the North Wind* being my first screenplay, I know I won't have much control, unlike Stephen King and other well-known writers. I will say that after chugging through the screenplay writing process, I fully understand why some of the novel has to be cut or changed to work on the screen.--and not every story will work on screen. Though I'm in agony when a movie deviates from my favorite book, I now understand there are valid reasons for this. It may be a few years before *Souls of the North Wind* reaches the screen. Believe me, you'll hear a delighted scream from the Blue Ridge Mountains when it happens.

Chase Von: How important is family to you, and what is your take on the state of our current world?

Chrissy K. McVay: A man I worked in a factory with once told me: "Build plenty of memories with your kids. Never put work ahead of them." Now that three of our four boys are grown and living their own lives, I know his advice was wise, and I'm so very glad I took it to heart. My husband and I passed on many hours of overtime to hike Pike's Peak with our children, take them kayaking or horseback riding through Garden of the Gods in Colorado. It's fine to build your retirement nest egg, as long as you don't neglect the golden years with your children. Too many parents I know today are caught up in the capitalism whirlwind—choosing to get caught in a six- or seven-day workweek to build up that 401K—while their children grow more and more distant from them in age, and emotionally. It breaks my heart. I don't regret all our vacations and long weekend adventures for one minute, even if I end up eating road-kill stew in my nineties.

Chase Von: What would you say if you were standing in front of a microphone that could be heard by every child on the planet, and regardless of what language it was they spoke, they would understand you? What positive advice would you give the children, if that were possible?

Chrissy K. McVay: *Slow down!* We've become a culture that runs around like rabid dogs, buying toys we can't take with us, etc. I believe this makes us cruel to one another, and is probably hazardous to our health. If we take more time to talk to one another, maybe we can focus on the good in people around us. I truly believe that a positive attitude can bring out the smiles in even the sourest-behaving folks.

Chase Von: Are there any stories that you are working on now that you want to give us a heads up about? And are there other things you enjoy other than writing? Hobbies? And what lies in the future, for Chrissy K. McVay?

Chrissy K. McVay: I'm currently working on a sequel *to Souls of the North Wind,* and my second novel *Only Eagles Know My Name* is in the final editing stages. I hope to have it ready for press by February 2008. *Only Eagles*

Know My Name is another Young Adult/adult adventure loosely based on the mysterious Anasazi culture of the Southwestern desert region. When I'm not writing, I love hiking with my family. The Blue Ridge Mountains of Western North Carolina have some great trails. I also have a sister in Colorado, so we've taken some great hiking adventures there, as well. My husband and I hope to one-day hike the entire Appalachian Trail. In the near future, I'd love to continue to concentrate on more screenplays. I have several different ones setting on several producers' desks (hopefully, not collecting dust). However, I'll never completely abandon the novel or short story. There's something about books that ignites a spark in my soul, and it's been there so long, I don't think I could put it out, if I tried––despite the struggle to get several projects finished in a short amount of time. It really is a labor of love, and I'll never give it up.

Chase Von: And how can our readers find you and more about you?

Chrissy K. McVay: I have a website on Author's Den: www.authorsden.com/chrissykmcvay, as well as a profile page on Amazon where I post questions to readers and news about my upcoming books and short stories. I'll post news about the screenplays on both sites as soon as it's available.

Chase Von: On behalf of the *Student Operated Press* and certainly myself, I am thankful and again honored to have been able to interview you, Chrissy. I really thank you for taking time away from the projects you're working on to share yourself, because I, personally, know how many things you have on your plate. So thank you so very much again.

Chrissy K. McVay: As a fellow writer, Chase, it doesn't surprise me that you've posed some excellent questions. Thank you for giving me the opportunity to shamelessly gab about myself. For more information:

http://www.authorsden.com/chrissykmcvay

****

"Too many parents I know today are caught up in the capitalism whirlwind––choosing to get caught in a six- or seven-day work week to build up that 401K––while their children grow more and more distant from them in age, and emotionally. It breaks my heart. I don't regret all our vacations and long weekend adventures for one minute, even if I end up eating road-kill stew in my nineties."
- Chrissy K. McVay, Author, Screenwriter

****

****

"If we take more time to talk to one another, maybe we can focus on the good in people around us. I truly believe that a positive attitude can bring out the smiles in even the sourest-behaving folks."
- Chrissy K. McVay, Author, Screenwriter

****

Interview with Jenny McShane

GORGEOUS ACTRESS, SINGER AND MODEL
by Chase Von

Photo by Donato Sardella

Chase Von: Hey, Jenny, and on behalf of the *Student Operated Press* and myself, I truly want to thank you for making room on your schedule for this. I've really enjoyed talking to you and I have to say, you could also be a comedienne. I'm still smiling when I think about our conversation. (Smile.) Before I get to any questions, though, thanks again for sharing yourself with our readers here at the *SOP*. I know you are really tapped for time and spinning multiple plates.

Poster courtesy of Michael Regen, Melee Entertainment;
distributed by The Weinstein Company; Genius Entertainment

Jenny: Hey, Chase...and I want to thank you and the *Student Operated Press* for having me. You're very funny yourself, you know. (Heh-heh.)

Chase Von: You've done so many incredible things in your life. Not only are you a much sought-after actress and model, but you also have your own band called Little Ruby and play at various locations around Los Angeles. But first, can you share with our readers what your childhood years were like? Where you grew up?

Jenny: Chase, I grew up in a very small town called Waseca in Southern Minnesota. The actual set of *Little House on The Prairie*, or the exterior they used, was in Mankato, Minnesota, which was fifteen miles west of where I grew up. I'll give this example so you get the picture: I was raised on a five-hundred-acre pig farm. I am the eldest of eight children...five girls and three boys. And if you think that's a lot, my father was one of twenty-two children! When the wind was blowing in their direction, neighbors used to call my father and ask if there was anything he could do about the smell. And yes, now it's funny but it wasn't then. LOL :) My brothers and sisters and I were raised helping my parents with farming duties that included some pretty gruesome tasks that weren't in a typical young girl's world. My father was in the 101st Airborne before I was born and used to tell me the way we worked was nothing compared to the Army. "We had it easy," he always told us.

Chase Von: Pig farm? (Smile.) Again you had me crying-laughing when you were telling me about your life there, but you look at it all now with a sense of humor. When we lived in New York, periodically we would drive down to Virginia to see "kinfolk" and us children could always tell when we were getting close because of a certain aroma in the air. It didn't occur to me then that there might have been other kids living there that were hating life. For the record, how many showers did you take before school? And what was it you would ask your Mom when the Avon Lady came calling? (Smile.)

Jenny: Well, Chase, I really did hate the manual labor and the way that I was raised then, but now I look back and know I am so fortunate. If ever I have to survive, I have that knowledge now. (Smile.) I was driving a tractor when I was only four years old! I also drove grain trucks and anything else that had to be driven, as I was the eldest. My father gave me a choice when I was in first grade: I could continue to work outside with him or do the chores inside with my mom. I chose outside with Dad. My sister who was a year younger took inside with Mom. Oh, and my mom had a friend that sold Avon. I always had Mom order the perfume that was on special in the large bottles because after pig chores, I always took at least two showers. I would also pour on a good bunch of the perfume before school. But I swear I could still smell "home," no matter what. Sad, huh?

Chase Von: I'd have to say *yes* and *no*, Jenny...definitely not what most people have lived through, but for the record, I've interviewed Shawn Richardz, Kitty "Kitania" Kavey, Darcy Donavan, Barbara Evans, Debra Garrett, Leah DeVon, Alina, Audrey Michelle, Kimberly Prendez, Vanessa Jay...and I could go on, but you are certainly another one of THE most beautiful women in the world.... The day after talking to you, I was at the store, and I thought of you as I bought some Spicy Pork Rinds. (Love those things...Smile.) Prior to talking to you, that would have been the last thing that would have come to mind... Heh–heh :) Ok, sorry, but I also have to say this: If you are an example of what women look like from the pig farms, men reading this that used to speed up when driving by are going to be slowing down and visiting awhile. *You're Gorgeous!* (Smile.) Can you tell our readers how you went from that life to the life you are currently living, and various jobs you've held prior to landing on the big screen with some of the most recognizable and talented individuals in that profession, in the entire world?

Jenny: Well, first, Chase, let me share this: I'm not so sure about men reading this and deciding to stop rather than step on the gas pedal. I remember once a football game was canceled, so I was at home--up to my knees in pig s••• with my rubbers and bibs on--when my dad pointed all the football players to the barn. Those guys never looked at me the same after that! Then one summer I rode my bicycle to town and asked the city council to sponsor me in the *Miss Teen Minnesota Pageant*. They gave me a check, which I showed my parents. That was my first time in the "Big City" when I was sixteen. It was such a pleasure to hang out with the beautiful city girls. In the interview, the judges asked me what the worst thing I had ever had to do on the farm was. I told them I knew the answer but didn't want to say. They wanted to know, so I proceeded to tell them I had to castrate pigs. Well, one female judge nearly fainted. (Smile.) Needless to say, I came in third out of 276 contestants.

Jenny McShane
Photo by Anthony Moore

On the way home, my father asked me what was said in the interview, as one of the parents had told him that the most points were accrued in that part of it. I told him the same thing... After the teen pageant in Minnesota, my dad's sister helped pay for a modeling school. I look back on this now and laugh, as I really needed the information I learned. I had no idea about how to dress or apply makeup, etc. *I didn't have a clue!* My parents didn't let me wear makeup or nail polish or anything like that. I finished modeling school and was signed by a small modeling agency in Minnesota. The agent there was wonderful to me and booked a lot of jobs for me that helped to pay for my college at St. Thomas. That same agency in Minnesota also referred me to an agency in Chicago, which was also very wonderful to me. While I was in Chicago, a photographer who had photographed me for several catalog jobs told me I should pursue acting, because when he photographed me, he felt I had such an interesting character and that it wasn't necessarily that of a model. I remember that conversation really making me sad, but I love and appreciate it now. That day he told me that modeling is a very hard career, much like dancing, as it tends to be very short lived. If you can be an actor, you can work until you're a hundred and also make a much better living. That same photographer found me in Los Angeles years later when I was working with the William Morris Agency. He came to Los Angeles where he became a very highly sought-after photographer for headshots. He'd done headshots of Sean Penn, Drew Barrymore, etc. His name was Helmut Lange. Unfortunately, Helmut died while I was filming in South Africa back in 1998.

Chase Von: Amazing how mere words can change someone's entire path in life, though, isn't it, Jenny? And I'm sure if you could have said something else in your first beauty contest you would have won; sounds like you got penalized for being honest. Another thing that you were telling me that had me laughing so hard I had tears in my eyes is about your interview on the Howard Stern Show. What again was your answer to him when he asked you if you were enjoying New York? And if you had gotten a chance to visit Central Park to see any of them cute little squirrels? (Smile.)

Jenny: Chase...are you talking about when I said, "*Yes*, I did see some squirrels in Central Park and I was wishing I had brought my Winchester."? Howard had actually asked if I had ever eaten any road kill, should we call it? I told him I'd had raccoon and squirrel on occasion. Then Howard asked me if I had liked going to Central Park when I was in New York and I said, "Of course, I love it there as it reminds me of Minnesota and the farm." So he then asked, "What do you do when you see a squirrel in Central Park?" I said, "I wish I had my shotgun as things are very expensive here." Well, they are you know, Chase! (Smile.)

Chase Von: Ah, Jenny... country girl to the core. Heh-heh :) I think we better get off the animal subject. I've learned that some people don't think "vegetarian"--old ancient American Indian word for "bad hunter"--is amusing. But before we do, there's an article here at the *SOP* by Ashley Judd who is on the warpath against Sarah Palin. And although I'm not a vegetarian by any means, I still think what Sarah has done in regards to animals is appalling. I myself remember seeing a video and, seriously, after seeing the treatment of some of the animals, almost stopped eating meat altogether myself. *Horrible!* But shooting wolves from the air and cutting off their left front leg and various other things she has allowed or supported are sickening. Recently I watched *Dancing With Wolves* by Kevin Costner and they have this slaughter scene in it where people had shot buffalo for no other reason than to take their hides. Maybe it's my American Indian heritage, but I believe there is a natural order to things. If wolves didn't eat deer then there would be too many deer, and I am kind of glad frogs have mosquitoes on their menu. (Smile.) One could even argue that salad shouldn't be eaten either, because it, too, is a living thing. And how fair is it to eat something that couldn't run away if it tried? (Smile.) Sorry, not trying to make light of a very serious subject, but it does go both ways. Insects eat plants too. And then there are plants that eat insects. Ever heard of the Venus Fly Trap? What's that all about? Before we go on, have you seen this? Some things you just can't make up! And are you a vegetarian? And what are your views on the subject? For me, it just boils down to: don't kill more than you can eat. And be thankful for the life given to sustain your own... And for those that want to read the entire article by Ashley Judd, who I truly do think is wonderful:

Gruesome News of Sarah Palin`s Cruel Aerial Wolf-Killing
http://thesop.org/index.php?article=14958
Sarah Palin Pardons Turkey - While others killed behind her (Note: Not for small children).
http://www.youtube.com/watch?v=rJXFfTpPWlI

Jenny: No, Chase, I'm not a vegetarian, but, like you, I don't believe in senseless killing either. I was raised by a real hunter––my father. But Dad never killed or hunted for pleasure. Anything he caught or killed was to provide for his big family. And as you know now, it really is a big family. I still love deer meat and know that the deer fed my large family many a delicious meal. When it's winter in Minnesota, there are not any fresh vegetables. I can't imagine there are too many vegetarians in Russia either. I did my first starring role in a feature in Russia. While there I met people raised in weather like me. And I think to be a vegetarian you have to live in the right climate or near a grocery store that imports fresh produce. Like here in LA, I imagine is good for that, for those that prefer that lifestyle. Plants that eat insects? Chase, are you saying someone might be biting into a salad someday and it might bite them back? (Smile.)

Photo by Anthony Moore

Chase Von: Now that's strange, Jenny... Earlier tonight when we were talking again, you brought up when you were on set and someone was telling you a story about Donald Sutherland. And I was, like: Isn't he the one who played in the movie *Invasion of the Body Snatchers*? *(Though I'd written part of this question before we spoke again)*... It's like I brought up the subject before we even had that conversation. (Smile.) And wouldn't it be strange if an intelligent life form of plants showed up and didn't care if people were eating meat, but got really p.o.'d if they saw someone chomping on asparagus? Heh-heh... Enough on that though... *Your resume is outstanding!* You appeared in *The Watcher* with Keanu Reeves--who, incidentally, also stars in one of my all-time favorite movies, *The Matrix*--*Nash Bridges* with Don Johnson, *Shark Attack* with Casper Van Dien, *Renegade* with Lorenzo Lamas and *The Fallen Faithful*, starring Sonny Marinelli and Mark Margolis. You were also in *Wayne's World II*, with a cast that included Dana Carvey, Mike Myers, Heather Locklear, Christopher Walken, Drew Barrymore, Kim Basinger, Tia Carrere and the late Chris Farley. It would take up the rest of this page to name all the other notables in *Wayne's World II*, but it also has Jay Leno playing himself and Steven Tyler of Aerosmith who also played himself. (Smile.) You're also in *US Seals*, *Cyborg III*, *Hit the Dutchman*, directed by industry legend Menahem Golan, and written by Alex Simon. Your other film credits are: *Never Say Die*, *Monsoon*, *Outlaw*, *Megalodon*, *Stag*, *Rangley Beach* and you also star in *Furnace*, a horror film that was just released last year, directed by the very talented William Butler and featuring Michael Pare, Ja Rule, Danny Trejo, Paul Wall, Cowboy Troy, and Tom Sizemore. And that isn't all you have accomplished as an actress: you've also appeared frequently on shows as a guest star...*Silk Stalkings* and *Too*

Something, to name a few. Who are some of the people you enjoyed working with the most? Who haven't you worked with that you would love to? And what has been your most demanding role and was that because of the challenges, physically or emotionally or both?

Jenny: I have loved all of the performers I have had the opportunity to work with. The one performer who was really enlightening was Don Johnson. He really pushed me to deliver such a great performance. Don came from a small town just like I did. We had a common bond on that experience. He knew I was not a professionally trained actor and called me on it. "Where did you go to acting school," he screamed, "––on the farm?" I wanted to say, "Yes," but didn't. I loved the episode I did on *Nash Bridges.* I played my guitar and sang a rendition of "Desperado." I finger picked an acoustic guitar, no less. As for most demanding and who I would love to work with that I haven't yet? Hmmmm...there are so many people I would love to work with, I can't name them all. And I love to be challenged, so they may seem demanding at the time, but we get better by constantly challenging ourselves. (Smile.)

Chase Von: One thing my dear friend, author Betty Dravis, noted about you, is you're like a chameleon. (Smile.) She said that you're always beautiful, but you can change your appearance so much one has to look twice to be sure it's you. How much say do you have in how you will appear on the big screen and do you think being able to look so differently has added to the longevity of your career and kept you from being typecast?

Jenny: I had the very fortunate experience of working and starring in one of my first films in South Africa: *Never Say Die,* opposite one of my favorite actors I have worked with to date, Billy Drago. The director of the film was Yossi Wein and it was produced by Avi Lerner. I was very young

Photo by Dave Edwards, CEO of Daily Celeb.Com

at the time and the character I played was an army sergeant's daughter who had gotten caught up in a cult similar to the cult in Waco, Texas. On the second day of filming, the director said I would be a movie star if I could remember one thing: Change myself with makeup and hair and costumes...but when he saw me walking from a half mile away he should still know the person walking was JENNY McSHANE. I never forgot those words. He said I should watch John Wayne movies or Clint Eastwood movies so that I could see what he was trying to communicate. Yossi Wein (director) said, "Movie stars keep a piece of themselves in every character they play. Remember that *you*, Jenny McShane, are walking in a character's shoes and the audience wants to see both. When you see Clint Eastwood walking from a half-mile away, you know it is Clint Eastwood." I have tried the best I can to keep my own walk, personality and humbleness in all of the characters I have played to date.

Chase Von: I always try to ask a tough one, Jenny, so here's yours and you don't have to answer, if you don't want to. Your movie *Shark Attack 3* has a cult-like following. But there is one particular scene where an actor says something to you that was supposed to be edited from the film, but got left in. Because it is of adult content I won't linger on that, but it got a lot of attention and you yourself had absolutely nothing to do with it. Do you think that publicity has helped or hurt you, because most people have already heard this, though I can't remember who said it, but something to the affect of: "*The only thing worse than bad publicity is no publicity.*" And there are a lot of people that seem to think any kind of publicity, bad or good, keeps a person's name in the limelight. But again, no fault of your own...and suddenly it's just out there. Your comments? Because I think this is a perfect place to set the record straight, and for those that want the truth. Note: *THIS MATERIAL IS NOT APPROPRIATE FOR CHILDREN, FOR ADULTS WHO WISH TO VIEW, the link is as follows:* http://www.boreme.com/boreme/funny-2007/shark-attack-3-script-p1.php

Jenny: Wow, that is a very tough question. I was raised in a very strict Catholic home and am one of eight children. I have tried to take films that upheld the standard in which I was raised. Some of the roles I have played are very upsetting to my parents because of their content. I really feel strongly about making my family proud of my work and craft. Growing up, my parents only allowed us to watch one hour of television a night after our chores and homework were finished. My parents had to approve of the show and sit with us to watch it. I was able to watch every John Wayne movie or any "cowboys and Indians" movie there was without getting permission. I feel that the movies and shows I was allowed to watch have affected America in a very good and moral way; to know that strong and good will prevail. The line the actor said in *Shark Attack 3* was said as a joke to make the crew-- working long hours in Bulgaria--have a laugh. I was so in shock when the actor said the line that I walked out of the take with no response. *The words that were said had never been said to me in my life!* The editor of *Shark Attack 3* cut that take in and it was purchased by Lions Gate without being viewed, based on the success of the *Shark Attack* that I starred in with Casper Van Dien. That movie has made so much money for Lions Gate, and they should thank the editor who put the take in the final cut-- wherever he is-- for all of the money that was made by this. It was also ironic that the actor who said that to me was helped so much in his own career by the line. The actor's name is John Barrowman. John is an extremely talented actor who had been on a television show created by Aaron Spelling, playing Casper Van Dien's brother, ironically enough. But getting back to that, though, because of that accidental line being left in, John Barrowman received a lot of press--especially in London where he has won Tonys on the West End for his singing. John is an incredible singer and won his first Tony for *Sunset Boulevard* opposite Patti LuPone. I am very happy that the mistake helped him to be catapulted in his career. I have never worked with an actor who can be what old-school performers call a "superstar"--meaning they can sing, act and dance. I was told in the beginning of acting that you had to have all of those talents to get a studio deal.

Chase Von: Again, I think that was something you had absolutely no control over, but just like you told me on the phone, growing up on the farm--much as you hated it and as your own father said--gave you a work ethic that you, perhaps, wouldn't have had otherwise. And also, things in life happen that test your will sometimes. You have persisted and look at you now! (Smile.) And who would have thought that "one line" would be a blessing? I know when I was working on my last book, Murphy's Law seemed to kick in to the tenth power. I had it just about finished and was up in the wee hours of the morning working on it when I got an email message from a friend (who shall remain unnamed): It was an update on what this "famous" person was doing. I said, "Well, let me check this out... I clicked open the message and my screen faded in and out. I was like, "That's strange!" And then my computer just went haywire; I lost my manuscript, and another computer on the "slain" list. (I let my friend know and she, of course, apologized.) It wasn't her fault, but there I was...frustrated again. *But I persevered!* I'm of the belief that when you really want something, often if not all the time, fate will throw things in your path to see how much you *really* want it. Is that something you, yourself, have experienced, or how you view it? Because that one line--although initially, you might have looked at as being negative--has had a silver lining attached to it for you both. (Smile.)

Jenny: I definitely am a firm believer that if you want it you get it. I have gone to church to pray for every part I really wanted and it worked every time! I know that you are not supposed to ask for monetary things or cars, etc., but I just *really* wanted certain roles. I often think that when I don't get a role, I didn't want the role bad enough...if I wasn't willing to head to Saint Charles's or Saint Monica's to get it. I believe that everything that happens to you was meant to happen. As I am getting older, I look back on everything that has happened in my life and have no regrets. I have always followed my gut instinct, even in friendships and business dealings outside of acting. If I am not feeling good about a person or an opportunity I change my direction. I feel I have this "light" that I don't want to waste on someone who doesn't work in that "light." I would rather get an ice-fishing house and sit beside my dad on the lake than have stress or bad feelings. I am happiest when I can love and trust my environment and who is in it.

Chase Von: What are some of your favorite meals? And how do you stay in such fantastic shape?

Jenny: My mother was a fantastic cook. We didn't get to go to the restaurants very often, as you can imagine, because that would be some bill with eight children. My

Jenny McShane, Shark Attack 3, Lions Gate Films, Executive Producer Avi Lerner
Photo courtesy of Michael Regen, Melee Entertainment

father's friends, however, used to (coincidentally) show up at our house around dinnertime. I have to honestly say that in my career as an actress I have been to some pretty fancy places, but I have never tasted anything that was better than my mother's home-made cooking. My mother was also an amazing baker. Her cookies and cakes were always hidden in secret places, and "finding the stash-- quick" was a pastime of my brothers and sisters when Mom and Dad had to leave the house for whatever reason. (Smile.) My mom was an expert at baking a cake that was so delicious I can't even write about it or I will have to fly home to get it. I never had sushi before I came to Los Angeles and am a very big fan. My parents were obsessed with fishing growing up, especially my father. I always loved fish and craved it, especially fresh fish that was just caught and filleted and dumped into the frying pan. You can never have fish that tastes as good! *Fresh from the catch is amazing!* My Mom had mastered a beer-batter coating for her fish. I still love it when I go home and Dad has been out fishing and I get the fresh catch. My mother also made a "mean" spaghetti and meatballs. I always requested spaghetti and meatballs for my birthday dinner. I have made that for many of my friends in LA. I get a lot of respect when people taste mine. I am even thinking of creating my recipe so you can buy it in the frozen section at the grocery store because I have mastered the recipe my mother used. I guess, thinking about that, I would have to get Mom's consent to proceed with this venture. I love spaghetti and meatballs so much, I have found an LA restaurant that is close to the recipe: Maggianos. I was so excited when I landed *Furnace* in Nashville and found a Maggianos near the hotel, I asked one of the actors, Michael Pare, if he liked Maggianos. Michael is from New York and went crazy when he found out Maggianos was nearby. During the filming of the movie, I reserved a table

every night... What was that other question, Chase--
something about exercising or staying in shape? You must
have asked me about food first. (Smile.) But in a way, I
sort of answered this before; being raised on the farm I
have a really strong work ethic. I of course swim, and run
my dog and other things, but I was also really fortunate to
meet a physical trainer after my first three films.

Photo by Peter Makolovich

His name is Dion Jackson. Dion trained Jim Carrey, Dustin Hoffman, Belinda Carlisle, Jennifer Lopez, Natalie Ratano, Joan Severance, Pamela Anderson, Julia Roberts and a host of others. Dion's workout takes place in his home. He has you do fifteen minutes on the stair master, fifteen minutes on the treadmill, fifteen minutes on the bike and ten minutes of jumping rope. When you are done with cardio you proceed to the back of the house, which overlooks a beautiful outdoor garden. In the back you lift weights on all the same weight machines that would be in a gym. After the weights, you proceed to a wooden floor for sit-ups, push-ups, leg lifts, etc. The end of the workout is a massage on a massage table with a device that reminds me of my father's electric sander. Dion has a workout that is addicting. You feel so amazing you can't wait to get back the next morning. When I am not working, I also workout with all of Dion's teachings at a gym called *The Boulevard* in Beverly Hills. Working out makes you feel strong and capable to fight anything that comes your way.

Chase Von: Are there any future projects you're working on you can share with our readers? Also for those in LA and those visiting that are fortunate enough to get to see you and your band, Little Ruby, perform, what can they expect from that experience? I read where you began singing as a child, with your father playing the fiddle. (Smile.) And I am really touched you loved the country song I wrote, called "I'm Your Friend," which as you also know is pretty much just gathering dust. But again, how can people learn ahead of time where you are performing? And what will they come away with after having the experience?

Jenny: I've got a web page where I try to keep people up to date on what I'm doing, and I can't go into it now, Chase, but there is another band I might just join...but it's sort of hush-hush for now. And I love country music and really do love that song of yours. Thanks for blowing the dust off it. (Smile.)

Chase Von: What are some of the causes you feel very strongly about and support?

Jenny: Cancer! I've lost someone that was like a little brother to me...and it can kill so quickly! It was like I found out one day he had it and the next thing I knew I was at his funeral! There has got to be more that can be done about fighting this disease. I have learned through losing dear ones who were close to me, that we have to get up in the morning and live each day like it was our last. Natasha Richardson was one of my favorite actresses. The accident that just happened to her was so very sad. It seems to me that she was happy and was spending her last moments with her beloved family. We just can never know when our time is going to be up, Chase. I also give to and support charities that are close to me, though I don't want to broadcast which ones. (I think you have to keep some of those between you and you-know-who.) (Smile.) Though I will say, every year for the last four years I have supported *SOBER DAY,* which was begun by the great Robert Shapiro after losing his son.

Chase Von: How important is family to you, and what is your take on the state of our current world?

Jenny: *Family is everything, Chase!* I come from a very large one and for me that means I'm very lucky because there are more of us to love one another. I also think having a loving family makes one able to get along better with the rest of the world. I believe I mentioned before my father has twenty-two brothers and sisters, but one of his sisters is also one of the heads of the Franciscan Nuns,

Sister Ramona Miller. Also my Grandfather Alvin Miller Senior's sister is a nun, as well. Her name is Sister Iria Miller, and my Grandmother Lucille Miller's sister was a nun, also: Sister Marianne Kahnke, who we, unfortunately, lost last year. There are eight children in my family. I am the eldest, then Rebecca, Reginald, Lucas, Lance, Muriah, Karee and Candice. My parents are Alvin Miller Jr. and Donna Miller and I also want to mention my Grandpa Alvin Miller Sr. and my Grandma Lucille Miller, the parents of my father and the ones who had the twenty-two children. We lost my grandparents in the last two years... My Grandpa is responsible for my storytelling techniques...but then again if I had twenty-two children, I think people would listen right away! I also want to mention my beau, Jonathan Brayley, because he is family to me, as well. He is so supportive and is quite an inspiration himself. As an editor he has worked on *Troy, Rockstar, Harry Potter II, Sopranos, Bratz, Robosapien,* produced by Avi Arad (*Iron Man*), and is currently directing and editing a television show. My "Beau" also edited *Played* along with Matthew Booth, which was produced by Executive Producer John Daly and starred Val Kilmer, Gabriel Byrne and Mick Rossi. Mick Rossi is the one who wrote it and it won many awards, and John Daly is the one who produced *Platoon* that was directed by Oliver Stone, *The Last Emperor*, and he himself won thirteen Oscars for best movies. Unfortunately, he also died of cancer...recently, which is another reason I really want to find a cure for that disease. Also my sisters, Candice and Karee––believe it or not, Chase––did a song that was used in John Daly's film, *The Petersburg Cannes Express*. The song is called *"Rather Be Blind."* My beau Jonathan is also working on something else I can't share with you right now, but we think it's going to be big!

(Smile.) But for more about him, visit this link: Jonathan Brayley:
http://www.imdb.com/name/nm0106280/bio...

And I should have mentioned this earlier, Chase, when you asked me about my own music: I have two sisters, Karee and Candice, The Miller Sisters, who have been singing in bands for ten years, starting in Minnesota, moving through Nashville, Nevada and Alaska. They have mostly done rock-and-roll covers and written original country tunes, but now in Teton Valley they are experimenting with Bluegrass. Candice plays guitar, Karee plays mandolin and they have killer harmonies. Check them out online at: www.millersisters.net

See, entertaining does run in our family! (Smile.) And If I could blow their horn, they have opened for Buddy Guy, Michelle Branch and The Wreckers. One exciting gig they had was singing for Lisa Marie Presley's fortieth birthday party. After hearing the girls sing on New Year's Eve in Jackson Hole, Wyoming, Lisa asked to meet them backstage. Then later, music producer Michael Lockwood--who was her fiancé at the time and is now her husband-- hired them for the party; he paid for the band to play and travel to Ojai, California where the party was held. (Smile.)

... As for the state of our world, that honestly worries me, Chase. We, as a nation, are facing some very difficult times and I really do hope we pull together like "family" because we *have* to!

Chase Von: That's quite a recommendation for your sisters, Jenny, and having their song in a movie by someone that won thirteen Oscars is fantastic. And is your "Grandpa Miller" the one responsible for you being so funny? Sorry for your loss, but he certainly left a great piece of himself behind to live on in you! (Smile.)... What would you say if you were standing before a microphone that could be heard by every child on the planet, and regardless of what language they spoke, they would understand you? What positive advice would you give the children, if that were possible?

Jenny McShane

Photo by Dimitri Halkidis

Jenny: First, Chase, I would like to say that I love this question and I hope everyone who reads it, tries to answer it themselves in their own way. I can think of so many things to say, but what I'll say for now is: don't be selfish and be willing to learn about others. I started out in what is really "the country," but because of all my traveling, I've found that people are pretty much the same everywhere. And the more you learn, the more you grow, and learning about others you might think are different than you makes you grow even faster. Also try to be nice to everyone and "dream." Because one of those people you are nice to might surprise you and help you--when you least expect it-- to get closer to your dreams.

Chase Von: Where can our readers find your music to purchase? And your different websites and links where they can also learn more about your movie projects and events...or shows where you might appear?

Jenny: The best place to find me is at my official website: http://www.jennymcshane.com Here's my MySpace link as well: www.myspace.com/jennymcshane I can also be reached through Mary Putnam Greene, my manager, and Bruno Frasca, my guitar manager/instructor.

Chase Von: Jenny, on behalf of the *Student Operated Press*, thanks so much for sharing yourself with our readers. I look forward to talking with you again. I know when people look at your photos--especially men who may not have previously known of you--they are going to be thinking: *her beauty is literally breathtaking! (Smile.)* And it certainly is, but having spoken to you, I know you are also a *comedienne* and I can see why Howard Stern loved having you on his show. (Smile.) You're a riot! And you have such a lovely heart... Life is, indeed, too short to be serious all the time. So "Love and Light," and I'm looking forward to speaking with you again and listening to your coming audio with Judy. P.S., Carpal tunnel syndrome from what? (Heh-heh.) Our little secret... (Smile.) And also, when you speak to TIC next, please give my love and thanks for introducing us; another between-you-and-me "thang." (Smile.) I am truly glad they did.

****

"My father was in the 101st Airborne before I was born and used to tell me the way we worked was nothing compared to the Army. 'We had it easy,' he always told us."
- Jenny McShane, Actress, Singer, Model

****

Jenny McShane, Shark Attack 3, Lions Gate Films, Executive Producer Avi Lerner
Photo courtesy of Michael Regen, Melee Entertainment

Jenny: That doesn't have to be our secret, Chase! I have a hard time with the fancy cell phones. Or we can keep that a secret and we won't tell anyone you don't know how to

"Text" people either. (Smile.) And I'm glad they introduced us, as well. See what can happen when one person is nice to another? And thanks so much to you, Betty Dravis, and the *Student Operated Press. You guys really do rock!* Love and light back at you all! – Jenny :-)

Photo courtesy of Chaunce Hayden, CEO
and owner of Steppin' Out magazine

****

"Also try and be nice to everyone and 'dream.'
Because one of those people you are nice to might
surprise you and help you--when you least expect
it--to get closer to your dreams."
- Jenny McShane, Actress, Singer, Model
****

Interview with Sara McDonald

POET AND ARTIST
by Chase Von

Chase Von: Sara, on behalf of the *Student Operated Press* and myself, I want to thank you for doing this interview. I haven't yet read *When Rainbows Fall* but I have read *Stellar Expressions* and I really enjoyed that one. Recently I read and reviewed Alicia Keys' book, *Tears For Water,* on Amazon, and I have to admit I found some similarities in the ways you both express yourself. Although I do think you come across from what I can only say is an "older" perspective. In the introduction she states, and I quote: "I called this *Tears For Water* because everything I have ever written has stemmed from my tears of joy, of pain, of sorrow, of depression, even of question. Every single word has come from some form of my tears. I use them as water to nourish me, quenching the thirst for understanding myself. I don't mind drinking tears for water." The reason I share that is I would like for you to share with our readers why you, yourself, believe you write, and if you can relate to the reason Alicia Keys gives.

Sara: First off, I appreciate this amazing opportunity to be interviewed by the great Chase Von. :) Interesting, you speak of Alicia Keys' *Tears for Water* as I own it and read it frequently. I can definitely relate to her reason for writing. I believe writing, for me and most poets, is the greatest form of expressing your experiences, spirit, mind, and soul to yourself and–if you so choose–an audience. I believe the more I write, the more my strength grows. And reading back on poems, I can reflect on that growth.

Chase Von: Well, this is more like talking to an old friend than an interview, you know, Sara. (Smile.) We've been through a lot together, even though we connected from a great distance. I will always be grateful for your assistance with my own book, *Your Chance To Hear The Last Panther Speak,* and I also hope it makes you feel good sometimes to know that you are listed in it not only as a friend, in acknowledgements, but also as co-editor, even though you told me repeatedly, I didn't have to do that. I am, however, someone that tries as best I can to recognize whoever has assisted me in any way I can. I also don't know--with all the issues I was having at the time I was trying to bring it to light--if I could have done it without you. Though I've thanked you in private many times, it's great to have a forum to thank you again publicly. So again, talented and very "computer-smart lady," I thank you again. Now can you share with our readers how your younger years were, growing up, and when you first found yourself writing and how those writings eventually led to you being the author of two books?

Sara: Yes, it is like talking to an old friend, an interesting, conversational read for all! :) I am indeed grateful for being able to be a part of your project. I told you repeatedly that you didn't have to include me in the co-editor acknowledgements because the act itself was truly an honor to do, but the recognition is still very much appreciated. And you're very welcome. To answer your question about my younger years, I was always very creative. I started off drawing and painting and throughout the years have developed a love of all arts (theatre, music, fine arts etc.). Writing started for me at around fourteen. I just found it so soothing at times to just sit down and write out my feelings or experiences in a creative way. With dramatic arts and drawing and painting, you are somewhat limited either by the script or the muse, but with writing poetry, it's like capturing a concept in a bottle and spinning it your own unique way. The first ten years of my writing was just sitting in hard-copy form in a box. One day I decided that I would type every one of my poems up (dating back to 1995) and shortly after (since I type so fast–thank you, Lord), I had 300+ poems on my computer. I decided I would like to work on a project I could be proud to say I had completed for myself, so that is when *Stellar Expressions* came together. *When Rainbows Fall* is a collection of my more recent works and I'm putting more energy towards marketing and selling this body of work.

Chase Von: I would like to think I am not the only one, but my first reaction to seeing your picture was: "Tupac has a sister in Canada?" Whoever Tupac's father was did some traveling! (Smile.) On the serious tip, you and him have such similar eyes it is uncanny. You're a very lovely woman, by the way, and considering all the comments I know you get, you don't need me to tell you that. But how often does that question come up--you know, because of the physical resemblance--of whether you two are related? Perhaps personal, but my wife met Tupac before he was really huge... and got his autograph. Someone she was seeing at the time got jealous and threw it away. I guess fate must have felt badly for her and then allowed her to meet me to make up for it. (Smile.) But really, I would think on a daily basis people that are just meeting you must do double takes and then say, at least to themselves, "Where have I seen those eyes at?"

POETIC JUSTICE

Sara: Ha! Thank you so much! Honestly, I'm not sure how many people think that, but I have had a few people mention that to me. I have a poster-size charcoal drawing I did of him a few years ago up on my wall, and I took a picture the other day and stood near it. Upon looking at the picture, I can now see why people have said this. It's an amazing compliment to me because I have such a huge adoration for his work. To me, 2pac reeked of creativity, knowledge, wisdom, strength, courage, and faith. I can only hope that's what people see in me too. As far as your wife's autograph that was thrown away, I have no words for the man that did that (no wait I do, he should be shot...lol).

Chase Von: You are also a very talented artist, Sara. Did you include in your recent book, *When Rainbows Fall,* any of your own creations? And will you be doing any art shows in the future? You know you could combine the two if you wanted to. A book signing and an art showing all at the same time. (Smile.)

Sara: *Chase!* It's like you've been reading my mind with these questions! In *When Rainbows Fall* I wanted to keep it strictly the written word. I have formatted the book to be quite a unique piece of artwork all in itself, so I felt there was no need to include my drawings as I did in *Stellar Expressions.* And yes, I *will* be doing an art show in the near future. I won't give away all the details, but the overall concept is "Art for All Senses". Stay tuned--it may be coming to a city near you. (Smile.)

Chase Von: I know you admire Tupac immensely and your writer's name now--Poetic Justice, I believe--comes from the movie him and Janet Jackson were in. I also remember when you had--or still have, I don't know-- another name, but a writer's name that states your admiration more clearly. (Smile.) Can you expound on why you are so impressed with his legacy of work, as am I, but also on other writers that you admire as well?

Sara: Yes, my name does come from that movie as well as that I feel I do words *justice*...in a modern-day world where we make acronyms for everything and language is simply being crushed by technology. Why I'm so impressed with his legacy of work? Oh, good question! I'd simply re-use the word you used: *legacy*. As I mentioned earlier, he was a compound of every element that I find most admirable in a human being, but vulnerable enough to allow his words to come to light for all to hear. He just brought a sense of true raw emotion and reality to all of his bodies of work. Honestly, I admire any artist who emits that energy through their work because realness is what reaches and resonates through people...Other individual writers I admire: Maya Angelou (of course!), Augusten Burroughs, Walter Mosley, Alicia Keys, Common. And those I am so proud to say are my closest friends such as Moka Only, Jeff Spec, Narai Dawn, Jena Fair, Omar Khan, Ishkan, Birdapres, Sichuan... I have a large creative circle. MySpace's Rhymesoulnice, Sirhavoc, Deepoet, Brian, and, of course, *you!*

Chase Von: You and singer Jena are friends, as well. I remember when I found that out and thought, *Small world!* Her song, "Can Anybody Spare Some Change," or I think the short title is just "Spare Change," still touches me in ways I can't begin to describe. I mention her because I'm wondering, are you going to branch out into lyric writing, as well? I've seen some of your short stories, so I already know a novel from you is certainly not out the question either.

Sara: *Ah, the lovely Jena!* Yes, she, funnily enough, will be the first owner of my second book. Agreed, she is truly an *amazing* talent... Other people have asked me about song writing, as well, and right now I can say: time will tell. I often don't think I'll ever do certain things, yet I have now crossed them off the list...lol... I would like to; I'm not quite knowledgeable in the structured song-writing format yet.

Chase Von: I haven't heard from Erica Rose for a spell now, not that I hear from her often anyway, but I do remember her sharing with me that she co-wrote "A Woman's Worth" with Alicia Keys; and in the credits of Alicia's book, she does in fact give her credit, which gives me all the more respect for Alicia. I know also Erica Rose--who is a talent in her own right as well--is touring now with Alicia Keys and that they, too, are great friends. Considering how talented you and Jena are, I can just see something like that in the future happening with you two, because I know you both are down-to-earth people, also. And if you did help write a song for her, she would certainly recognize that publicly as well. But have you ever experienced any friction in the writing world? I know I have on occasions--and how, if so, do you deal with it?

Sara: I can't say I've experienced any friction in the writing world. Sometimes if I collaborate on a piece with someone, you can butt heads regarding concept or wording, but I don't collaborate with anyone that I can't settle that with amicably. After all, it's all for the greater good: a creative masterpiece. I don't generally tolerate friction or negativity, so perhaps that's why I don't experience it much. I learned a short while ago that I steer my own course, so I veer away from that road altogether.

Chase Von: How important is family to you, and what is your take on the state of our current world? And who are some of the people you consider your heroes?

Sara: Oh, three questions in one! :) Family is very important to me. I've been blessed to be able to make great friends from all over the world who are now known as my extended family. The only thing that I find more important is creating and maintaining a welcoming "home," and that is what I think the world needs more of today. I'll leave it up to the readers to decipher that one. :)...My heroes? As it says on my MySpace page: those who can change and those who possess the power to make change (when change is needed) *and* happy people. I look up to those who can look at their life every single day and say, "I couldn't want for anything else."

Chase Von: What would you say if you were standing in front of a microphone and could be heard by every child on the planet, and regardless of what language they spoke, they would understand you? What positive advice would you give the children, if that were possible?

Sara: My initial response when I read this question: *cry and pray* (and I did both of these upon reading the question). My positive advice to give children: never be afraid to be you and live your dreams, because they can come true.

Chase Von: Where can our readers find your book, *When Rainbows Fall,* as well as your first release, *Stellar Expressions*? Can you share your MySpace and any other websites where they can learn more about you and your writings, and also see some of your artist creations?

Sara: Currently, you can order *When Rainbows Fall* directly off my personal MySpace page:
www. myspace.com/whenrainbowsfall

The first ten will be limited-edition books with a personal touch courtesy of *moi.* :) Starting in the summer, it will be available through the webpage as well as Lulu. com...*Stellar Expressions* sold out through www. myspace.com/stellarexpressions but is available through Trafford Publishing (ISBN: 142510872-5).

My personal My Space page is:

www.myspace.com/thuglifebiatcho24

and also features excerpts from both books in the "Blog" section, and "My Pictures" section features most of my recent artwork.

Chase Von: And what is the reason you decided to title your latest book *When Rainbows Fall?* I couldn't let you go without asking that. (Smile.)

Sara: The title of the second book, *When Rainbows Fall,* actually derived from a poem I never wrote. I came up with the title based on the idea that everything that falls was risen or rises first, but never wrote a poem to depict this. So I decided I would use that title for the collection.

Chase Von: Can you share one of your shorter pieces here?

Sara: No-just kidding. :)

11:49 pm

A road freshly tarred black
Makes for mysteriously sleek interference
Like the 7:30 am alarm call
Leaves an unsightly wound

Hope is your umbrella for this rainy day

A few seconds of delay gives chance for light to create
a vast field of dreams in which you will lay
For now the goal is your target practice

Awarded by your own shine
You will, at some point in time,
stop skating a figure eight
And be so enveloped in the moment
to not notice the change in your fate;

Now, you are simply gliding

Chase Von: On behalf of the *Student Operated Press* and myself, Sara, I again thank you for finding the time to do this. It's a fine line, I find, when I'm interviewing talented individuals who are also friends. I hope I didn't cross any. I do know that you have been through some really hard experiences in your life and that the strength of your character is displayed in your writings. I hope our readers go the next step and bless themselves by reading your works, particularly women, who, I think, will truly relate to what you are courageously sharing with this world of ours. Going to sign off here, like I always do, and wish you continued success in all you do so...love and light to you Always, Buddy. :)

Sara: And again, thank *you*, Chase for the truly amazing opportunity. No crossing of lines at all, you really do an amazing job. Thank you for your kind words and for spreading the news about my new book *When Rainbows Fall*. To all readers, I appreciate you taking the time to get to know me and my work through this interview. To learn more, just visit www. myspace.com/whenrainbowsfall. 'Til next time–love & light to all! Sara

****

*"Family is very important to me. I've been blessed
to be able to make great friends from all over the
world who are now known as my extended family.
The only thing that I find more important
is creating and maintaining a welcoming
'home,' and that is what I think the
world needs more of today."*
- Sara McDonald, Poet, Artist

****

By Poet and Artist, Sara McDonald

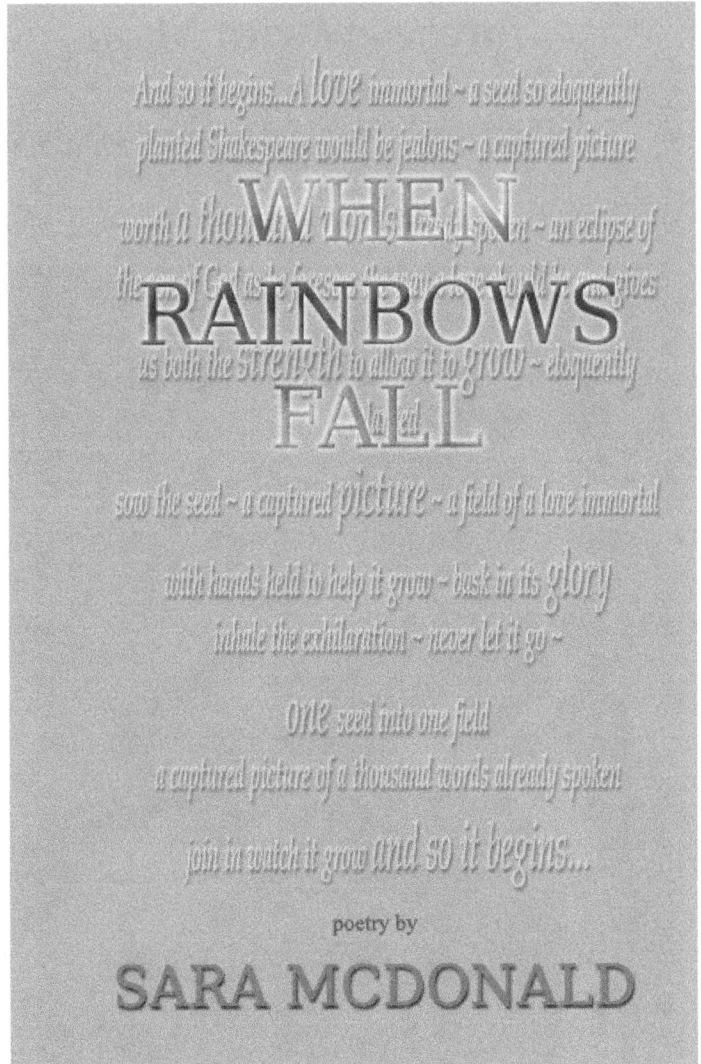

****

*"My positive advice to give children: never be
afraid to be you and live your dreams,
because they can come true."
- Sara McDonald, Poet, Artist*

****

Interview with Nhojj

INCREDIBLE FOUR-OCTAVE SINGER
by Chase Von

Chase Von: Nhojj, this is a true pleasure! So on behalf of the *Student Operated Press* and myself, I really want to thank you. When I got that music gift from you, I figured why not ask him for an interview? Worst-case scenario, you would be too busy, so I was pleasantly surprised when you wrote back and said, "Let's do it!" So again thanks for sharing yourself with our readers.

Nhojj: Thank you so much for extending the invitation. Things have been really busy this year with the release of the new disc *Soul Comfort,* but this has always been my dream, so I'm counting my blessings.

Chase Von: You've led a very interesting life. Growing up in Guyana and then moving to Trinidad and Tobago before making your way to the U.S. and New York. I've read that your father was a minister and you began singing in church at the mere age of six, with your sister playing the organ, as well. And that you were appearing on radio stations and eventually even performed for the presidents of Guyana and Trinidad....What were your younger years really like, being a performer at such a young age, and was there any difficulty transitioning from that lifestyle into the American way of life?

Nhojj: It's interesting you should ask me about growing up in Guyana, I just returned from their 2nd Annual Fashion Week. It was pretty amazing to be back, to perform and to visit some of the places from my childhood. Growing up in Guyana was pretty normal. I went to school, studied, got into trouble, enjoyed my friends, got teased, cried, laughed, and dreamed. Performing was just another facet to my life as a child. I was really excited to move to New York––it was like a big adventure, full of possibilities––so I was looking forward to it, which I think played a big role in how easy the transition was. I think the only thing that took some time to adjust to--and sometimes I feel as if I'm still adjusting--are winters. *I love the heat!* ...lol...

Chase Von: I know you have a huge, worldwide fan base, but how supportive are the people of Guyana and Tobago and Trinidad of your successes? And do you get to return there, because I would imagine you still have family there also yes?

Nhojj
Someday Peace Love & Freedom

Nhojj: Right now most of my fans live in the USA and Europe. I want to spend more time over the next few years cultivating and re-establishing a following in the Caribbean in general. I'll be performing at the Barbados Music Awards in January, and I think that would be a great step in connecting with music fans there. I don't get back as often as I would like, partly because most of my family lives in the US, UK or Canada.

Chase Von: The way I learned about your music was from a friend and fantastic fellow-poet Vennie, author of the soon to be released poetry collection, *Dusted Shelves*. She wrote me one day and said, "Chase, you have to check this guy out!" *I'm glad I did!* Initially, I thought of Maxwell, then I thought of Prince, and then I thought of a variety of other people who are all great...but you have your own unique sound that is distinctly *you*.

Nhojj: Thank you, and I'm glad Vennie connected us. *Thank you, Vennie!* I remember when I first heard Maxwell, I got so excited, because it was a bit of validation for me: we had such similar voices. Believe it or not, growing up I didn't listen a lot to Prince, I listen to him now; I'm actually watching a live performance of him as I type...lol... But all the comparisons have been very encouraging, as an artist. You know this because you are an author: there is so much pressure to conform, to give up your dream, so these give me strength to continue pressing on.

Chase Von: Dozie, who I've interviewed as well, occasionally uses instruments from Africa in his music, and I was wondering--with all the many references to your Caribbean sound fused with Reggae and Jazz and R and B--if you incorporate instruments that are from your native lands?

Nhojj: *Someday Peace Love & Freedom* was inspired by my experience growing up in the Caribbean and it expresses more of a West Indian sensibility and perspective. We didn't use any local instruments, but we did use the musical style, the vibe and the feeling. I like trying different things with each project, so *Soul Comfort* has a different vibe. But on the flight back from Guyana, I was listening to the steel pan radio station. The steel pan originated in Trinidad & Tobago. I was really inspired, so I'm sure you'll hear more of it in future projects.

Chase Von: I was born in Japan, have lived in England growing up and various other places, being a military,

unspoiled child, more commonly known as "military brats." (That brat part still mystifies me.) (Smile.) But do you think your being from another place other than the United States and the many other places you have traveled to and performed at, allows for your music and your lyrics to have more of a universal appeal? Because your music is being well received all over the entire globe. And do you think if you weren't as well traveled as you are, you would still be able to achieve that?

Nhojj: I'd never connected the two before, but I think it is true, traveling exposed me to different cultures, views, forms of expression, ways of being...and my whole experience informs my work in subtle ways even I don't know. But at the fundamental level, I believe this is a gift that I've been given. Traveling shaped it, molded it, and made it richer, but I think I was born this way.

Chase Von: One of the things that blows people away is your four-octave range. You've been compared to Stevie Wonder, Marvin Gaye, Bobby McFerrin, Maxwell, Prince and I could go on... All are legends in their own right! *And like Prince, you're the whole show!* You're self-taught and you write your own lyrics, arrange your own songs, play all the instruments, on some occasions, and even produce it. I've also read that you prefer being independent, like a few of my other friends, because it allows you total control.

Recently I read where "Miss Control" herself, Janet Jackson, is disappointed with her sales and is planning on going more the independent route, as well. I still occasionally hear a mainstream song I like, but more and more, I find myself listening to yourself, Dozie, Barbara Evans, Willard Barth, Janice B, Kristin, Leah DeVon, Rachael Bell, Trish Andrews, The Artist C, Alice Marie,

Brian O'Neal, Alina, Jena, Lisa Lavie, and a host of other people who aren't with major labels...or if they are, just recently signed. My question though is this: If a major label said they would allow you creative control would you bite the bullet? Or are you totally against being with a major label? Because you certainly have the talent...and then some!

Nhojj: I play guitar and a bit of piano, but it's all forms of self-expression. I feel things that I want to express; I've learnt things from my spiritual journey that I want to share. Music is my medium, music is the tool I've been given to help shape the world. I've just accepted the call. I believe we all have seeds of genius waiting inside; we just have to have the courage to accept the call. If a major came along and gave me creative control––the room and support to grow as an artist and a human being––and I felt they truly believed in what I create and were committed to using their resources to support my music, I would bite the bullet. For me being an independent artist is not sitting around waiting for that to happen; it's taking control and using the many resources I have right now, and carving out a future that may or may not include a major. There are so many successful artists who have gone the independent route, and so many who have gone the major-label route. So we artists have options, and options are always good.

Chase Von: Not only are you a singer who is getting accolades the world over for your initial CD *"I've Been Waiting For You,"* as well as your other release, *"Some Day, Peace, Love and Freedom,"* but you also are an actor. You appeared in a stage play called *The Making of The Black Man*, directed by Sean, which I hear got all kinds of positive reviews. And you also sing some of your original music in it, as well. With your original look––and

apparently women are digging not only your voice but also you, yourself (Smile.)--do you see yourself pursuing more roles and perhaps tackling the movie industry, as well?

Nhojj: *Absolutely--so many things, so little time!* I don't have the time right now to audition and pursue acting the way I would want to. The disadvantage of being an independent artist is that I'm also the manager, the secretary, the booking agent... But that is changing, and help is on the way, so soon, hopefully, I will be able to get back to acting.

Chase Von: The list of awards you have garnered already is mind-boggling! "1 Fusion" was on MySpace NY Charts for six weeks! "Neo-Soul" was on it for an incredible twenty-five weeks! You were also nominated the Best Male Performance for the Fresh Fruit Festival 2004, Outstanding Male Album Nomination for the Outmusic Awards 2004, and Honorable Mention at the 13th and 14th Annual Billboard Song Contests for 2006 and 2007! You have two film sound tracks, *Finding Me* and *Blue Print* and your acting credits include *Out of Dreams*, a play, *Twirling Earl & City Sights* which is an animation, *Jesse O, I Think I'm Falling in Love,* a music video on Logo TV, *Fabulosity and Downsizing the Gods* for New Fest, and *The Making of the Black Man,* which was with Fringe Festival... On your fourth CD, *Soul Comfort,* you worked with Carl Evans who has worked with the amazing Stevie Wonder and the legendary Barry White, David Stark who has worked with the Super Freak himself, Rick James and Teena Marie who I love! (smile) And you filmed an *Intimate Evening with Nhojj,* an unplugged performance with Emmy-nominated director Bill Cote. And you're also performing there with incredible jazz guitarist Marcelo Cardozo... Who are some of the people in the industry you would love to work with and would love to work with again? And who are some of the people you consider mentors and role models?

Nhojj: I would love to work with Me`shell Ndegeocello, Jamiroquai, Stuart Matthewman who produces Sade and Maxwell and Trevor Horn (Seal's early producer). I love working with Marcelo. We've been performing together for about five years now, and *Soul Comfort* is the second time I've worked with Jon Evans. In terms of role models - Barack Obama is my role model; he has done something that many people consider impossible.

Chase Von: How important was it to you because of your upbringing, to produce a Gospel CD and considering how well all your other music is doing, how well is that one doing? Will there be future all-Gospel projects, as well?

Nhojj: I felt it was a gift to my parents. Gospel music is very important to them and it's music I grew up listening to. I don't like repeating myself. Each project I've done has been different and unique, and allowed me to explore a different type of music, so there probably won't be another Gospel project. In terms of its success, it allowed me to tour Europe and Canada and the Caribbean, so it did really well.

Chase Von: Are there any future projects you have coming up you can share with our readers? Also any places you're going to be appearing at, so those in the area can check out your shows?

Nhojj: The next show I'm focusing on is at Cornelia Street Café on Oct 22nd at 8 pm. It will be an intimate set and, of course, the Barbados Music Awards in January that won't be an intimate set. ...lol... I've had a very busy year in terms of performing, so there won't be too much more between those two shows. I need to review the year and make plans for the new year. I want to do more online work, add more to my youtube channel. Next year will be an exciting year, more recording, of course, more touring, and a few surprises.

Chase Von: One thing I can certainly say about your music: it is mood changing. (Smile.) Just like our mutual friend Vennie says; she puts you on and instantly she is in another place mentally. With the soothing and mellow Caribbean and Jazz and Soul combination it obviously takes all listeners to another place, but is this something you do consciously, or is it just what comes from the man known as Nhojj?

Nhojj: LOL. I think it's a bit of both. I'm a pretty mellow person. In general, I like the simple things, like good company. I like to laugh, I like connection, seeing what we humans have in common...growth, empowerment. I believe we should make the people around us happy, better somehow. And my music is just an extension of who I am and what I believe.

Chase Von: What are some of your favorite meals? And how often do you get to enjoy them being on the road so much?

Nhojj: I love "soul food" (mac-and-cheese...yummy). I also love Caribbean food; I ate way too much while I was in Guyana, but generally I don't eat too much of these foods. I generally eat very simple foods, mostly vegetarian; my own internal ying and yang.

Chase Von: And I also see where you are a strong supporter of HIV/AIDS, drug addiction, disability awareness, Earth Day celebrations and peace and domestic violence. Are there any personal reasons you feel so

adamant about the worthiness of these causes, and I know they are all worthy and you certainly don't have to address them all, but let's just say, Disability Awareness? The reason I pick that one is because so many are coming back from the wars disabled and recently I met a model, actress and screenwriter who is a traumatic-brain-injury survivor (TBI) and she has accomplished some amazing things, despite that. Her name is Kitania "Kitty" Kavey and she's an inspiration to so many! I also suffer from PTSD myself.

Nhojj: I was reading this morning *Think and Grow Rich,* and in it the author tells the story of his son who was born with no ears and how out of this perceived disability, so much good came out of it. I think our disabilities are opportunities. Some of the most successful people in the world have disabilities, like your friend Kitania. I want to help shed a positive light on the way we view our individual experiences.

Chase Von: What would you say if you were standing in front of a microphone that could be heard by every child on the planet, and regardless of what language they spoke, they would understand you? What positive advice would you give the children, if that were possible?

Nhojj: Every morning find one thing, one thing that makes you happy, and tell everyone you know about it, or write about it, or draw a picture about it. And each day find one more thing that makes you happy, and don't let anyone stop you, because your happiness is your magical power.

Chase Von: Where can our readers find more of your music? Your different websites and links where they can also purchase it as well as the video links?

Nhojj: You can find my music on all the major download stores like iTunes, Rhapsody, Amazon, CDbaby.com and there are links to these on my site, www.nhojj.com, and my MySpace page www.myspace.com/nhojj

Chase Von: Nhojj, on behalf of the *Student Operated Press* and myself, thanks so much again for sharing yourself with our readers and honoring me by doing so. I do have one last question, though: What does the name Nhojj mean, if you can share that?

Nhojj: Nhojj is the name of my Spirit and it means peace and beauty. Nhojj shines through me.

Chase Von: Thanks for sharing that. I am sure many inquisitive minds wanted to know, as well. (Smile) Continued success with your music and acting careers and in all your pursuits, brother. *One love!*

Nhojj: Thank *you* for sharing your time with me, and continued success to you. *Love and light!*

****

"Every morning find one thing, one thing that makes you happy, and tell everyone you know about it, or write about it, or draw a picture about it. And each day find one more thing that makes you happy, and don't let anyone stop you, because your happiness is your magical power."
- Nhojj, Singer, Musician, Actor, Songwriter
****

****

*"Nhojj is the name of my Spirit and it means peace
and beauty. Nhojj shines through me."*
- Nhojj, Singer, Musician, Actor, Songwriter

****

Interview with Shannon Grissom

MULTI-TALENTED WOMAN
by Chase Von

Chase Von: Hey, Shannon, and on behalf of the Student Operated Press and myself, I thank you for doing this. I know when we spoke, you were in your gallery hard at work, so thanks so much for taking the time out from your busy life to share yourself with our readers.

Shannon: Thank *you*, Chase, and the *Student Operated Press* for having me here.

Chase Von: Shannon, you're one of those people that do so very many things, it's hard to pick where to start first. (Smile) But let's begin at the beginning. What was your childhood like? Where did you grow up and when you were young, did you ever envision you would be doing all the things you are doing now?

Shannon: I had a wonderful childhood. I grew up in Almaden, a suburb in San Jose, California. My mother was a teacher and my father worked at IBM. Both of my parents were really creative and they encouraged any creative activity. In addition, my mother was also a music major with perfect pitch. Music was a big part of our life. Mom would play piano and we would either sing with her or play our instruments. I'd play the clarinet, my twin sister Cheryl would play her flute and my little sister Jill played the French horn... *Nope!* I did not see me where I am today. When I was little I wanted to be a pilot and rock star. I'm still working on those two. I think I'm going to let the pilot dream go. (Smile.)

Chase Von: I've seen some of your art and it is fantastic! I really loved the picture of your grandmother; you captured the soul in her eyes so vividly. And you actually did that by using a black-and-white photo. Were you told her eyes were blue, or did you actually know her? I know I have relatives I've seen black-and-whites of that I didn't get to meet in person. And how long does it take you to do a painting that requires such detail?

Shannon: I was so lucky to be able to have great relationships with all of my grandparents, and lucky that both grandmothers lived long lives... It takes me about a month to do a portrait, but I also work on about five pieces at once. That way I'm always in the mood for one of them. I always want my energy to be positive when I approach the canvas.

Chase Von: Well one thing I found out while talking with you is––and that, too, is amazing––you weren't born with a paintbrush in your hand. (Smile.) I guess back then it was a silver spoon... Heh, Heh :) But when did you start painting? And what drove you to be so passionate about it? And what would you say to anyone that has a dream that they keep putting on the back burners because of events in their perceived "nows" and what is happening in the present in their lives? I know when I wrote my first book, *Pink, Blue and Green,* and even my most recent one, *Your Chance To Hear The Last Panther Speak,* I burned some midnight oil--*and then some!* And I guess what I am saying is that people who find time to pursue their passions--despite of, and in addition to, what the other things in their lives might be demanding of them--have more of a shot at living their actual dreams. And on top of that, even if it doesn't materialize into fame and fortune, at least they won't have to look back on their lives one day and think, *I didn't even try!* My friend Willard Barth, inspirational singer, life coach and songwriter, calls it *expanding your comfort zones.* You have done that *and then some!* (Smile.)

Shannon: How about silver-plated?...lol... I painted a bit in high school but did not take formal lessons. I did not start painting in earnest until I was thirty-two. I took an Adult Ed class and knew right then that I was supposed to be an artist. I went out the next day and had business cards printed. Oh, I wasn't very good, but I knew where I was going. Ever since that class I've made painting a priority. I would get up at three am to paint before work. After work I'd be too tired to create. I still paint first thing every morning...You have a great point about expanding your comfort zones. I am really a shy person. All these things that I have accomplished have been *way* out of my comfort zone. I just did them anyway. Sometimes *shaking,* and sometimes not so great, but I put myself out there anyway.

Chase Von: Have you ever thought about what your life might be like now, if you didn't go after your dreams?

Shannon: Oh yeah... I thank God every day that I have been blessed with creativity and perseverance! You see, I know what I was like before I was creating. I was not happy. *Painting saved my life!* I quit drinking when I started painting. I could see there was going to be problems had I continued down that road.

Chase Von: Having spoken to you on the phone, it's easy to tell how, with your lovely personality, you can keep an audience engaged. Have you always been so people-friendly, or did that part of your personality evolve when you became an internationally known public teacher with your own art show? And how hard is it for you to handle your celebrity status?

Shannon: Thanks, Chase. I've always been good one-on-one with people, but the group dynamic is a learned skill. The first Chamber mixer I attended, I could only last a half-hour. I was afraid to speak to anyone. I made myself stay a half-hour longer each time I went, until one day I could attend the whole event. Now I look for people who appear as scared as I was, and I talk to them. As for handling celebrity status, I make sure I get enough time by myself. The grandkids keep me grounded. They don't care that I'm on TV. *I'm just Grammy!* And I still take out my own garbage. (Smile.)

Chase Von: Where can people actually purchase your original artwork? Do you have auctions at your own personal gallery or do you travel and share your artworks across the country and world, as well?

Shannon: They can purchase original art at my studio. I have traveled with my art, but am not currently on tour. I'm hunkering down this fall and winter to complete my books and CD. Prints and other merchandise are available at http://www.shannongrissom.com

Chase Von: Well, now you're a composer, a singer, an author, a painter and the host of your own art show that has won, or been a finalist in W.A.V.E., from 2003 until 2007. Your show is seen and syndicated in Washington, Tennessee, Idaho, California, Arizona, New York, New Mexico, Illinois, Oregon, just to name a few--and carried by so many stations, I'm going to have to ask our readers to check your web links so I don't get carpal tunnel syndrome from typing them all. (Smile.) How does it make you feel--knowing how late in life you started painting--to be the host of your own television show and teaching others how to do what you feel so passionately about?

Shannon: It makes me feel great. I feel like I am here to inspire others to create. Whether you are a cook or a gardener or a painter, my show gets your creative juices flowing.

Chase Von: Since I know you're a singer and composer, as well, do you ever sing any of your original songs for your audiences? And what is this about: if you don't like a painting you do on your show, you just throw it out right there? (Smile.)

Shannon: *I'm so excited--I'm working on my first CD!* I've not performed it live...yet. It is coming soon though. I'll let you know when I make my first appearance. As for throwing out paintings, I do it all the time. The feedback I get from the audience is that it gives them permission to not be perfect.

Chase Von: I draw a little myself but in your own words, how do you think that art contributes to the lives of us all and the title of your show, *Give Your Walls Some Soul,* of course, captures some of that meaning, but if you could expound a bit more on it for our readers; what it personally means to you on an in-depth level?

Shannon: The energy and passion of artwork becomes a life of its own. My goal is to touch every viewer's soul.

Chase Von: How did you come up with the idea of Sock Monkey? And what inspired you--who have already done so much in your life--to write children's book?

Shannon: Sock Monkey was my mother's idea. A couple of years after she passed away, I entered a competition that required you to paint a fish and a pear and relate it to someone you knew. I saw the Sock Monkey and thought I'd do a tribute to Mom. Also in the painting is a black-and-white photo of her as a child, as well as a kazoo. You can see, I took great liberties with the fish. I didn't want the smell in my studio, so I painted goldfish crackers. *Hey, they didn't say what kind of fish!* Additionally, besides the gift of music, Mom had the gift of humor. My first Sock Monkey painting was titled, "I Will Remember You." I've done thirty-six sock monkey paintings and that first one continues to be a favorite.

Chase Von: Who are some of the painters, singers, composers and authors you truly admire and look up too? And who are some of the individuals in your life that have been key mentors and people that truly encouraged you to pursue your talents and dreams?

Shannon: Oh, it's so hard to choose. Of the painters, Vermeer and Sargent resonate most with me. As for authors, I love the humor of Mark Twain and the candid view from Steinbeck. Composers Clementi and Pleyel. And contemporary Diamond's... *Jonathan Livingston Seagull* is brilliant. Key people in my life have been my parents, my sisters and my husband Dwight. Michael Linstrom and Janet Vanderhoof have also really impacted my painting. Doug Jones has really impacted my business. I am really blessed. I feel that everyone is conspiring to help me succeed.

Chase Von: Jumping back to Sock Monkey. (Smile.) Is Sock Monkey going to be your only children's book character? Or are their characters in the Sock Monkey story that are going to have stories all their own?

Shannon: There will be more Sock Monkey characters and their friends will be diversified.

Chase Von: Has Sock Monkey ever made any guest appearances on any of the children's shows? And if not, is that something you perhaps see in the future for him? I watch a lot of children's shows and one is really just two hands with eyeballs on them. Had me at the edge of my seat. (Smile.) Also, is there an actual Sock Monkey available to buy? I can certainly see people using it to read bedtime stories to their children. And what's the chance of Sock Monkey having his own show and his own CD and his own career? I'd like to be a part of that. Although my kids don't dig them now, I came up with some pretty original songs when they were kids that are a bit embarrassing now. (Smile.) One was "Do the Bunky Dance," and I bet just from the title, your toes are tapping already but, my daughter now grown, detest that name Heh, Heh :) It was really cute back in the day though. (Smile.) There's a song in my book, also, called "I Bet That You Like Them Too." It's about peanut-butter cookies, and I would be honored if Sock Monkey sung it! (Smile.)

Shannon: Your songs sound wonderful. Yes! I can see an animated Sock Monkey show and it makes me smile. *And if I can see it and feel it, well then it can happen!* Thus far, he's been camera shy. Yep, I think he is going to have his own empire. As for purchasing Sock Monkeys, there are many wonderful monkey-makers out there. You'd be surprised when you Google: sock monkey.

Chase Von: How important is family to you, and what is your take on the state of our current world?

Shannon: Family and good friends that are like family are really important to me. The only thing that matters at the end of the day is the people you love and the people that love you. As for the state of the current world, I can't speak to that. I shelter myself from world events in order to keep a positive slant on my painting. I am however very involved locally. Here I can make a difference--*and I do!* I'm on the board of the local YMCA and am president of the Culinary and Hospitality Foundation of San Benito County. Both groups are very youth oriented.

Chase Von: What would you say if you were standing in front of a microphone that could be heard by every child on the planet, and regardless of what language it was they spoke, they would understand you? What positive advice would you give the children, if that were possible?

Shannon: What would you do if you knew you couldn't fail? (From Eleanor Roosevelt.) The only failure is in not following your dreams. There is always a way! And the way will be shown to you once you begin, and it's up to you to move toward it. Don't ever give up.

Chase Von: Where can our readers go to learn more about you? Your television art show *Give Your Walls Some Soul*, your CDs, your books? And are there any future projects you have in mind, like modeling? Or acting? (Smile) As they can tell by your pictures, not only are you multi-talented, you are also very pretty. And being someone that has actually spoken to you, I for one know you aren't really shy. (Smile.)

Shannon: Oh, Chase, thanks so much. You are so kind. They can visit http://www.shannongrissom.com to see my paintings, books, music and merchandise. In a few months I'll also be developing creativity teleseminars. Here's some other links as well. (Smile.)
Shannon's Web TV CHANNEL
http://www.shannongrissomchannel.com
Everybody's Favorite Sock Monkey
http://www.monkeymadeofsockies.com

Chase Von: On behalf of the *Student Operated Press* and myself, Shannon, I truly thank you for finding the time to do this. I'm wishing you continued success and best wishes to you and yours, including Sock Monkey. :) He's really a cute little fellah. (Smile.) So thanks so very much again and blessings to you always.

Shannon: Chase, thank *you* and the SOP for taking the time to interview me. It is always so nice to talk with you. Blessings to you, Chase, and all of you out there.

****

"What would you do if you knew you couldn't fail? (From Eleanor Roosevelt.) The only failure is in not following your dreams. There is always a way! And the way will be shown to you once you begin, and it's up to you to move toward it. Don't ever give up."
- Shannon Grissom, Artist, Singer, Songwriter
****

****
"The only thing that matters at the
end of the day is the people you
love and the people that love you."
- Shannon Grissom, Artist, Singer, Songwriter
****

303

Interview with Debra Garrett

LOVELY ACTRESS AND MODEL
by Chase Von

Chase Von: Debra, on behalf of the *Student Operated Press* and myself, I thank you, I know you said you would get back to me when filming wrapped up, but I'm still both surprised and grateful that you did. You have so much going on, so it is truly appreciated.

Debra: Thanks, Chase and the SOP, for having me as your guest.

Chase Von: I, of course, want to know--as I imagine the readers do--whatever you can share about your new movie, but before we get into that, can you share what your childhood was like? I see where you were born in Virginia, but you've lived in New York, California and

Japan, as well as Florida. What was it like moving around so much when you were young, and are you like myself, a "military unspoiled child"? (Smile.)

Debra: No, not at all. I didn't move until I was eighteen. I grew up in Newport News, Virginia, but the reason I moved to so many locations afterwards, was to pursue acting, and also because my ex-husband was a major league baseball player. Oh and, Chase, don't you mean "military brat"? (Smile.)

Chase Von: Born in Virginia? Both my parents are from there, as well, although my dad is deceased. From what I remember, it's quite close to where Walton's Mountain was. Well, then again, it's a mountain so it's probably still there. Heh-heh :) Do you have relatives there, and do you think we might be related? Because you have some high cheekbones... Do you have any American Indian in you, in particular, Blackfoot and Cherokee? And how supportive are your family and friends of your chosen profession now?

Debra: Yes, many of my relatives are all in the Tidewater, Virginia area, mostly nieces and nephews, and I have Cherokee Indian in me... Everyone is very supportive and wants me to succeed, and have stated that they believe I will... More than I believe, but I trust them. And I doubt that we're related... ha-ha

Chase Von: I'll check the family tree when time permits. (Smile.) How old were you when you realized that acting was in your blood? I know when I interviewed Shawn Richardz and Barbara Evans, they both knew from a very young age.

Debra: I was working as a bank teller in Newport News and the manager wanted me to do a modeling job for the branch. They shot photos of me in an ad and turned it into a lifelike standing poster. You know, those big, tall cutouts of your entire body on cardboard? Well, the branch was downtown Newport News, so all the Newport News shipbuilding and dry-dock workers banked there, and they all would want to come to my window and see my big lifelike poster. Ha-ha :) I was sixteen at the time and always loved movies, so I guess you could say that's when it really hit me to go into modeling and acting. Later while in Georgia, a photographer actually came up to me––you know the classic story, but it is how it really happened. (Smile.)

Chase Von: You're, as the readers can tell by looking at your pictures, a very beautiful woman. How much modeling have you done in your career, and are you like Shawn, who continues to both act and model as well?
And I hear you have also appeared in numerous commercials. What were they, and is it possible some of our readers here are going to say, "That's it! That's where I remember seeing her lovely face!" (Smile.)

Debra: I have modeled off and on, really seriously since I was twenty-three, although I got into it, as I said, at sixteen. But I have worked in New York, Atlanta, Florida...and I did a lot of print in Florida and New York, as well. Mostly beauty or lifestyle, not too much fashion. As for commercials, I did, however, work with Coca Cola, Levi Strauss, JC Penny, Sprite, Meineke Muffler, British Caladonia Airlines... The thing was: I always put my children first; they always came before my career. In order to raise them in a place where they could have a normal life, I had to be away from where some of the major roles and modeling assignments were being cast, like New York or Los Angeles, but I was still able to find quality work.

Chase Von: I've interviewed other actors and actresses like Shawn Richardz, Jason Seitz and Kimberly Prendez. Kimberly has also written, directed and starred in her own film, *Until Next Time,* and is also working on another one as I type this. I don't know the name of that one just yet. Successful people do what my friend Willard Barth calls *expanding your comfort zones.* So do you ever see yourself either writing scripts or, perhaps, some day being behind the cameras directing?

Debra: I am already co-writing now, so writing scripts is definitely not out of the question. Directing, however, is something where I think the best ones have either acted for many years and totally understand the whole of the picture and, also, how to get the best out of the actors and actresses, as well as have a natural gift for it. But you never know what could happen. (Smile.)

Chase Von: From the brief clip that I saw of your new movie, it looks like the movie itself has quite a few action scenes. In the clip, you pull a gun out of the small of your back and facedown the bad guy to protect your younger brother. And from the looks of the blow you throw to his throat, you're no stranger to fighting. How much actual fight training did you do prior to the shooting of this movie, and do you perform all your own stunts, or do you have a stunt double?

Debra: I box four times a week, so I am pretty well trained in self-defense. As for the stunts, in this one I do all my own stunts, but I imagine on future projects there will be some things I will have to let those truly trained do, although I would do them all if I could. *I love action—it's* exciting and challenging. (Smile.)

Chase Von: The director of this film is a rising talent on the scene. How did you enjoy working with this mysterious man, who for now shall remain nameless?

Debra: That's right, Chase! (Smile.) I loved working with him! He's tough, knows what he wants and goes the extra mile to get it. I can't tell you any more than that right now, but I will say he is fantastic. And I would love to work with him again as action films are his specialty. *He won't remain nameless for long!* (Smile.)

Chase Von: You started your acting career in New York and studied at the prestigious Lee Strasberg Theater. You then took a ten-year break away from acting to do real estate development in Florida. Now you're back, pursuing your true love: acting. How hard was it for you to step right back in there and hold your own after such a long hiatus away from the craft? Or is acting like riding a bike: once you've done it you don't ever forget?

Debra: It was hard, it is ambitious to do this, but what I had learned in the past was there and I felt comfortable... so sort of like riding a bike. I have always loved being in front of the camera whether its print or film, it is just something that I love to work, and the camera has been kind to me, probably because it knows I love it...lol....

Chase Von: Well, one thing for certain is even if you took a break away from acting, you still kept up your appearance. You still look fantastic! I also see where you're an avid angler and also saw the video of you when you went deep-sea fishing with your friend. (Smile.) Is she also an actress and do you ever share the fish you catch? (Smile.) Also, I know you love so many sports, but what sports do you actually participate in? I saw where you enjoy hiking as well as swimming, boxing, golf, snow boarding, snow skiing, yoga, basketball, football, so is there anything I missed?

Debra: My friend in the video is an artist, and a great friend, Alisa Jeecrystal. And yes, we share the fish, although Alisa really loves raw yellowtail, so I try to give her a little more. (Smile.) She is a world-renowned painter of wildlife, huge fish. *Just Google her name!* And you left out baseball, Chase, but I swim, box, play golf, snow ski, yoga four times a week, and play basketball and pool. Sports has always been a huge part of my life, so it just comes naturally, and I have to keep in shape for the job, so it's a good thing I enjoy it so much.

Chase Von: There's a movie out now called *Into The Wild* based on a book by the same name. It's also directed by incredible actor Sean Penn, and I have to say--having seen the movie--he is an incredible director, as well. It's a tragic story, but perhaps one that appeals to me because of my poetic side. When I was in the military I went through a Cold Weather Survival School and I remember one day there was a guy that wouldn't get out of the tent. The instructor was like: "Who's in there?" The answer came back, "Private Yusafool!" The instructor said, "Like Private who?" This time the guy said, "Private Yusafool! And you`se a *fool* if you think I'm getting out of this damn tent!" (Smile.) Lots of funny things happened there, but one night we had to create our own structure and survive it. That's why I like snow--*on post cards!* (Smile.) But the reason I bring this up is you have a really adventurous spirit. Could you ever see yourself stepping off in the actual wild to survive for a period of time?

Debra: I love going deep into the Everglades on the airboat looking for alligators and filming them, but my idea of camping is a room at a hotel. Ha-ha :) I am not a big fan of snakes or creatures that are awake at night! So as adventurous as I am, I still like to be clean and comfortable and around people...lol...

Chase Von: Are there any future projects you are going to be working on you can share with our readers? And who are some of the top actresses and actors, in your eyes, both past and present?

Debra: *Morgan Freeman!* Oh I would love to be working with him! I also love Sean Connery, Steve McQueen, Ashton Kutcher, Bernie Mac, Kiera Knightly, Cameron Diaz and Kate Beckinsall. I have a project in the works, but it is still in a developmental stage. However, it is a comedy that is a spoof of a very famous film, so we shall see how it all comes out. It has a few of my friends giggling already. (Smile.)

Chase Von: I already know you love fish. (Smile.) But what are some of your other favorite meals and how often do you get to enjoy them? Also do you have a thing for cougars? (Smile.) They're a near cousin of something else, if you know what I mean. "Last Panther"... Heh-heh :) And what are some of the charities you are involved with and/or feel strongly about?

Debra: *Sushi, and often!* (Smile.) I do love to eat, so I enjoy every meal. I just eat very healthy. Lots of fish and chicken; try to keep my body weight very lean and mean...lol... And a cause I truly support and feel extremely strong about is the Cancer Society. I also support the Red Cross and Salvation Army. I think they do a terrific job. Personally, I would also like to stop the seal slaughter in Canada and help with all the hunger in some of these other countries. We, as Americans, have so much, and it saddens me to see people so destitute in today's time. Oh, and I just think cougars are beautiful creatures, but panthers are, as well. There are lots of panthers in Florida. (Smile.)

Chase Von: How important is family to you, and what is your take on the state of our current world?

Debra: Family is the most important thing in life to me. Without my family, I would be lost! They are all supportive and keep me grounded... Our state of the world: *Wow, it is worrisome!* I have seen a lot of change, but nothing as dramatic and as quick as it is changing in the last decade; some great and some not so great. It is a very unstable time, and I am concerned about our leaders.

I also have a lot of concern with the state of many other countries, such as the recent issues between Russia and Georgia.

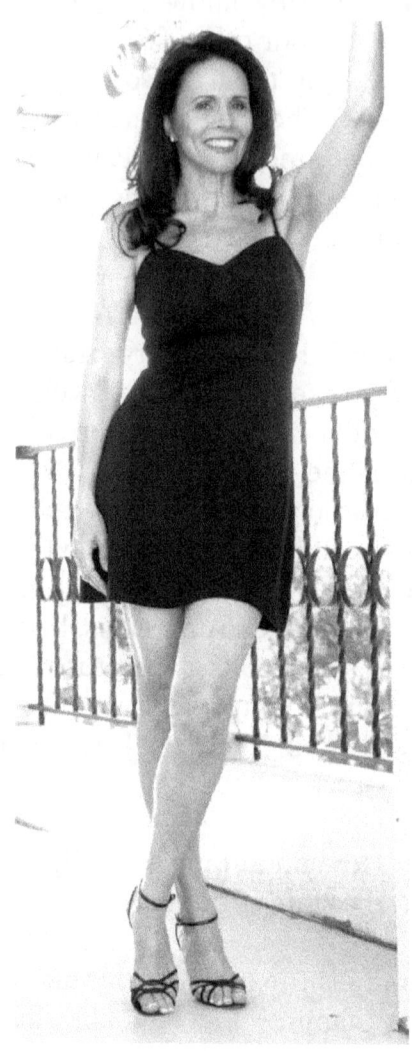

China and North Korea have always been a concern on multiple levels for me, as well. Hopefully though, after this election, more positive changes will come and more rapidly.

Chase Von: What would you say if you were standing in front of a microphone that could be heard by every child on the planet, and regardless of what language it was they spoke, they would understand you? What positive advice would you give the children, if that were possible?

Debra: I would tell them to always try and respect their parents, appreciate their family and try to get a great education. I would also want to tell them to play a lot of sports to keep themselves very healthy, because I believe it helps you to be more successful in life. I would tell them to follow their dreams, try and learn as much about how to solve many of the hunger problems and end wars, and keep their faith in God. Lastly, I would encourage them to stay drug-free because it really ruins relationships and their lives.

Chase Von: Can you list the web links where our readers can find you and learn more about you? And, also, are there any other future projects you're working on you can share with our readers besides the ones already mentioned?

Debra: The best one is: http://profile.myspace.com/index.cfm?fuseaction=user.viewprofile&friendID=102258523 or just Google my name, Debra Garrett, and it takes you to anything about me. Here's a direct link to our movie clip on youTube, as well. http://www.youtube.com/watch?v=KGCCkUkUjQU

Chase Von: On behalf of the *Student Operated Press* and myself, Debra, thank you so much for coming through on this interview. It's a pleasure sharing you with our readers, so once again I appreciate you giving me the opportunity to do just that. Love and light to you, and maybe one day I can share one of the fish you catch...by candlelight or something. (Smile.) That sounds so romantic--except it would be my wife, my kids, my dog, and me. Heh-heh :) You might want to haul in a few of them. (Smile.)

Debra: And much love and peace to you too, Chase, and thank you! Now next time I take a big sport fish out deep-sea fishing, I will send you an invite, or maybe you would enjoy being surrounded by dozens of fifteen-foot 'gators...lol...

Chase Von: Debra, let me give that some thought... Ah... *No!* (Smile.) But again thank you, and continued success in your career.

Debra: Thank you again, Chase, and my thanks to the SOP as well.

****

"I would tell them to follow their dreams, try and learn as much about how to solve many of the hunger problems and end wars, and keep their faith in God. Lastly, I would encourage them to stay drug-free because it really ruins relationships and their lives."
- Debra Garrett, Actress, Model
****

Interview with Donna M. Solitario

HEART TOUCHING POET
By Chase Von

Chase Von: Donna, how are you? And on behalf of the *Student Operated Press* and yours truly, I thank you for finding the time for this. The school year has just kicked in, and with you being a teacher, I know your hands are full, so thanks again for finding the time to share yourself with our readers.

Donna: Thank you very much, Chase, and the *Student Operated Press* for having me here on this interview. I am thrilled that you asked to interview me. In fact, I am honored. I am also very happy to share myself with all of the readers.

Chase Von: Your book touches on a myriad of subjects, but before we get into that, I know you certainly didn't have the best childhood. Can you tell us where you grew up, what it was like coming from an abusive home? And how you found, through writing, you could not only heal yourself of addictive behaviors but also help others who find themselves in the same place?

Donna: I grew up in a small town in Massachusetts. Coming from an abusive home was painful. I felt alone much of the time. Being a child, I did not understand the abuse that took place in my home. Writing helped a great deal to heal from the abuse, and to let go of unhealthy behaviors. It enabled me to release the pent-up emotions I held in through the years. Writing enhanced my life because I was able to let go of my past. Through writing, I have been able to forgive my parents. I realize now that they could not give the unconditional love, which every child needs because they did not have the tools to do so. I learned to become my own parent by honoring and loving myself. Forgiving my parents has brought me peace. Many of my family, friends, students and readers have told me that my story poetry book has enabled them to take a look at their lives and behaviors. I think that the connection I make with them is what motivates me to continue writing my books. This is especially true when any one of my readers, youth, or adult, makes positive changes for themselves.

Chase Von: I posted a bulletin on Amazon--which is how we ended up connecting. I titled it: What are your three favorite poems of all time? (Smile.) It's not the most popular one on there, mind you, but I am surprised it has gotten as much activity as it has. I am also meeting great poets and that of course includes you. (Smile.) Who are some of the poets that you most admire?

Donna: Thank you so much for the complement, Chase. It was a pleasure to meet a great poet like you on Amazon. I loved the poems that you shared with me. They touched my heart. You have an incredible talent for writing poetry and song lyrics. Some of the poets I admire are *you*, Chase Von (smile), along with Robert Frost, Emily Dickinson, Edgar Allen Poe and Elizabeth Barrett.

Chase Von: Where did you come up with the title for your book: *Embrace The Light*?

Donna: My title *Embrace The Light* describes who I am today. I try to see the good in people and life. Being in the dark much of my younger years from child abuse, and some domestic abuse and alcoholism, I was always searching for love and light in my life. I never really knew how to find it. Unfortunately, I turned to alcohol to ease my pain. Today I have twenty years of sobriety which I am very grateful for. I never gave up, and I am happy to say I have found happiness and peace. When I turned my life and will over to the care of God, His love and grace healed my heart, mind, and soul. For me, poetry is a gift from God. My gift to Him is to reach out to others through my poetry and share it with them. I believe that God works through others.

Chase Von: In getting to know you better, I've learned that you gave a poem one day to an at-risk student to inspire him. And after that other students were asking for poems from you as well. I know you were tremendously touched by the reaction you got from them and all the positive changes you saw in them upon receiving your poems. But how did you write poetry for each individual student that you knew would touch that particular student in a desired way? Instinct? Gut feelings, or just your knowledge of them as individuals?

Donna: Yes, Chase, I did give a poem to one of my at-risk students one day when he appeared to be down. I wanted to cheer him up. I was touched deeply when I saw him the next day. He was happy and also made the poem into a card for his girlfriend. The other students began to ask me to write poems for them. I believe that God has blessed me with insight and empathy for others. This enables me to write poems for them while reinforcing their strengths and encouraging them to become accountable for their limitations. When I give a poem to a student, friend, or reader, I feel blessed when it brings out the best in them.

Chase Von: I know six of your creations have been published in anthology books and you are a poet ambassador who has won five Editor Choice Awards. But when was it that you decided to go from writing poems to actually putting them in a book? And were your students the primary reason for that, or was that something you intended to do all along?

Donna: I was extremely excited when six out of my seven poems published in anthology books won the Editors Choice Award. One poem that won was for my four grandchildren titled: *I Love You When*, another poem was for a teacher that I worked with. She lost her sister and brother-in-law in a tragic accident. The title is *Mama*. Being a poetry ambassador has been extremely rewarding. I love to inspire youth to write poetry and motivate them to publish their poems, as well. When I hand out a poem to one of my students and it helps them in some way, it melts my heart. I would have to say, *Yes, my students were the primary reason I wrote my poetry book*. It is wonderful to see the light in their eyes when they can relate to the poems. The outstanding connection I have made with my students has led for a passion to touch more youth and adults. When I inspire others with my poems it, in turn, inspires me.

Chase Von: I often ask these questions of the people I interview. I went from wanting to write a book, to writing one, to becoming my own publisher, to publishing others, and now I am also mentoring student writers here, and not only contributing my own works, but doing interviews such as this one. (Smile.) I also started out writing poetry, and then--although I still write poetry--added song lyrics to that, and later, quotes and then branched out into short stories. I think I might tackle a novel one-day. Heh-heh :) And I am also reading a book on scriptwriting, as well. But what else do you plan on doing? Are you going to stay strictly poetry? Or do you see yourself expanding into writing stories or actual novels as well? And how long will it be before your second book titled *Coming Home To My Heart* is released?

Donna: I think that it is wonderful for your many accomplishments, Chase. My book *Coming Home To My Heart* will be released sometime this year. I am hoping by winter. This will be another poetry book that will include child abuse, motivation, and inspiration, along with some family, friends, love poems, and spirituality poems. I plan to write an autobiography to help others who have been through similar experiences.

Chase Von: Who besides your students have been some of your biggest supporters and motivators? And also who are some of the people you yourself consider mentors and that aid you in becoming a greater writer?

Donna: God has inspired me to write. I believe this is where the gift of writing comes from. Colleagues, such as teachers, have inspired me to write, also, and to continue writing. Other inspiring authors have motivated me to write my poetry also. I come from a musical background, and my grandparents were singers who sang in weddings and church. This had a huge impact on me. I admired them for it. They were kind and wonderful people. My mother inspired me with her opera singing. She was also a piano teacher. I tried to follow their footsteps when I was young and spent hours in my room making up songs. I had an aunt who wrote poetry for children, also. Family and friends also told me I had a gift of writing poetry, which inspired me and motivated me even more to continue writing.

****

"Have faith in God and yourselves. Listen and take suggestions from your parents and teachers. To have a good friend you must be a good friend. You are special in your own unique way."
- Donna M. Solitario, Poet
****

Chase Von: Is there a relatively short poem you can share with our readers so that they can have a taste of your skills? (Smile.) And can you also give a little history about it to, so we know the inspiration that was initially behind it?

Donna: Thank you, Chase, for asking me to share one of my poems for you and the readers.

The Space In-Between My Heart

The space in-between my heart
Feels alone and terribly dark
It lays hardened yet quite protected
Its surroundings are dull and extremely infected
With a coating of dust which covers it interior

A dimmed light is shattered in the rear
The components are covered with a mist
Portraying visions of love that were missed
Spurts of water seeps to drown memories sounds
Emptiness fills a cushion all around
Attempts of filling the space are made
But shattered dreams leave a large trace
My heart feels weary from this dreary space
So it sheds love and light to take its place

This poem describes what it was like for me living in an abusive home and growing up. Through recovery and writing I have been blessed to find love, light and peace.

Chase Von: That was beautiful, Donna. (Smile.) Thanks so very much for sharing. How important is family to you, and what is your take on the state of our current world?

Donna: Family is very important to me. I have two grown children and four young grandchildren. They are my heart. I enjoy spending every moment I possibly can with my grandchildren. It brings out the child in me. It's as though I am getting a second chance at my childhood. We have a lot of fun together. I am very close to them. Even though I was abused, I forgive my parents. I really believe that the disease "alcoholism" played a huge part in the way they have treated me. It is pointless to hold onto resentment for people who are sick. I pray for them and try to be there for them.

Chase Von: What would you say if you were standing in front of a microphone that could be heard by every child on the planet, and regardless of what language it was they spoke, they would understand you? What positive advice would you give the children, if that were possible?

Donna: Have faith in God and yourselves. Listen and take suggestions from your parents and teachers. To have a good friend you must be a good friend. You are special in your own unique way. Follow your dreams and make good choices. Eliminate the negative and assimilate the positive. Believe in yourselves; you hold the key. Forget the drama and begin to honor who you are: a true star. Be a leader, not a follower. Give to the world and the world will give back to you. Your future is untouched, so be all you were meant to be.

Chase Von: Where can our readers find your book? And can you also list the various websites that you have, so they can learn more about you? Also, I am aware that your next book, *Coming Home To My Heart,* is on the way. Are there any future projects you're working on that you can give our readers a heads-up on?

Donna: I hope to become a radio show host to inspire youth and adults in the near future. I plan on writing and publishing an autobiography book and continue writing poetry books. The easiest way readers can find my book is through my website. The title of my book is: *Embrace The Light*; a woman's story through poetry to touch your heart. Donna M. Solitario website:
http://outskirtspress.com/PoemsFromaWomansPoi
ntofView
Amazon Link: http://www.amazon.com/Embrace-
Light-womens-through-
poetry/dp/1432710257/ref=pd_bbs_sr_3?ie=UTF8&s
=books&qid=1222063640&sr=1-3

Embrace the Light, a woman's story through poetry
to touch your heart
Also available at: Barnes&Noble.com

Chase Von: On behalf of the *Student Operated Press* and myself, Donna, thanks so much for squeezing this in. I know we will be in contact, but thanks again for sharing yourself with our readers. Wishing you love and light and continued success.

Donna: Thank you so much, Chase, and the *Student Operated Press* for having me here for this interview. This has been very exciting for me, and I am truly grateful for this wonderful experience. It has been a pleasure to meet you. Also thank you for the wonderful person that you are, Chase, and for inspiring me and others to "embrace the light" so that we can "embrace the world." I wish you the very best for your continued success, while making the world a better place. (Smile.) God Bless you and yours. *Love & peace.*

****

"Follow your dreams and make good choices.
Eliminate the negative and assimilate the positive.
Believe in yourselves; you hold the key.
Forget the drama and begin to honor
who you are: a true star."
- Donna M. Solitario, Poet
****

Embrace the Light

A woman's story through poetry to touch your heart

DONNA SOLITARIO

Interview with Clint M. Byars

AUTHOR OF DEVIL WALK
by Chase Von

Chase Von: Hello, Clint. On behalf of the *Student Operated Press*, thanks for finding the time to do this. I have my own reasons as to why I am so moved by your story. But what I would like to know first is: what were your younger years like? Where did you grow up, and was religion something you took seriously?

Clint M. Byars: Thanks for hooking this up; I'm always blessed when people are interested in my story. I grew up just south of Atlanta, GA. I had a relatively normal childhood; some of my family members were into not-so-normal businesses but, for the most part, life was like most others'. I was not raised in church--I probably went to church a dozen times before I was 21. My parents believed in God but religion was never discussed or pursued. I got into drinking around twelve and started doing harder drugs around fourteen.

Chase Von: Having read your book, I personally think it validates some of my own experiences. But there are those who think that people who share stories such as yours aren't right in the head. (Just being blunt, which is my nature at times.) I also happen to think, if you believe in the Bible, then the story of Jesus taking demons out of a man and running them off a cliff should be taken literally. Demons are spirits, and spirits cannot die. Where do you think they are now? And is it possible that women cutting the children out of other women is part of their doing, along with all the other insane things we see daily in the news?

Clint M. Byars: I hear myself tell my story sometimes and think how bizarre it is. If people don't believe it or think it was just a bad trip, then I don't blame them. I usually only hear from people who have had similar experiences, but who never realized the truth of their situation until they read my book. Demons are all over the place; they're in the bars, streets, schools, governments, and churches. They basically seek out places and people who will listen to their lies. I think we'd be astounded if we could see how much influence they have. The problem with demonic influence is that people don't usually know the truth of who Jesus is in them. The only power a demon has is suggestion. They hang out and lie to us; it's up to us to believe it or not. In the tragic case of a woman doing what you described, all a demon has to do is stand there and say things that make that mother believe she's unfit to raise that child and due to the fear she's already feeling, she'll then believe that demonic lie and take action based on a lie, motivated by fear. I want to reiterate that they have no power other than what we give them.

Chase Von: You have a part in your book that really hit me: where you say you were looking back in time, and you saw Jesus on the cross. And although he was beaten and broken, you looked at his eyes and realized he was looking directly at you. And it dawned on you that--way back then--he already knew that what he was doing was for you, specifically. Can you expound a bit on that for our readers?

Clint M. Byars: God says that he knows us before we're in our mother's womb. None of us are mistakes. I'm not saying that he chose to birth you in the situation you were born into, but there's something going on there where the essence of you was in his mind. It's like parents who are planning to have kids. They may not know what the child will look or sound like but that really doesn't matter, they already have love for that unborn child and are anticipating loving it for the rest of its life. I'm a father and I can remember daydreaming about how great it was going to be to take my son fishing or to a ball game. It was like that with God: He couldn't wait until we got here so He could love us for the rest of our lives.

Chase Von: Prior to writing this book, did you ever consider yourself a writer?

Clint M. Byars: Not really. I had written some poetry and I was always good in those kinds of classes in school, but never really imagined being a writer. I knew I needed to get my story out, so I kind of did it out of necessity. I have since fallen in love with writing. I've written a screenplay and I'm currently working on two more. I am also working on my next book about what happened to Jesus during those three days He was in the grave and what it looked like in Heaven when He came out victorious on our behalf.

Chase Von: One of the things that really startles someone reading your book, initially, is that you are highly intelligent and that when you write, it is exposing that intelligence. For me, it makes me happy that someone is not only writing about a subject that I feel truly needs to be addressed, but also in a manner that approaches what you are speaking of in a way that even the well-educated can't dismiss. How much schooling do you, yourself, have and do you think that in order for this all to be taken seriously, it takes someone who, such as yourself, is very articulate and well spoken to break down the barriers?

Clint M. Byars: Well, thanks for that compliment. I have to give credit to God. I wrote this book in about five or six sessions of about two to three hours each. It just flowed out of me. I remember reading back and thinking, *Man, did I just write that?* With that said, I have an associate's degree in science and a bachelor's degree in theology. I constantly read and love learning. I suppose it helps in some cases to sound intelligent about this topic. I have actually had a few psychologists and other professionals contact me for advice, which they used in their practices with clients they couldn't previously help.

Chase Von: I understand they are going to be making a movie based off of your story. When is that going to take place and will you be on the set as well, to make sure it holds to the truth of your story?

Clint M. Byars: That is such a slow process; I wish I had an answer for *when*. I do, however, plan to be on set as much as I can. The producer has a great vision for the purpose of the film so I believe it will hold true. We'll see.

Chase Von: This is a tough one, but I have to ask. Is Jesus the only way to heaven from your perspective? More wars have been fought throughout history in the name of religion than any other thing. So many are born in countries where Islam is what they first sink their teeth into, or Buddhism, or you name it. How is it that what someone is born into is not right for their soul's salvation? And since I am asking tough ones, are we--meaning humanity--in your view, in what is often referred to as *the last days?*

Clint M. Byars: I believe the perfect sacrifice of Christ is the only way to eternal life. Many people *have* been killed in the name of religion and the misunderstanding of a man's teachings, but when it comes down to the sacrifice of a sinless man and the free gift of righteousness as a result of that sacrifice, there's no other way for our spirit, soul and body to be made acceptable for the direct, eternal presence of God. The problem is in religion; if we could spread the message of the Christ instead of the message of a religion, no one would turn Jesus down... As far as "last days," it certainly seems like there are lots of signs pointing in that direction.

Chase Von: How important is family to you, and what is your take on the state of our current world?

Clint M. Byars: Family is the most important. I think the world is in the state it's in, aside from original sin, due to the lack of love and identity we *should* receive from our family during childhood. We have a world full of insecure, fearful people who don't feel loved. That's a breeding ground for what you see on the news every night. Love is what *family* should be about. We're all family so Jesus was right: love your neighbor as you want to be loved. In addition to that, Jesus said the world would believe in Him when they see believers loving each other instead of fighting over doctrine.

Chase Von: Your book is a very intense read, exceptionally well written, and yes, quite scary for some who understand what you are really addressing. Why is Satan a *paper lion,* as you call him, and how can people who do believe in these things not fall under his power, in this conflicted and complicated world we live in today?

Clint M. Byars: Satan is a paper lion because he has no substance. He's a weak, torn, battered entity that floats around the winds trying to find a place to land. Jesus totally stripped him of authority and power when He came out of the grave. Jesus kicked Satan out of Heaven when He went home, which means that God the Father no longer hears his accusations against you. God's not using Satan against you, and Jesus stripped him of all that he had. So what's left? He runs around trying to find someone ignorant enough to believe his lies. The problem is, most of us are ignorant about who we are in Christ and the fact that we were raised with Christ, seated in Heaven above principalities and powers. That's just Biblical terms for demons and fallen angels. The way to not fall under the influence of their lies is to know the truth. The truth just so happens to set you free.

Chase Von: What would you say if you were standing in front of a microphone that could be heard by every child on the planet and, regardless of what language they

****

*"Satan is a paper lion because he has no substance.
He's a weak, torn, battered entity that floats
around the winds trying to find a place to land.
Jesus totally stripped him of authority and
power when He came out of the grave."*
- Clint M. Byars, Author

****

spoke, they would understand you? What positive advice would you give the children, if that were possible?

Clint M. Byars: Don't lose your innocence because of your elders' offenses. I would also tell them that God is a good God and what you see around you is not His original plan, but they could help bring back His intention through love and forgiveness.

Chase Von: How can our readers find you? Can you list your websites and other means by which they can find you and learn more about you?

Clint M. Byars: The best way to reach me is through www.clintbyars.com. I also own a clothing company that can be seen at www.glorygear.com.

Chase Von: On behalf of the *Student Operated Press* and myself, Clint, I truly thank you for taking the time out to do this. Your story is something I, personally, believe should be read by believers and unbelievers alike.

Clint M. Byars: Thank you for helping me get my story out. Be blessed.

****

"We're all family so Jesus was right: love your neighbor as you want to be loved. In addition to that, Jesus said the world would believe in Him when they see believers loving each other instead of fighting over doctrine."
- Clint M. Byars, Author

****

****

"Don't lose your innocence because of your elders' offenses. I would also tell them that God is a good God and what you see around you is not His original plan, but they could help bring back His intention through love and forgiveness."
- Clint M. Byars, Author

****

Interview with Jason Seitz

RISING NEW ACTOR
by Chase Von

Chase Von: Jason, on behalf of the *Student Operated Press* and myself, thanks for finding the time in your busy schedule to do this. You're really doing some amazing things, and it has been evident in every communication I've had with you that you're a ball of energy. People are going to think I am making this up, but even when we correspond in writing, it comes through. Can you share with our readers some of your philosophies? Also, are those philosophies things you live by, that keep you energetic and so positive in your thinking?

Jason: My philosophies most definitely are guidelines by which I live. For what other reasons would I have them? Beyond acting, I've made it a point to always work on becoming a better person. Sure, I fall off track...*all the time!* But there hasn't been one experience that's set me back so far that I wasn't able to rebuild my foundation, or utilize it to become a better person.

Chase Von: I hate to bring this up, but your father passed away in 1995. I've had to deal with some losses in my life, too, people I've served with as well as family members and close friends. I can tell you from my own experience, losing someone often makes a person--at least for a period of time--almost immobile. Did you go through a period in your life when you weren't quite as optimistic as you are today? And I couldn't help but pick up on how you truly established meaningful relationships with your teachers. I firmly believe that we have blood family, and we have extended family. So sometimes a role that is absent in our own families--or that they are incapable of fulfilling--is represented by another individual outside of the family. Did teachers in your life, in some regard, not fill, but rather help with the loss by keeping your mind active and involved in the positive things life has to offer?

Jason: As much as I loved my teachers, when it comes down to it, although people have the power to influence, the choice to maintain a positive outlook is your own. One of the things I've been blessed with is an amazing mother and father. To date, I've never met anyone as cool as my dad; and second to that, there's no one I have ever met who pays more attention to me than my mother. Unfortunately, I grew up with a very large lack of male attention. This happened because my mom and dad got divorced when I was one year old, and the man who became my stepfather had serious issues with loving me. As I'm sure you can imagine, when my father passed away, it got even worse. My dad once told me he believed that I was the only thing he ever did right--which is so far from the truth, but he really believed it. He had the IQ of a genius, was incredibly creative and charismatic, and such a strong person. Even though he wouldn't live long enough to discover what it might be, he always knew there was something special about his good son, Jason Seitz.

Chase Von: You pursued acting quite early in life, packing your bags and moving to Seattle, Washington to do so. You also worked very hard at it, and at some other jobs not remotely related to acting, as well. You can honestly say, having been a shoe salesman, that you didn't just suddenly appear on the scene. We don't have to get into the number of toilets you've cleaned, either, unless you want to. (Smile.) And don't get me wrong...all work is honorable, so I am not taking any shots at anyone in whatever they do. Cleaned my share, as well, as a private in the military... What I *am* saying is that you dreamed of more, and even while doing those things, you still had the ambition and desire to reach for your dreams--and you're achieving them. You received a speaking role in *Elephant* (2003), directed by Gus Van Sant; and not only that, but it

Photo property of Jason Seitz

took home the Golden Palm Award from the Cannes Film Festival. I told you I had to ask Kimberly Prendez, an actress friend of mine, what that meant. (Smile.) Her response was something to the effect of, "That's huge! That's not just big, that's the biggest!" I congratulate you on that achievement, but I also want to know: How did achieving that feel, especially in contrast with what you previously had to do?

Jason: Aw, thanks. I'd like to make something clear, though. As much as I was the key player in my scene, I was not the star in *Elephant*. Gus is notorious for hand picking talent, even his extras. And when you sum that all up, even though I may not be the star, Gus cast me as a principal actor; and, what could be more special than that? You mention some of my previous jobs. Once I discovered I was an actor, every job I did after that was in support of my acting. Thankfully, I was never forced to miss auditions because all my managers supported me, as well as the cleaning clients I had. When I was informed that *Elephant* won the Cannes Film Festival, my jaw dropped. It was at that point that I knew there was no turning back from here. One of my very first acting appearances--and the film took home the largest festival award there is.

Chase Von: You're not only an actor--and one who is rising up in the ranks, with roles in *Elephant* and the strong cameo in the 2007 film *Rolling*, as well as work in a Landmark Feature *Emilio* scheduled for release in 2008-- but you're also quite the poet. "1st Place Winners," a piece you wrote, is an excellent poem that I think should be circulated throughout the high schools of America, as well as the colleges. It really drives home what happens out there on a daily basis. Do you foresee your writing eventually leading to books of poetry? Novels? And, in your profession, perhaps some screenplays or movies?

Jason: Nah, I write poems just for fun. This piece was very different and had an extremely powerful twist. I've always believed that everything has meaning *if* you bring meaning into it. If I can guide someone in the direction of expanding his or her mind with a poem, I find deep satisfaction in that.

Chase Von: Tell our readers what it is you love about acting. You have so much energy and determination, I am sure you would succeed at anything you put your mind to. But for you, acting is your calling. What drew you into this world where you are quickly becoming a force to be reckoned with? And is there a role out there you would love to play--something you think would further challenge and strengthen your acting abilities?

Jason: Why don't I list a few actors whose work I look up to? Topher Grace, Scott Mechlowicz, Joseph Gordon-Levitt, Gary Oldman, Seth Green, Jack Nicholson, Elijah Wood, Emile Hirsch, Johnny Depp, Shia Lebouf, Jim Carrey, Jon Abrahams, Martin Short, Giovanni Ribisi, Freddie Highmore, Anton Yelchin, and of course, James Dean. The reason why I act is *communication.* I've always been interested in sharing my perspective, but during my youth there was always something in my way. On the other hand, God has always given me a powerful way with words so, naturally, I needed to communicate. Right now I'm looking for roles that expand my pigeonhole type. When you're starting out it's important to take whatever you can get, but I'm definitely paving the way for more. I also love fantasy films. I love parts that have some type of trouble, substance abuse issues or even mentally challenged types of characters.

Chase Von: How important is family to you, and what is your take on the state of our current world?

Jason: I already talked about family above, so I'll just skip to the state of our current world. I think people need to talk to other people more. On a personal note, I find religion to be anti-productive. Let me start with saying I think it's great to have a group of people with similar interests and beliefs. However, I feel the wise man knows that God speaks separately to each and every one of us, using catered forms of communication that match the needs of our unique and specifically handcrafted spirits.

Religion gets in the way of that. It separates humanity by putting everyone into groups when most of us already have what is really important in common: our belief and love for God.

Jason Seitz and Gus Van Sant

Chase Von: What would you say if you were standing in front of a microphone that could be heard by every child on the planet, and regardless of what language it was they spoke, they would understand you? What positive advice would you give the children, if that were possible?

Jason: I would tell them to understand that each and every one of us was made to be different, and that it's okay to be yourself; to believe that everything happens for a reason, even if you can't figure out the reason; that everyone's thoughts, ideas and emotions are always specific to their own experiences--which obviously means everyone's thoughts, ideas, and emotions might potentially be different. I would also tell them to remember that nobody is like you, and because of that alone, you are special; to, at all costs, find a way to be comfortable with yourself and set goals that will help you become the person you want to be. If they stick to those goals, they can accomplish their career dreams as well, and will find value in every experience, because it is those experiences that shape the person they are today.

Chase Von: Where can our readers learn more about you? Can you share your links and web pages? And what projects are you working on now that we can expect to see in the future? And can you also tell our readers the names of them, if possible, so they can be on the lookout for them?

Jason: Sure, you can reach me on my official MySpace page at www.myspace.com/actorjasonseitz; or visit my website, www.jasonseitz.com. At this point I still maintain them both. It's not super high-tech but they're great resources. Just search for me as you would any other actor and you will find more things than I could mention here. Things are really slow right now, Chase. I'm reading the script of a film I just booked called *The Pentagon Memo* but, with the WGA strike, some casting directors have temporarily closed their offices, several shows have been canceled, the Oscars are going to be without their WGA writers, and agents aren't interested in new clients.

Chase Von: I really do hope that gets resolved soon. Is there a possibility you might just share "1st Place Winners" here with our readers so they can see that you are certainly a deep individual as well as an accomplished actor at the young age of twenty-one?

Jason: Sure, Chase, just as long as everyone understands it has an official Jason Seitz copyright.

1st PLACE WINNERS

"Come on! Give me a hit, I just want to try!
Sure kid, go ahead, but prepare to be high.
Prepare to be a loser, in the world of drugs.
Rarely having someone beside you, to give you warm and reassuring hugs.

Prepare yourself kid, to scrounge for food.
To fulfill the craving, of whatever drug you use.
Prepare yourself, kid, for a world of hurt and sorrow.
A world of hate and backstabbing, bitches and ass holes, who don't care about tomorrow.

Go ahead kid, throw your life away...
You realize you can do this by liking your one hit today?
Prepare yourself. Go home high.
Do it often, and don't be surprised if your Mom ends up giving you the big bye bye.

So you're out on the streets now with all of us here.
The home of the 1st Place Winners, of the losers, every year."

by Jason Seitz
All rights reserved

Chase Von: On behalf of the *Student Operated Press* and myself, Jason, I really want to thank you for finding the time for this interview. I'm wishing you continued success and, who knows, you've already won the biggest Film Festival there is, so is there an Oscar out there with your name on it?

Jason: What a powerful day of acknowledgment that will be. I love the journey.

Chase Von: Thanks again, brother, and I look forward to seeing your star on Hollywood Boulevard; you keep working as hard as you are and it is a done deal. Stay blessed, and wishing you an amazing New Year.

Jason: Thanks, Chase. Happy New Year to you too. It is an honor to be the first *Student Operated Press* interview of 2008. Feel free to contact me, anytime.

Jason Seitz in scene from the critically acclaimed movie "Rolling."

Photo property of Jason Seitz

****

"I would also tell them to remember that nobody is like you and, because of that alone, you are special; to, at all costs, find a way to be comfortable with yourself and set goals which will help you become the person you want to be. If they stick to those goals, they can accomplish their career dreams as well, and will find value in every experience, because it is those experiences that shape the person they are today."
- Jason Seitz, Actor

****

Interview with Violette L. Reid

TALENTED WRITER, POET
by Chase Von

Chase Von: Hello, Violette, on behalf of the *Student Operated Press* and myself, thanks for finding the time to do this interview. You have your hands pretty full with quite a few projects and are doing some really amazing things. In addition to having published your first poetry collection *Violette Ardor,* you are releasing a fantasy novel called *The First Chronicles of Zayashariya: Out of Night* in March 2008. In reading up on you I find that, like many of the people I have interviewed previously, you have been writing since you were a pre-teen. And to date, you have more than 1,200 poems, as well as twenty-five short stories. *You're a writing machine!* (Smile.) When was it that you realized writing would become such a major force and ingredient in your life?

Violette: Greetings, Chase. Thank you for taking the time to interview me. I consider it a true privilege. I am not sure when I realized writing was so important to me. At first it was just something I liked to do when I was bored, and the older I became it became as natural as breathing. Now I cannot conceive of never lifting a pen again... as a bard or creating new characters to tickle people's fancy. I realized that I had a story to tell and my weird imagination was limitless. I guess I truly became interested in becoming a career writer after I graduated from college.

Chase Von: You were brought up, and still currently live in Georgia, and also attended Clark Atlanta University where you earned your B. A. in English. I know when I first saw pictures of you, my first thought was, "Who does she look like?" It didn't hit me instantly, but after studying them for a while, it occurred to me that you look so much like Halle Berry. Am I the first to say that? Or, did you often, in college and perhaps even now, have people tell you that? Because, since there is only one Halle Berry, your husband has to consider himself a very lucky man to have you. (Smile.)

Violette: LOL I have heard that a few times, but I do not see the resemblance. I take it as a supreme compliment because she is one amazing-looking woman.

Chase Von: You write about a plethora of topics: supernatural, horror, thrillers, mild erotica, romance, fantasy, poetry, and I could go on, but you, obviously, have no limits in what veins you will allow your talents to be utilized. As a fellow writer, I am always curious about other writers on this point. How is it you find your inspiration? As for me, I always feel like I am catching things. I will see or hear something, or have a feeling, and it is more like I am remembering than really creating anything new. It's like a part of the puzzle will reveal itself, and I feel compelled to find and capture all the remaining pieces. How is the creative process for you?

Violette: When writing prose, I simply sit down and write and allow my imagination to take me where it pleases. It is almost like *possession.* I am surprised by the things that I write and how the story unfolds. When writing poetry, I have to feel an intense sensing or have a strong desire to spill my emotions upon paper. Poetry, for me, is raw and unedited. I hate to change and correct my poetry after it is written because it seems to lose its sincerity.

Chase Von: Who are some of the writers, both past and present, that you admire? And, was there anyone in your younger years that caught your attention and thus sparked your interest in writing? There was no person for me, per se. I stumbled on it by accident and didn't even know that I had really written a poem. It just felt right. But were you exposed to, maybe, a Maya Angelou or a Nikki Giovanni or someone of that caliber, and decided you wanted to do what they do, as well? And you, also are an artist, so the question's the same except: Are there also artists that you admire?

Violette: My favorite writer is my husband Latif Reid. He is the most incredible poet I have ever encountered. The things he comes up with are just mind-boggling.. Famous writers that I admire are: Maya Angelou, Anne Rice, Terry Brooks, Langston Hughes, Countee Cullen, R. A. Salvadore, Tim LaHaye, Jerry Jenkins, Orson Scott Card and just about all the poets of the Harlem Renaissance. Believe it or not, I am not big into art. I like to see beautiful things; occasionally, I walk through museums and go to art shows. I appreciate it, but I do not follow artists. I just like to paint. I'm not sure how good I am at it, but I enjoy creating. There is no person in particular that I want to write like or aspire to be. I always want to develop my own voice and be as original as I can be.

Chase Von: In the past, I have had people that state openly they don't like poetry, but say they loved mine. Have you also had the same experience?

Violette: I understand why people would love your poetry. It is very refreshing and heartfelt. I enjoyed your book, myself.... Yes, I have had many compliments on my poetry. It makes me feel wonderful, but it is not the reason why I write it. Poetry is my heart's song. It will sing, regardless of who is around to hear it. *I love poetry.* But truthfully, it is hard to read a whole lot of poetry. There are so many writing styles and vague images and abstract emotions. Sometimes, I feel that many poets are not true poets. Many just write rhyming words with no meat to the poem, or they become spoken-word masters, mastering their voices instead of the poetry...or they write prose in sentence fragments or simply rant and call it poetry. Poetry is about raw passion and sincere feeling. A thing of beauty and immaculate words being strung together into a precious piece of jewelry that is not only original, but also unparalleled. Poetry is also about opinion and this is just mine. LOL

Chase Von: I won't put you on the spot, as I have done many times with this question: What is your favorite poem that you, yourself, have written? (Smile.) To me, my writing creations are like children and it's hard to pick a favorite, but is there a short one in your vast collection you would like to share, so our readers can get a taste of your   works?

Violette: *Wow—-that is hard!* My favorites are: "Lost," "A Poet's Words," "God," "The Rape of Christianity"... I could go on forever; I am a vain creature...LOL... But, here is a short poem about my husband who is a hip-hop lyricist from New York:

My MC

He sits on a rock in the midst of Central Park
as the skyscrapers peer over his shoulders hoping for a
glimpse of his words
He palms a pad in one hand as the other spills ink
upon paper absorbing true lyrics of poetic phenomena
I see his lips humming the beat that drums through his
brain
as his head nods and feet beat against concrete
An MC
with vivid visions of microphone victories
galloping through his psyche
lyrically crushing those who dare to contend
against the might of his tongue and pen

He sits
heart pumping against his shirt
The hurt of the world mingling with birds singing
as his page flips
and those juicy lips leaking poetic poison
drowning within the noise of the city
VL Reid 2006©

Chase Von: You also own your own newsletter called "Peach Publishing." How long have you been doing that, and do you also promote other up-and-coming writers?

Violette: I have been doing "Peach Publishing" for about five years now. Of course I promote writers, and I do it for free. Networking is a wonderful thing and we all need as much exposure as possible. The newsletter is read nationwide and in the UK, Africa and India. I have received submissions from all over the world. Check it out on www.violettereid.com. It is updated monthly and is dedicated to writers and artists. I am constantly amazed by the creative literature and art submitted to me. I feel blessed. Maybe one day the newsletter will get more exposure and many more people will become aware of all the unheard talent floating around.

Chase Von: How important is family to you, and what is your take on the state of our current world?

Violette: Family is *everything* to me. I have been blessed with the most wonderful family in the universe, and I thank God for them all every day. Our world is in a state of peril. We all are so lost, morally corrupt, sexually retarded, heavily medicated and ridiculously violent. Of course, there is still beauty, kindness, love and hope in the world, but sometimes I fear for my children. I try to instill in them as much of God's word, hope, faith, kindness, compassion and love in them that--when they get out on their own--they will not be caught up in this crazy whirlwind we call the world.

Chase Von: What would you say if you were standing in front of a microphone that could be heard by every child on the planet, and regardless of what language it was they spoke, they would understand you? What positive advice would you give the children, if that were possible?

Violette: Love God and yourself. Love your mind, spirit, skin, hair, body and your uniqueness. God made you perfect and beautiful just the way you are. Nothing needs to be added and nothing needs to be taken away. Let no one tell you different. Never compare yourself to anyone. You are unparalleled. Hold yourself to your own standard, not anyone else's. Live to your fullest potential and love everyone like you deserve to be loved.

 Chase Von: How can our readers find out more about you and your works? Can you share your links and web pages? And, are there any future projects you are working on you care to share with our readers? Or any upcoming book-signings you want to make them aware of?

Violette: You can find out more about me and my work at www.violettereid.com. I am always working on new stuff. You can get all of my updates on www.violettereid.com Also, visit my MySpace: http://www.myspace.com/violette_peaches, and add me as a friend!

Chase Von: On behalf of the *Student Operated Press* and myself, Violette, I want to thank you for taking the time to do this. I imagine one day you will be famous enough to be on the same stage as Halle Berry and people, other than myself, can marvel at the resemblance. (Smile.)

Violette: Thank you so much for interviewing me. It was a true pleasure sharing with you. You are too kind. :)

****

"Love God and yourself. Love your mind, spirit, skin, hair, body and your uniqueness. God made you perfect and beautiful just the way you are. Nothing needs to be added and nothing needs to be taken away. Let no one tell you different. Never compare yourself to anyone. You are unparalleled."
- Violette L. Reid, Poet, Author

****

Interview with Nick Valentino

HORROR WRITER
by Chase Von

Chase Von: Hello Nick. I truly appreciate you agreeing to do this interview with me. I know you have various projects on your hands, so the *Student Operated Press* and I really thank you for finding the time. I came across you on MySpace, and I remember thinking to myself--when I started reading some of the chapters you had posted-- *Stephen King has some "serious" competition here!* You had posted, I believe at that time, two chapters of *Fallon,* and I have to tell you, you certainly know your craft. Later, you posted an additional two chapters and, true to form, it was exceptional. You also had another short story that I thought was excellent, as well, and could have been the building blocks for another novel. How did you initially get into writing to begin with? I believe I read somewhere that you started out by telling stories to your kids. And have you always written horrors?

Nick: Actually, I think you may have me confused with Richard Adams, the author of *Watership Down*. He told his children bedtime stories about a group of rabbits trying to survive in a land suffering from over-development; subsequently, these tales were woven into one of the most wonderful stories I have ever read. My storytelling began with what is now the second book of the trilogy entitled *The Adversary*. The tragedies of Columbine had an effect on me, and I couldn't understand what reasons the perpetrators had, besides ignorance and weakness, to cause such immoral acts. I began to write a story about kids that actually believed what they were doing was right by means of moral justification. In doing so, I brought in my two favorite things, God and the Devil. Not God and The Devil incarnate, per se, but agents of both in order to guide and distract them accordingly. From there I stumbled upon a character that captivated me, and instantly took center stage. This was Fallon, a young girl kidnapped by a trapped, fallen angel that understood her natural divine abilities and stole her for his own devious purposes. When I began to write about her, I found that she was my girl. She was the one that made everything perfect. She was the dichotomy of good and evil and had to act on both of those things that ran through her supernatural body.

Chase Von: Like I said before, you are an excellent writer. What really got me was the attention to detail. Some people tell stories and you feel as if they are skimming the surface. Others have vast knowledge on the subject and you can tell that they did extensive research prior to even picking up a pen. Chrissy K. McVay has a book called

Souls of The North Wind, and she told me she had spent a few years studying the Inuit culture in order to write her story. I know you have a true love for all things Japanese, as do I because I was born there. (Smile.) But how much research time did you put into learning about the Japanese culture, traditions and history, so that everything in your story rings of such authenticity?

Fallon by Will Routon

Nick: As for Geisha, (or Geiko), I spent a lot of time doing research on them. I have only been to Japan once and I yearn to go back. I have very little first-hand knowledge of Japanese culture; it is all garnered from things I have read and researched. The book, *Geisha: A Life* By Mineko

Iwasaki, gives a lot of insight of the business life and strict upbringing of Geisha and I applied a lot of that to half of Fallon's formative years. She needed that to become her full self.

Fallon Full Body Prototype by Will Routon

Chase Von: In regards to *Fallon,* you have some truly well defined characters. I don't want to give too much of the story away, but can you share with our readers the basic premise of the story?

Nick: As for the first book, *Fallon,* I think the short synopsis I have on my web page is the best example without giving too much away: "Kidnapped as a baby, Keiko Tanaka is taken to Japan where she is given the unusual name Fallon by her kidnapper, a tall mysterious man named Aleser. She learns the arts of the geisha and begins to unravel her power that is far beyond the natural abilities of man. She grows up in the strictest of environments while uncovering her supernatural abilities throughout her youngest years. With much tragedy constantly surrounding the geisha house, Fallon is moved at the age of seven, to the hidden mountains of Japan, where she is taught the darkest arts of mankind and learns her true identity."

Chase Von: You have actual depictions on your page of the characters in *Fallon*... very nicely done, I might add. Having learned that you are also an artist, are you the one that created the depictions of the characters? And also, like I told you before, I really think you have a movie on your hands with this one. Are you also considering that? Doing a screenplay? I think it would make a fantastic picture.

Nick: All of the characters *in Fallon, The Adversary* and *The Triumvirate* were designed by me. The art was almost completely done by an artist from Los Angeles named Will Routon. I described the characters to him, and he put them on paper as if he were reading my mind. It is one of the strangest experiences I have had in quite some time. I told him certain things and he made them come to life, visually. I am shaking my head now thinking about it. The one other image of Fallon was made by Alex Eckman Lawn, who does a lot of art for the zombie thriller comic books, *Awakening.* As for a movie? I don't know... I imagine if the right things happened, I would be interested. I would want it to be done right. I would so hate for it to turn out under budget or cheaply made. Let's say I would want it to look more like *Donnie Darko* than... say...*Transformers.* Does that make sense? To get back to the question, I am not really focusing on making it a movie, but I do see it as a movie as I write it.

Chase Von: What are some of the other things you like to do...hobbies, interests? I take it you're a hockey fan, from seeing some of the snapshots on your page...and, also, your statement about the Red Wings. (Smile.) And since you live in Nashville, you're a big country music fan, as well. I've written a couple of lyrics for some country songs, by the way. Happen to know anyone there you could...like, show them to? (Smile.)

Nick: Well, believe it or not, I grew up quite a metal/punk kid here in Nashville. I was in a metal/hardcore band for a long time, and eventually, my passion for writing books took over from my passion for writing music. I hate to say it, but I never enjoyed country music, as to me it was kind of the corporate giant that infected Nashville. As for the songs you have written, send them to me; there are thousands of publishing companies frothing for the next country hit here. As for other things, yes, I am a Nashville Predators hockey fanatic. I fell in love in 1998 when the Predators came here, so you can catch me at almost all of their games. I only enjoy other sports mildly, but there is something about the intensity, skill and violence of hockey that sucks me in. On a recent trip to England, I saw a lot of really unbelievable street art by Banksy, Faile, Space Invader and Hush. That inspired me to start doing stencil art. I really see it as a "side project" for my life. It is an artistic escape where I can blank out and make something tangible. It seems to dominate my web page, but my main focus is always writing.

Chase Von: Writer, artist...so you're very multi-talented. I also know you have a true love for comic books. I, too, have a love for comic books. Although I am sure it doesn't equal your interest, I still buy occasionally, of course, Ta Challa The Black Panther, Wolverine and I followed *Conan The Barbarian* for years. I also like Elektra. (Smile.) Who doesn't? And *Daredevil* or *Matt Murdock*, as well. As a kid, I really dug *The Fantastic Four* and *X-Men*, and still do. But one of the things I don't think a lot of people who don't read comic books know, is that some of the storylines are really not for kids. I also think that is how kids, or some of them, learn quite a bit about the adult life. What's your take on that, and are you also working on storylines for comic books as well, and do you do both the art as well as the stories for your comic books?

Nick: I have always had a bit of a fantasy that I would write a series of comic books or graphic novels that would accompany these three books. They would mainly focus on backstories of minor characters that also had some powers of their own and played some part in the larger novels. That is where the novella, *A Weapon Ripens*, came into play. I wanted to write about some of the smaller characters in the first two books. They were too odd not to have backstories. Although this might not give their entire backstories, it lets the reader (and myself) know that they are not just some magical being that appeared out of nowhere. They had or have a life, too, and a connection to the other main characters. I am a big fan of the show *Lost* that is brilliantly written--character- and mystery-wise-- and I do my best to incorporate some of those elements into what I write. While I read comic books like *X-Men* and *G. I. Joe* when I was younger, I really enjoyed the smaller characters with the shorter-run comic series. Still, to this day, *Firestar* and *The White Queen* still take center stage for me. I think characters like that are the ones that have really influenced me. Now that I think about it, maybe in bigger ways than I ever imagined.

Chase Von: When I read your first two chapters of *Fallon*, I couldn't wait to read more because you are truly an exceptional writer. But what I want to know is: that by sharing a few chapters and having me--and I am sure so many others--who couldn't wait to see if you were going to post another chapter, (Smile.)... Well, has that made it better for the popularity of your book? Because you sort of teased your audience with your talents. I know other writers who have done that, as well, and, to me, it's a win-win situation. The readers get a taste and sometimes get hooked. But the bottom line, just to be blunt, is that if you sucked, it would also be a reason for them to pass on this book when it comes out. How has the response been from those that you shared some of your work with before it was completed?

Nick: It has actually been received quite well. There is nothing like having someone tell you that something you have written gave them the chills. As a new writer, that was one of the biggest compliments I could have ever received. I don't want to give it all away, but I am interested in, well, like you said, testing the waters and seeing what people think. So far, besides one woman saying that I was glorifying Eric Harris and Dylan Klebold (which, for the record, I am not in any way, shape or form endorsing them or their actions), everyone has been quite excited and happy about what they have read. I wanted it to be sort of a trailer for the books. Sure it works, but I wanted to see what people thought. I have no real formal education in writing, I just write what I feel and what I think real people (or deities) would say.

Chase Von: I know you admire Clive Barker and J. K. Rowling, but who are some of the other authors that you admire?

Nick: Clive Barker was my first love. Literally, I love everything that man has ever written. J. K. Rowling is hard for me to fathom. She is so perfect in every way--writing wise. No, I don't know her. I simply can't understand how a person could write such a truly amazing set of seven books. I admire Richard Adams greatly, as well. *Watership Down* has affected my life in very strange ways. When I was a child, they used to show the cartoon every Easter. Yeah, that is a bit twisted. The major networks, basically, showed it because it was around Easter and it was about talking rabbits, but the message of survival and the character development was overlooked by the masses that watched it just because it had rabbits in it. Well, *that* and it was a good little story. I also have a great respect for Hayao Miyazaki who is more of a filmmaker than anything. *(Spirited Away, Howls, Moving Castle, Nausica and The Valley of The Wind, etc.)* He is brilliant. I must share that he actually sent one of his animators to sit at a bus stop in Japan all day to sketch women's skirts as they flowed in the wind to capture what they might look like while flying. While that might sound a bit like a stalker, that kind of dedication to detail and realism is a dream of mine to reach one day.

Chase Von: Stephen King wrote *The Green Mile,* a story that wasn't really horror, but still a huge success. Are you ever going to venture out into other areas of writing, or are you going to stay strictly with horror? Like him, it is obvious to me, and anyone that has ever read your works, you could write just about anything, and it would still be incredible.

Nick: I like to keep things dark. When I write, I often write to strange music, played way too loud. I really enjoy writing to music as it helps me get into a zone; it puts me in a place and helps paint a surrounding that normally is not there. I listen to everything from Black Metal, which is overly fast, to orchestral music with a very dark message, such as "Cradle of Filth" and Chthonic, to older Tori Amos, to bands like Godspeed You Black Emperor and A Silver Mount Zion. All of these groups paint a dark picture and it helps me see what I am writing. They become sort of a soundtrack to what I write. Have you ever seen *The Never Ending Story?* It is the feeling of "The Nothing" which is a black cloud that rolls across the earth, enveloping everything in its path and ending the world, as we know it. In a way, the music is like that... I have strayed from the point. Yes, I have other stories in the works. My favorite at the moment involves a family of witches in the 1800s that possess a Golem. No, not Golem of *Lord of the Rings,* but a true Golem of the Kabala. When the family is murdered by fearful locals, their young girl relies on this family friend, which is a Golem to roam the world and attempt to make a real life for herself amongst people that are not like her at all. I like the idea of developing her in a world that is completely opposite from how she was brought up. I might throw some real world occurrences in there as well...maybe something exciting involving the Civil War.

Chase Von: How important is family to you, and what is your take on the state of our current world?

Nick: My family is the world to me. Sometimes I feel like a bit of a freak compared to most of them, but in the last five years or so, they have embraced my ambitions and I am proud to say that I bounce ideas off of my father. I like to hear his honest opinions; whether good or bad, we understand each other and I value his open-minded opinions. Even when I write about some pretty disturbing things, he never judges what I am writing. As for the world, that is hard to say. Maybe a more specific question would help. Politically, I respect our soldiers more than anyone in this world, past and present. The fact that men lost limbs and died face-down in the bloody mud so I have the right to write the books I want, and say the things I want, and vote for the people I like, is something that literally is the most amazing thing in the world.

Chase Von: What would you say if you were standing in front of a microphone that could be heard by every child on the planet, and regardless of what language it was they spoke, they would understand you? What positive advice would you give the children, if that were possible?

Nick: Do what you want. Do you want to be a fireman? Do it. Do you want to be an astronaut or fighter pilot? Do it. There is nothing that can hold you back if you focus. I have wasted way too much time being distracted by what life throws at me, and I would wish none of those distractions on anyone. Go out and do what you want and let nothing stand in your way. *Have fun! Follow your dreams!* Not that there is anything wrong with being an accountant or having an office job, but if you want something and you dream to achieve something, do it at all costs.

Chase Von: How can our readers find out more about your books and your other works? Can you share your links and web pages? Also, how can people learn more about your artwork? And are there future projects you are working on you care to share with our readers?

Nick: My new website, done by designer David Gates, is: www.valentinoempire.com. This is dedicated to both the books and the art.
My book MySpace is:
www.myspace.com/theadversarybooks
My more personal MySpace is:
www.myspace.com/hazeltherabbit. This is where you can find out much more about me as a person, if someone so desired. If I may be so bold, I would like to share a few other people's sites that I encourage anyone to visit as well. Alex Eckman Lawn (Artist)
www.alexeckmanlawn.com
David Gates
(Web & Graphic Designer) www.myspace.com/dunnydave
Inert Nashville
(Art and Culture Blog) http://inertnblog.blogspot.com

Chase Von: On behalf of the *Student Operated Press* and myself, Nick, I want to thank you again for taking the time for this interview. I know you have many things going on, so it is truly appreciated you found the time for this. Thanks again, and best wishes with your career and also to your family, brother.

Nick: Chase, you are a great person and I am honored to

know you. You have been there since I started this mess (Smile.) and I appreciate your friendship. It has been a pleasure, and I have really had a good time talking with you.

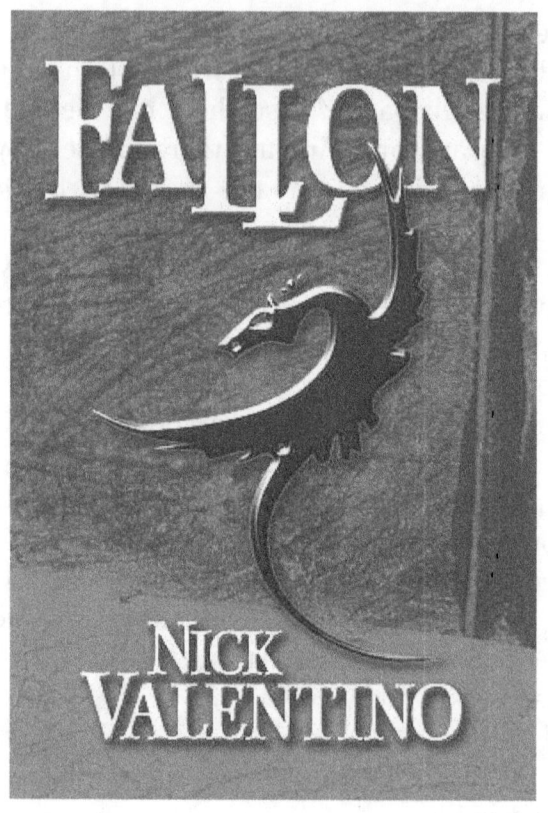

****

"Go out and do what you want and let nothing stand in your way. Have fun! Follow your dreams! Not that there is anything wrong with being an accountant or having an office job, but if you want something and you dream to achieve something, do it at all costs."
- Nick Valentino, Horror Writer
****

Interview with Aberjhani

AWARD-WINNING POET
by Chase Von

'CONNECT SAVANNAH', Photo by Darryl Reynolds

Chase Von: Aberjhani, this is quite the honor for me, as I too am at heart, a poet. And arguably you are now one of the best and most recognized poets in the contemporary field beyond any doubt. So this is, also, in many ways a humbling experience. I first want to thank you for finding the time to do this interview with me on behalf of *the Student Operated Press*.

Aberjhani: Thank you Chase, I always appreciate an opportunity to dialogue with fellow poets and to share whatever insights I can with reading audiences.

Chase Von: Growing up, I initially didn't want to read the works of other poets. I started writing when I was twelve or thirteen and thought that if I read the works of others it might influence my style. Pretty opinionated for a kid, huh? (Smile.)

Aberjhani: It really is extraordinary that at the age of thirteen you felt you had a definitive literary style that you didn't want altered by reading the work of other poets. Apparently you came here knowing to some degree who and what you were meant to be so far as poetry goes.

Chase Von: But eventually I was given a book by Kahlil Gibran, and to be frank with you, it was like receiving a treasured gift. My brother-in-law gave it to me and it was like the entire collection in one book. I had that book for years and considered it as more than just a book; it was like an old friend. One day I was working at the ports in the Marine Corps and had brought it along with me to fill up some of the dead time. You having been in the Air Force, I am sure, are familiar with the hurry-up-then-wait syndrome. But I had to do something, so put the book down and when I came back it was gone. Over the years, few have moved me as Kahlil Gibran has moved me. I got into Javan, and later befriended an incredible poet by the name of Ed Roberts. I've also been amazed at some of the newer poets on the scene and people that have been around for a spell that I am just now discovering. *Taalam Acey is incredible!* Wisdom Supreme is also exceptionally gifted and Zora Howard, Marcus Jones AKA, Morpheus and Neo The Poet, (NeoSoulJah) are off the chain! Bryant McGill has a way of saying things that just reach out and grab hold of your intellect and makes you think deeply. And there are so many others that are off the charts. I don't recall when first I read your works, but I have to tell you: *I got the feeling when I was reading that Kahlil Gibran had returned!* Your style slightly differs but the same spiritual depth and almost musical way that he had of making words sing from the very pages is what you do also.

Aberjhani: I definitely share your passion for Kahlil Gibran's work. The first time I read *The Prophet* I felt like I had journeyed to a secret world reflecting the hidden truths of this one and had to stop to catch my breath after every page. Much later, I discovered a book called *Beloved Prophet,* which is a collection of love letters between Gibran and one of his main benefactors, Mary Haskell, who lived in Savannah toward the end of her life. I have to admit that gave me a sense of connection with him that I kind of treasure. And I agree that there are a lot of very fine poets out there today producing some great work. You can count me among the visitors to Taalam Acey's MySpace page.

Chase Von: When did you start writing and has your style morphed into what it is now or has it always been in the same vein so to speak?

Aberjhani: As for when I started writing, that would have been as a teenager during the Black Arts Movement in the 1970s. That was when Black America first rediscovered the Harlem Renaissance and started republishing classic books like Jean Toomer's *Cane* and Zora Neale Hurston's *Their Eyes Were Watching God.* But also, by that time we had some of the revolutionary works by writers like Eldridge Cleaver and Nikki Giovanni. To me, their writings said all the things I was too terrified to say out loud as a teenager in the South of the 1970s. Ironically enough, though, one of my primary motivations for actually picking up a pen and starting to write was the character John Boy, as portrayed by Richard Thomas, on the old *Walton's* TV show. He used to write about his family, their struggles, pleasures, and what have you. So I started writing in these huge yellow legal pads that I used as journals to help me clarify and direct the conditions of my life as an adolescent. My style has evolved over the years pretty much in direct correlation to my growth as an individual human and spiritual being.

Chase Von: Who are some of the people that you look up to and admire when it comes to writing?

Aberjhani: I admire pretty much any writer committed enough to the craft to make a serious study of it and exercise the discipline necessary to produce worthwhile work. But there have actually been quite a few of those, so I have to admit that some do stand out for me, including John Edgar Wideman with whom I was blessed to appear in the pages of *Essence Magazine*, November 1997, Phillip Caryl, the great Toni Morrison, Alice Walker, Gabriel Garcia Marquez, Ja Jahannes, Louis Reyes Rivera, Amiri Baraka, the extraordinary Ben Okri, Sapphire, Edward P. Jones, Junot Diaz, and quite a few more. In fact, I have a good number of book reviews on my Amazon.com profile and at my Creative Thinkers International site of the writers and poets I appreciate the most.

Chase Von: You were born in Savannah, Georgia, and then apparently moved around quite a bit in your younger years. Were you a military brat? (Smile.) I understand if so, I hate the term myself! But for me, moving so much indirectly caused me to develop a love for books. That is, after I learned how to read and got past failing first grade.

(Smile.) Oh? So you got jokes? Just kidding. What were your younger years like? Did you also get into reading early on because of all the moves, and develop a love for the written word because of the difficulty of making lasting friendships when you are only in a place for a short time, while books are there whenever you pick them up? I know I, and many others, did.

Aberjhani: In terms of different cities or states, my life was fairly stable as a child because we lived in different parts of Savannah, but I didn't relocate outside the city until I went off to college at eighteen. Books were more like my refuge from poverty, racism, and the intense drama that can come with being part of a large black southern family. Because I wanted my education to be something more than the memorization of textbook materials, I chose, after starting out in Savannah, to attend colleges in Florida, St. Paul, Philadelphia, and San Francisco. After my tour of colleges and universities, I further supplemented my education and career by serving in the U.S. Air Force for eight years, two at Eielson AFB in Alaska, four at RAF Lakenheath in England, and two years of reserve duty out of Charleston, SC.

Chase Von: By the time I was in first grade the second time (Smile.) we had already lived in Indiana, Virginia, New York, and England. What role would you say all the different environments you have had to adapt to played in your becoming a world-known writer?

Aberjhani: Travel allowed me, foremost, to break out of the repressive psychological and social conditioning that came with growing up in poverty and a racially oppressive environment. Once I hit the road, I was able to enjoy experiences beyond those allowed, if you will, within my native region during that particular time. By getting to know people from different places and with diverse life experiences, I developed a greater appreciation for the basic humanity that defines us all, as opposed to the socially, politically, and economically imposed categories that make us susceptible to things like discrimination and prejudice. The ability to recognize that basic humanity and celebrate it through poetry, short stories, journalism, and even the *Encyclopedia of the Harlem Renaissance* has certainly played a major role in my literary career.

Chase Von: How did your time spent in the military enhance your writing?

Aberjhani: Thank you for that question! My time in the military marked my beginnings as a professional writer. I was very fortunate in that I was able to serve as a military journalist/editor with the base public affairs office. And the thing about being a journalist with a weekly deadline, in the military, is that you learn how to write whether inspired by a particular muse or not. You know there's a job to be done and an entire base population counting on you to get it done because they need the information you're providing...so you do it-- *period.*

Chase Von: And how do you think that time spent serving your country affected you overall as the man you are today?

Aberjhani: Of course, one of the most obvious benefits was the experience of being a working writer in uniform. The development of skill, focus, and professional expertise that came with it proved priceless for me because after leaving the Air Force, despite my experience, I was not able to get a steady job as a journalist in my hometown. Prior to joining the military, I had an innate sense of self-discipline that became even stronger while serving, and that helped me in a big way as a bookstore manager for some thirteen years. That self-discipline and ability to apply my energies toward a specific goal was also crucial when I became a caregiver for my mom while simultaneously working on the encyclopedia.

Chase Von: *Your list of awards is astounding!* Your name is listed in a byline besides the great W.E.B. Du Bois himself. You have also won the Best Poet and Spoken Word Artist in the 2006 Connect Savannah Readers' Poll. The Poet of The Month, January 2007, at The Writing Forum. You're the recipient of the Irene Tromble McAlister Literary Prize, and the Critic's Pick for Best Savannah Author in the *Creative Loafing Entertainment Magazine's* Best of Savannah Year 2000 poll. And you have also been selected for inclusion in *Contemporary Authors* (published by Gale), which since 1962 has been the most authoritative reference on world authors. Did I miss any, and do these things just happen with you putting yourself out there? Or do you have to enter into contests and win to be recognized?

Aberjhani: I don't enter literary contests because I tend not to win them. (Laugh.) The awards that have come my way--including the Choice Academic Title and Best History Book awards--have all been bestowed by people and organizations who decided that my work provided something valuable for the reading public and for that reason deserved greater recognition. But I have to tell you that I received my greatest award when I gave a presentation for the Poetry Society of Georgia. It's the oldest literary organization in the state and many of its members at that time were senior poets who used to joke about needing new blood to stay alive, so they were happy when I was an active younger member. Anyway, after my presentation, I got a standing ovation, which, by itself, was deeply moving. But then this one poet (the great Patricia

Photo by John Zeuli

Robinson King)--who at the time I think was almost 80-- sitting in the front row, looked at me and said, "I don't usually stand because these old legs of mine make it difficult, but I'm going to stand for you." I shook my head and said, "Oh please don't," because she used a walker and I knew it was painful for her. She couldn't clap her hands because she was holding onto her walker, but that great poet insisted on standing and nodding to acknowledge her approval of my work. I cried over that for a year.

Chase Von: You have authored or co-authored the following that I am aware of: the *Encyclopedia of The Harlem Renaissance* (Facts On File Library Of American History), *I Made My Boy Out Of Poetry, Blood Kin, A Savannah Story, The Wisdom Of W.E.B. Dubois* (Wisdom Library),"*The Harlem Renaissance Way Down South,* and *The Hanging Man Dreams.* Are you currently working on any other projects you can make our readers aware of?

Aberjhani: Two of the titles you named only contain introductions by me. *Blood Kin* is an amazing historical novel for young adults by newcomer Robert Micklesm and *The Hanging Man Dreams* is an excellent volume of poetry by the brilliant David Hightower.

Chase Von: Thanks for the clarification.

Aberjhani: Believe it or not, my own current projects include three books: the first is Christmas When Music Almost Killed the World, which is my first novel and just published in November, 2007. For a long time, the working title of the novel was *The Black Skylark Z-Ped Music Player,* named after my Authors Den website, but readers should know we dropped that title after some mid-race changes in publishing options. The second book is *The Bridge of Silver Wings*, a volume of poetry that I've been working on for more than a year now. Even though one book is fiction and the other poetry, they actually have a lot in common since song lyrics make up a good portion of the novel. Also, both have cover art by Luther E. Vann, which is something I'm a bit proud of because Vann is one of the preeminent artists of our time. A third book, a very important work of creative nonfiction called *The American Poet Who Went Home Again,* is not out yet, but currently under publication consideration. So we'll have to wait and see how that one goes.

Chase Von: *Christmas When Music Almost Killed the World* is a very strong--and if you don't mind me saying so--an unusual sounding title for a novel. Can you tell me what it's about?

Aberjhani: Hmmm, you're the first interviewer to ask that question, so I need to make this a good answer, don't I? (laughs) It's about what happens to a young man named

Danny Blue after his girlfriend, an art student named Valerie Hyerman, appears to have been found dead with Danny Blue unconscious and unclothed beside her (this book is rated PG-13 btw). In the course of trying to make peace with her death, Danny Blue finds himself drawn into the schemes of two superstar musicians with very different intentions towards the world. One, named Jimmy Redfyre, is a vampire-like figure who uses his music to manipulate people's minds and lives and persuades them to do some totally uncool things in his name. The other superstar, named Ruzahn, is a kind of prophet-poet who uses his music for a different effect. On top of all this, Danny and his friends have to deal with a group of fanatics who are trying to use the memory of his girlfriend and her art as the basis for their cult beliefs. The title of the novel comes from an event that takes place during the holidays.

Chase Von: I know John Berendt's book *Midnight in the Garden of Good and Evil* is based on true crime events in your hometown. Is your novel also set in Savannah and based on something that really happened there?

Aberjhani: As a matter of fact, this story takes place in a town similar to Savannah on a planet similar to Earth, but actually not Savannah or Earth. [laughs] I think the term used to describe such places is called "parallel world." Although some people thus far seem to want it to be my hometown Savannah very badly because the city is mentioned in the *Uncut Goodies* series, which are outtakes from the novel, published recently on the Internet. (Talk about something controversial!) But those who read the novel notice both details and obscurities that could only make sense on a parallel earth, the existence of which according to modern physics is a very real possibility. We can say that certain aspects of this novel serve as metaphors for specific conditions in our world, but shouldn't say the story is any kind of attempt at a literal representation of this world.

Chase Von: With Russell Simmons's *Def Poetry Jam,* a lot more poetry and spoken word artists are getting some notoriety. Alicia Keys has also helped in that regard, as has Jill Scott, Jewell, and a few others. But having read some reviews, it seems there are some people who think that poetry should be left to the poets. I, myself, applaud all who write poetry because it––in itself, by the baring of the soul––opens one up for criticism. So those that criticize others, like singers or actors who try their hand at it, can do so, but I think it helps bring attention to it, overall.

Aberjhani: Poetry has become extremely important as a medium of self-expression and self-empowerment, providing many people with a crucial tool, or voice you might say, for addressing some very horrendous issues and some extremely sublime experiences. To me, for that reason, anybody who feels the urge to write poetry should certainly do so, no exceptions whatsoever. However, that having been said, probably not everyone who writes poetry should worry about publishing it or presenting it within a public forum unless that forum is designed to accommodate what they have written. This is significant because poetry didn't just arrive here with the modern spoken-word movement. It's been around since the first unknown, uttered prayer centuries ago, and is part of a global oral and literary tradition and art form with definitive qualities and standards. The fact that those qualities and standards are extremely flexible is one of the things that make poetry what it is, but it's also the recognition of those elements that determine one's abilities as an authentic poet. Poetry as personal expression, can and should be whatever an individual wants it to be. Poetry as literary art is an applied balance between aesthetic precision and individual mystery, and those who achieved that particular level are the ones who have been my teachers.

Chase Von: But facing facts, poetry is still the lowest genre in writing that there is. I, myself, had the lofty goal of reestablishing poetry on the literary map. (Smile.) However, it is obvious I am going to need someone to help me achieve that, and you are definitely a few light years ahead of me in that regard anyway. But do you, like myself, think that people are beginning to realize on a much larger scale, that poetry is important and that it does deserve equal billing in regards to other literary works, such as novels, mysteries, science fiction, horrors, dramas and the like? It has always baffled me that the one genre that is precisely about what people are feeling, is the one that is not given the time of day, for the most part. I still feel that there is something very wrong with that, and that it is just one of the indications of why society has many more things to do to right itself.

Aberjhani: Poetry has often been described as "the flower of language" precisely because of its concentration of imagery, philosophical nuance, and emotion, so it's really only the last-place genre in terms of the literary marketplace. And even that has changed substantially due to the guerilla marketing tactics of spoken-word artists who sell their CDs and chapbooks at readings or out the trunk of their cars. So it may not be getting top billing in the bookstore sense, but during the past decade it has become extremely commanding at the grassroots and folk level overall.

Chase Von: Your works are like what a lot of people have said about mine, meaning *eclectic!* You write about everything! I have read some works by you about love and angels, and other works about vampires that have the same dreamy feeling and otherworldliness as writings by the great Anne Rice, who, incidentally, keeps coming up in my interviews for some reason. (Smile.) But she is an incredible writer. What inspires you to write? For me, I just try and catch good ideas when they come, but I am always curious as to how others find their inspiration.

Aberjhani: For the most part, just being alive inspires me to write because I find everything in this world, whether dog doo-doo funky, or classy and exquisite, to be irresistibly fascinating. On another level, I look at literature in general as a conversation between writers and readers of the past, writers and readers of the present, and writers and readers of the future. I like the eternal nature of that dialogue and my writings are my contributions to the conversation. I try to be responsible when making those contributions, but I don't always get there. Sometimes I just want to be my plain human self and cut loose with an unruly burp, fart, or howl, either of which I have learned can make some readers squirm with nervousness (Laughs.) and others laugh out loud. It's never my intention to make anybody feel nervous or threatened, but I have to be true to my own voice--just as you were determined to be at the age of thirteen--before I can be respectful of anybody else's. Then on a level that goes even further than that, I am greatly inspired by spirituality, and the poems in *The Bridge of Silver Wings* draw heavily on my meditations concerning angelic influences.

Chase Von: Can you tell our readers about how some of your words have been adapted to music?

Aberjhani: I was extremely blessed a couple of years ago to meet on Authors Den my fellow writers, Nordette

Adams and Mark "Rahkyt" Rockeymoore, two extremely gifted individuals. It turned out that Mark is not only an educator, novelist, and poet, but also a budding music producer. Even though the three of us have never met in person, he was able to set to music recordings of Adams and me reciting our work. The resulting CD is called *The Goddess and the Skylark: Dancing through the Word Labyrinth*. We experienced a setback with the distribution of the CD, but are working on correcting that and hope to make it available again just after the New Year.

Chase Von: How important is family to you, and what is your take on the state of our current world?

Aberjhani: Sir, those are two huge questions rolled into one. (Laughs.) Family is very important to me, which is why I, somehow, found the strength and will to take care of my mother at home for a decade... right up until six months before her passing, when I had no choice but to place her in a skilled nursing home for medical reasons. Family, community, and the world at large are issues I deal with in the book I mentioned earlier, *The American Poet Who Went Home Again*. Readers who might like a preview of that title should check out my creative nonfiction, *With Love A Letter from Yesterday to Today and Tomorrow*, as well as *The Day the Word N****r Entered My Life*, and any number of personal essays posted on my AD pages.

Chase Von: What would you say if you were standing in front of a microphone that could be heard by every child on the planet, and they could understand you regardless of whatever language they spoke? What positive advice would you give them if that were possible?

Aberjhani: I first would apologize to them for my own and my generation's failure to make our world a safer and more loving environment for them to live and grow up in. Some people might read that and go "Ah-hh, ain't he sweet?" But there's nothing cute about the fact that every single day in this world 18,000 children under the age of ten die from disease, war, domestic violence, and starvation. Among teenagers, 5,000 die every year from suicide--which is one of the subjects addressed in my novel--because they apparently can't bear the conditions of their lives. So how can we not apologize to them for that? How can we--and I'm talking about all the "we's" around this globe--not apologize for continuing to destroy the Earth of their future for the sake of business profits and political domination? I would apologize to them, and then I would talk about all the opportunities they have to save and improve their own futures. Or at least I would try to do that.

Chase Von: What are the best websites and other mediums where our readers can find out more about you and your incredible work?

Aberjhani: At the moment, the best websites would be Creative Thinkers International:

(http://www.creativethinkersintl.ning.com), Authors Den (http://www.authorsden.com/Aberjhani) and my Connect Author profile on Amazon.com. And, of course, the best way to truly know any given author is through his or her writings. In my case, as you pointed out earlier, readers will discover someone traditional enough to respect and honor values and ancestors as I do in *Encyclopedia of the Harlem Renaissance,* but also adventurous enough to step outside the assigned box and examine interesting possibilities through original literary visions, such as I hope I have done in *The Bridge of Silver Wings* and *Christmas When Music Almost Killed the World.*

Chase Von: On behalf of the *Student Operated Press*, Aberjhani, I truly thank you for finding the time to do this interview. I also wish you continued success with your writings, and hope that you will continue to bless us all with your incredible gifts. As a fellow poet who doesn't have near the reputation as you, I kind of feel the way I believe I would have if it had been possible for me to interview the great Kahlil Gibran during his lifetime. So I again thank you! As a poet, this interview is one for the memory books. (Smile.)

Aberjhani: It's certainly one I will remember and treasure for a very long time. Thank you again, Chase, for the opportunity.

****

"I first would apologize to them for my own and my generation's failure to make our world a safer and more loving environment for them to live and grow up in. Some people might read that and go 'Ah-hh, ain't he sweet?' But there's nothing cute about the fact that every single day in this world 18,000 children under the age of ten die from disease, war, domestic violence, and starvation. Among teenagers, 5,000 die every year from suicide–– which is one of the subjects addressed in my novel––because they apparently can't bear the conditions of their lives."
- Aberjhani, Author, Poet

****

Visions of a Skylark Dressed In Black

by Aberjhani

BPS E-Publishing

****

*"By getting to know people from different places
and with diverse life experiences, I developed a
greater appreciation for the basic humanity that
defines us all, as opposed to the socially, politically,
and economically imposed categories
that make us susceptible to things like
discrimination and prejudice."*
- Aberjhani, Author, Poet

****

Interview with Jennifer Wilkinson

LOVELY COMEDIENNE, ACTRESS
by Chase Von

Chase Von: Hey, Jen, when we spoke on the phone you confirmed it for me: you are an angel. On behalf of the *Student Operated Press* I want to thank you for finding the time to do this interview. Before we get into other things, what was your childhood like?

Jen: Thank you for your work and amazing poetry. I do love meeting like-minded individuals. Ah, yes, the age-old childhood beginnings. I have to say my childhood was a happy coming of age. I feel fortunate to have had parents who focused on instilling manners, hard work, and the value of relationships. I may have decided to go a little less *politically correct* than their liking, yet this may be a sign of the times--they didn't get it that it would just be me being totally real with people. Yet, back to the childhood, even being an only child, I did have to earn what I got. For instance, even with the means my parents had to purchase things for me, like a TV in my room as a teenager, they opted to have me work off anything like this with documented chores over time. I appreciate this as it shows we do not get any *freebies* and life is what we truly make it to be. My parents were strict and, although I moaned over the early curfews or disciplines given, looking back, I am so grateful--as this truly was a realistic picture of how the real world is. Things do not come to you, you work for them.

Chase Von: I`ve always thought that comedians have to be some of the smartest people on the planet, because you have to think outside the box and then bring it back in a way the rest of us can understand. When, as you were growing up, did your mind start to do that, and is it something that you can't turn off?

Jen: It is true. I can sometimes be a little too *on*. When I was about five or six, that's when it really started to click. I have a mind that is truly interested in human nature and like to--perhaps, at times--go a little too deep in understanding trends or how things work. I have learned that when you are speaking to people on a subject they are interested in, that may be the time to go "analytical." Yet for the most part it is more fun to speak to your target audience about what people like or know. When I was younger, adults got a kick out of how much I would share; yet now in the adult world we may all be on information overload--so to focus on people's interest makes more sense or you lose your audience.

Chase Von: When I was in my first war, we had to set up tents. I remember a sergeant that said to me, "Private? Can you work any slower?" I stopped. Everyone was looking at us. I looked up in the sky and then down and rubbed my chin. I then said, after I had dramatically given it much thought (smile), "You know, Sergeant, I hadn't really thought about it but...if I apply myself and use all the things the military and people like you have taught me, I really think it is possible... I could work slower." (Smile.) The troops fell out laughing. Even the sergeant, who at first turned red, started laughing. He used it to rally us back together and really start working--but *God, it was hot...* How do you think humor positively affects our lives, Jen?

Jen: Well, first of all, I can say this: God bless the troops! Without the bravery and action, we would not have been as safe and well off as we have been all these years. And yes, in hot weather and constant-alert conditions I can only say that to keep the humor is a measure of superiority; overall a sense of humor is essential to even the toughest of circumstances. It is not to say this *should* happen; yet if we can see the humor, I feel this is one of the keys to releasing any negativity we feel. So humor, for me, is something I continue to appreciate and celebrate, especially when we have justified reasons--instead of complaining.

Chase Von: I saw the video of you dancing. (Smile.) If folks want to know what I said in comments, they can visit there; but how do you stay so slim and attractive? What are some of your favorite meals, and do you have to stay away from them sometimes to stay in shape?

Jen: Oh, please... Chase, this is where I have to fight the battle of "thin is not so in." Actually, I have to make sure to eat five meals a day just so I am not a stick. So although I know it sounds fun, I know and appreciate that many men want a woman with a figure. So thank you, yes, I am blessed with not fighting the scale, yet I too want to have some meat. Actually, ironically, I am frustrated now as I have a tiny belly so I know it is time to hit the gym--and yes, I will be doing this three or four times a week so I can gain a little mass and be minus the belly again.

Chase Von: You've been in a few movies--and when I say movies, I am talking about real stars. How has pursuing your dreams and doing things like that made you realize that by following your heart, you are on the right path? And can you share with our readers some of the incredible people you have met?

Jen: Wow. I cannot tell you how blessed I have been. I think when amongst talent and those that have worked their way to great heights in the tough business of entertaining, the most important thing is to just be *real*. There are so many wanting the light, and too often those in the spotlight get bombarded with people trying for the short cuts or just the "give to me and walk away" approach. I have had so many brushes--or in some cases meaningful conversations--with those in the know who worked so hard to get there. I think all people want to be respected for who they are and not what you may get from them. If you are being *you* and you are driven, people of great talent are not afraid to help you out and respect that you still appreciate help. I do not think many make it without a mentor or someone who believes in them, yet this is not a handout, but a huge blessing or opportunity given from our own hard work and focus.

Chase Von: I'm married, but you are still very attractive. (Smile.) How difficult is it for you to live life and think that people are genuine, or just want to be with you because they know you are eventually going to be a huge star?

Jen: Nah, I tend to be drawn for the long haul to people that are genuinely being themselves. Yet, again, I also understand anyone wanting to find a way to his or her calling or passion and being unsure how to get there. All in all, I am aware that I'd love to be trusted with the job of entertaining full time, and want this. I also know it is not so much the "big star" destination, but work we ourselves give and put out that shows we may be even close to that responsibility. Really, this all is about the gift we have that really is applicable to our talents. So if someone is reaching out to me, ask anyone who has been watching if I am accessible. Frankly, I interact with anyone that is real to me.

Chase Von: What projects have you recently completed and what are some of your future projects that you can share with our readers?

Jen: I am excited that I'm getting more exposure to hosting shows. I am blown away! It has even involved my booking some celebrities or talent well known in the world of comedy. Early this fall there is a show I hope to have an opportunity to tie to a charity, also. I think it is nice when the comedy "voice" can also show their sincere interest in making a positive impact on the community or world at large. Heck, just making a room full of strangers laugh is indeed a contribution, in my book; so to tie the show back to giving earnings to a verified good cause demonstrates even further how much we can do for positive impacts. So I am focused on the back-end a little these days, and like the responsibilities this brings.

Chase Von: A lot of comedians have died, or taken their own lives. I was really blown away when I found out Bernie Mac died. I don't really know the specifics but comedy is not an easy profession. Is this something you think about, as well? Because to be on stage and crack a joke is one thing... but what you say sticks. How do you balance that out and know you are saying things you can live with?

Jen: Sure, sure. It really is tough. A comic that gets the most audience connection usually has been the most raw or naked. Real time... So a piece of ourselves and, certainly, our energy goes to illustrate the life experience in words and actions. Although comedy can be fun and silly, often--and what I strive to grow to--it delivers the frustrations or truths so that we can laugh even when it may be something you would never say out loud. Overall, if we do not have malice, prejudices or bias, we may say anything--and with that create a perhaps long-needed laugh at society as a whole.

Chase Von: Can you share with our readers any future projects you might be working on?

Jen: As I shared, I will be more focused on hosting shows and involved in the creative process for the audience experience. For now, I find this to be rewarding. For the long term, I would like to return to acting and earn my way up to a featured role as a complex character in a movie. I am always open for a challenge! In the past I have worked with Greg Wilson (http://www.imdb.com/name/nm1034313/), Hollywood Improv host K-von (http://www.myspace.com/kVoncomedy), *Comedy Central* comedian Ian Edwards

(http://www.comedycentral.com/comedians/browse/e/ian
_edwards.jhtml), the amazing Toogie Jackson (with
Darren Carter at
http://www.youtube.com/watch?v=_rN9O3V0AKQ), and
been recognized by some of the greats such as Richard
Jeni (*Comedy Central* and *The Mask* with Jim Carrey) and
Kyle Cease (*Comedy Central* favorite), and other amazing,
talented comedians such as "the great" Sandra Vals
(http://www.latinheat.com/news.php?nid=670); and this
is just to highlight a few. I do know I am leaving some out
for now, Chase. Getting to meet all this talent blows my
mind.

Chase Von: How important is family to you, and what is
your take on the state of our current world?

Jen: I feel that family, as we define that, is essential. We
may define our families as the ones we create if we find

our partner later in life. Yet, if we are open, we can develop a family-like system amongst friends. I myself have family, yet I do find it becomes redefined to extend outside the boundaries of blood relatives, too. The overall concept of having a select group keeping us humble, accountable and honest is the benefit of keeping consistent ties to those who love us. I do think that when people expand their needs to include others--for example the people they live with, work with and share communities with--we, individually, benefit from this. Next to financial or health struggles, there is nothing harder than being lonely or isolated.

Chase Von: What would you say if you were standing in front of a microphone that could be heard by every child on the planet, and regardless of what language they spoke, they would understand you? What positive advice would you give the children, if that were possible?

Jen: The overall message would be that the best we can do, despite what others might say different around us--parent, teacher, coach, friend or counselor--is to choose to do what we want to do. It is important to adhere to guidance, especially from those more experienced or vested in our success; however, if we also measure in our own natural instincts or desires to focus on what we want, I think we are living to our true purpose. The best part of doing what you really love is that money and security will follow, even though perhaps sometimes it may not always be logical. However, from my experience, I would tell the children to have several plans of action and to develop skills through education and hands-on experience, and to continue to master where we fit in and how we add value to the world as a whole.

Chase Von: Where can our readers find your movie links,

shows and other things related to your comedy? And the lovely and talented *you?*

Jen: Well, my goal is to post the new generation stuff by the winter of 2008, as it develops. I would say I utilize MySpace the best I can for now, until I decide the best plan of action. Do not be surprised in the next year if I create a central website to deliver the AOL, Google, Facebook and other sources into one. Yet, being a person who believes in "show me the money," I take baby steps until it seems a grand plan is necessary. So the best is to Google me, as I am certain this article will be at the top; yet for now MySpace is my main source: http://www.myspace.com/comedylovelaughs

Chase Von: On behalf of the *Student Operated Press*, Jen, thanks so much for giving us some of your time. You are a very lovely woman and a genuinely sweet one. Having actually spoken to you I can only hope that all your dreams come true, because you are a true sweetheart. I am wishing you love and light always; and thanks again for sharing yourself with our readers.

Jen: This experience is another blessing for me. Talking to you, Chase, reminds me why this is really an amazing journey to be on. Thank you for your light, always.

****

"The best part of doing what you really love is that money and security will follow, even though perhaps sometimes it may not always be logical."
- Jennifer Wilkinson, Comedienne, Actress
****

****

"The overall message would be that the best we can do, despite what others might say different around us--parent, teacher, coach, friend or counselor--is to choose to do what we want to do."
- Jennifer Wilkinson, Comedienne, Actress

****

Interview with MT Robison

ECLECTIC ENTERTAINER, MUSICIAN, ANGEL
By Chase Von

Chase Von: Hey there, MT! I want to thank you for squeezing this in your hectic schedule and sharing yourself with our readers here at the *Student Operated Press*. My dear friend Tina Devaney told me to check you out and I always listen to Tina because she has excellent taste. Another one she turned me on to was music-singing sensation Lisa Lavie. *So when Tina speaks, The Last Panther listens!* I was actually coming home from the store earlier today and they were playing Lisa's song "No One" on 94.5 FM here is Southern Cal. The show itself is hosted by none other than Kenny G, but since I haven't heard from Lisa in more than a minute now--and I know she is mad busy like yourself--I told T to let her know she's on the airwaves here, as well (Smile.) Now when I checked out your music, my first thought was: *sounds a lot like James Taylor!* Do you get that a lot? And thanks again for finding the time to share yourself with us here at the SOP.

MT: Oh, it's my pleasure and honor, Chase. Well, I have had a few people tell me James Taylor, but actually we asked MySpace friends that very question, and by far the answers were Bob Dylan and Tom Waits. I think the Tom Waits comes from my live performance... I'm a little crazy, like Tom, on stage...Ha-ha...Dylan, I don't know...maybe the sound of my voice.

Chase Von: There's quite a few things I want to get to, as you are a very interesting individual, but let's start here. Where did you grow up, how was your childhood and how did music get introduced into your life?

MT: I grew up in a little town in California, fifty miles from Los Angeles...called Colton. My childhood was beautiful, great parents, middle class, *Leave it to Beaver* kind of family for real. My mom was a musician and my dad was an artist, so they were always very supportive of my desire to make music. That started when I was about eight years old and saw Elvis... *That was it for me!* I knew then I wanted to be a guitar player and sing. Used to do my own little rendition of *Hound Dog* for my sister and her friends at her slumber parties. They loved it and I thought, *Wow--this is a great way to get girls to pay attention to me!*...Ha-ha-ha... Always a motivation for what we do. (Smile.) Things changed a bit when I got older, meaning the neighborhood got a little bit rougher, but the early years were great.

Chase Von: I also thought I read where you performed in the circus. I'm a two-time war veteran and not saying that to say nothing scares me...just to make a point. But there are a lot of people that have phobias about clowns. Were you a clown? I'm not scared of them myself, but I can't say I care much for them, either. Might have something to do with watching *Batman* as a kid and the *Joker,* which is a role that Heath Ledger took to the next level, although sadly, he's no longer with us... But I've seen some pictures of you that are in clown face that I think would make the *Joker* want you on his team. How did you become involved in the circus life, and what was it like traveling around in that world? Do you think it has expanded you as a performer? And if you were a clown, were you a funny, nice clown or one of the ones that people would be saying: *Stay back! Stay way back!* Batman––help! (Smile.)

MT: Ha-ha-ha... Yeah I could definitely be on the Joker`s team Chase! I've even had people say when I smile I look like the Joker. My references to the circus come from playing in many heavy metal bands in the eighties when the Sunset Strip in LA was a freak show. *So much fun!* We all wore tons of makeup, crazy, colorful clothes, and you never knew what you were going to see. Girls walking guys like dogs on leashes down the street, gypsies and crazies of all kinds... It was totally like the circus! However, I've never been a real circus clown! (Smile.)

Chase Von: Well that's cool, MT, 'cause, even though I don't have Batman's cell number no mo`, (really never had it to begin with), I am friends on MySpace with Garret T.

L shrader

Sato of the movie *Waste Land*, and Taimak, *The Last Dragon* and Jackie Chan and Tony Jaa so if someone was `A Scared of a Clown`, they could let me know and I could, ah...message them. Heh-heh. Darcy Donavan likes to think of herself as *Wonder Woman*; Shawn Richardz has a super-hero costume; and Kiara Hunter also has a comic book where she's a female bounty hunter in the future called *Hunter Girl*. I can get in contact with them, as well, (Smile.)... Now to something a bit more serious: I also read where you took a break away from music, although for so long, music was your life. Not to get too personal, but you are back on the scene now and making many waves again. Is there more to the story you can share with our readers about why you now refer to your fans not as fans, but as MT`s Angels?

MT: After many years in the business and so many close calls with success--never quite getting to that next level-- I became a little bitter. *I quit music to grow up and make money. Big mistake!* I was never more miserable in my whole life. Six pack every night just to tolerate being a grown up... I guess I'll always be a "Peter Pan." I need to be making music, even if I'm a pauper the rest of my life. It is what I was put here to do: write songs and entertain people. Take them on a journey, out of their worries for an hour or so.... That's my mission. I refer to my fans as angels because when I got some clarity, I realized that all of us could be an angel for someone. A kind word, a gesture of help, even a little smile can change someone's day, week or whatever. If we all helped one another in our own unique ways, more dreams would come true in this world. So my fans are Angels here on earth... Like our mutual friend Tina, she is a Mighty Angel! I didn't understand when I was young, but now I do. The music is about *them,* not me... My job is to make them feel, smile, cry, go somewhere new in their head... Take them away and enrich their lives... Make a difference... *That* is being an Angel.

Chase Von: My taste in music is what one might call eclectic. In fact, I've often been called that. I know you are versatile in a lot of genres, and I have to admit, this is the first time I have heard of "HillBilly Urban." (Smile.) But who are some of the people in music you truly admire and look up to?

MT: Oh there are so many! Wow--Robert Plant and Jimmy Page had a huge impact on me. They showed me what a true performer was all about, not just the music but the show. I'm very eclectic too, so from there I go to Elvis, Joni Mitchell, The Stones, Jethro Tull, Crosby, Stills, Nash, and Young, Allman Brothers, Queen, Tom Waits, Sara McLaughlin... So many....

Chase Von: You've been compared to Iggy Pop, Steven Tyler, The Eagles. (My oldest brother actually went to High School in England with original members of the Eagles. Teena Marie was also in his high school.) You've also been compared to Bob Seger, Simon and Garfunkel, JJ Cale, Lou Reed, as well as the legendary Johnny Cash... At just twenty, you moved to LA and formed your own original rock band called *Gangster.* You also had a huge following and attracted the attention of *Warner Brothers.* You've sang lead in many other bands, but also wrote songs for all the bands you were in and opened for Great White, Vixen, Blue Oyster Cult, Tray Guns of Guns 'n Roses, and Night Ranger. You also formed a pop-rock band with keyboard master and music director Alex Alessandroni, who was the music director for many well-known talents such as Bobby Brown, Christina Aguilera and Pink. You even attracted the attention of Randy Jackson--and I can't tell you how many times in my interviews the name of Michael Jackson comes up...or the Jacksons! And you've just released your own self-titled CD called *Promise*. What can you tell our readers about this music which is coming from someone with such a variety of backgrounds in music? And how does one go from a band called Gangster to Hillbilly Urban? Curious minds want to know! (Smile.)

MT: Well, I started out playing super hard rock and I grew up in a town full of Gangsters, so it just sort of fit. As I was working on my CD, I started joking with my producer, Mark Shrader, that I was going to call this music Hillbilly Urban. Mainly because I have a little twang in my voice and my musical roots came from the hills of Kentucky. My grandfather Claude Ward was an award-winning fiddle player a long time ago, and my grandmother Ivy Pearl could sing you country ballads that would make a dead man cry. So my music sounds a little hillbilly but I grew up in a very tough urban town.

Chase Von: One of my favorite singers is Rachael Bell, which is someone I turned Tina on to. One of Rachael Bell's favorite singers is James Taylor...and mine as well; I even have his Christmas CD. (Smile.) So I will be sure to let Rach know about you. But who in the music industry would you really love to work with? And where can our readers find out more about you and your various links to your websites... to purchase your music?

MT: I have always wanted to do a song with Sheryl Crow. She just has this thing that makes me want to do a duet with her... I love her vibe when she plays. Maybe it's a soul thing. (Smile.)

My official web site is: http://www.mtrobisonmusic.com

MySpace: http://www.myspace.com/mtrobisonmusic

My Promise CD is available at:

http://cdbaby.com/cd/mtrobison

And various other sites for digital downloads like, Amazon, iTunes, etc.

Chase Von: How important is family to you, and what is your take on the state of our current world?

MT: My daughters, Echo and Piper, are everything to me. *They are my heroes! Beautiful women inside and out.* I am so blessed with family love and support. L. Shrader is my ex-wife and manager; Steve Shrader is my wonderful bass player and my amazing guitar player Jesse Whytock has become like a brother to me. I have a beautiful older sister, Sherron, in Ohio. Oh, and the little girl Blaze, on my CD cover is one of my Goddaughters. We have a great family; I have everything a man could ever want... *The world?* I think if everyone would just help one person, everything would change. This world would change. In some places the hurt runs deep, so that will always be there. But just one angel helping another could change the very fabric of our world... I believe that!

Chase Von: What would you say if you were standing in front of a microphone that could be heard by every child on the planet, and regardless of what language it was they spoke, they would understand you? What positive advice would you give the children, if that were possible?

MT: No matter what the circumstances...*believe* in yourselves! You can do anything if you believe!

MT and Band, photo by L. Shrader

Chase Von: On behalf of the *Student Operated Press* and myself, MT, I really appreciate your taking the time to share yourself with our readers! I'm Black, Blackfoot and Cherokee Indian, and possibly, a little French, but when it comes to music, if I like it, it doesn't matter what vein it is in. And if I don't like it, it doesn't matter what vein it is in, either. I dug yours when I first heard it, and I am sure others will dig it as well. You're versed, it appears, in all forms of music, but like a Bruce Lee--who borrowed from all forms of fighting to come up with Jeet Kune Do--you're using your mastery of so many different styles to weave a magic all your own. Thanks for finding the time for this and one last thing: *What does MT stand for?*

MT: Mighty Tall? Brother, mountain? Mad Thadeous? Ha-ha-ha... You'll just have to keep guessing on that one! (Smile.)

Chase Von: Well now, MT, the readers and I here at the SOP are still clueless. And by not answering that question and how you did it, does sound a little like the Joker! Hmmmm... I'll just have to ask Judyth Piazza to ask you herself when you do your audio. ...Heh–heh... Continued success to you, Brother. "One Love," and when next you speak to T, tell her my thanks for suggesting you for our readers... and *rock* 2009!

MT: Thank you so much for giving me this opportunity to tell my story, Chase. Now you are an Angel... See how it works? Bless you, and may anyone who reads this be blessed and have a dream come true this year!
Love and light!- MT

****

"I quit music to grow up and make money. Big mistake! I was never more miserable in my whole life. Six pack every night just to tolerate being a grown up... I guess I'll always be a 'Peter Pan.' I need to be making music, even if I'm a pauper the rest of my life."
- MT Robison, Singer, Musician, Songwriter
****

L Shrader

****

"No matter what the circumstances...
believe in yourselves! You can do
anything if you believe!"
- MT Robison, Singer, Musician, Songwriter

****

Interview with Leah DeVon

LOVELY SINGING SENSATION
by Chase Von

Chase Von: Leah, it's so cool we connected the other day because you are one on-the-go Diva! It's been almost a year since I communicated with you... Least it feels like it. So on behalf of the *Student Operated Press*, I really appreciate you finding time to share yourself with our readers.

Leah DeVon: It *has* been a minute! Thank you for taking the time to do this interview with me.

Chase Von: You're really accomplishing some truly wonderful things in your career, but before we get into all that, what was your childhood like growing up in Florida?

Leah DeVon: I loved my childhood! I have an amazing family. I am actually the youngest of four girls!

Chase Von: How early did you know that singing was your calling? And was church a part of that for you in your early beginnings?

Leah DeVon: I actually started singing solos at my church when I was seven years old, so church was definitely a place for me to find my voice at a very young age.

Chase Von: And lastly, for this portion: What was going through your mind when you left for Georgia to truly pursue your dream?

Leah DeVon: That I must be crazy leaving the comfort of all of my friends and family, but I knew it was something that I was going to do.

Chase Von: You've been doing something that is really dear to my heart, and that is performing for the troops all around the world and also in war zones. How has that affected you on a personal level and has it changed your perceptions any...being in contact with those that serve our great nation in these most difficult of times? Meaning prior to doing this, what were your thoughts regarding our service members and now that you have done it, what are they now? Also, can you share some links here so more of our readers can see what Music For Troops is truly all about and shed some of your own feelings on how it is truly a great thing for our warriors?

Leah DeVon: I have such respect for our men and women in uniform. My heart gets very heavy just thinking about it. If I could travel the world and just perform for our troops, I absolutely would. I will tell you that they are the most appreciative audiences that I've ever performed for. If you would like to learn more about performing for our troops you can visit: www.uso.com or www.armedforcesentertainment.com. If you're a musician and would like to donate your music you can also visit musicfortroops.com. Both are such lovely causes to let our service men and women know we care.

Chase Von: I imagine you had to fly to many of the locations where you performed, and perhaps had to reach some of those in tactical vehicles, as well. If so, was that a unique experience for you?

Leah DeVon: Actually, we were supposed to go to Diego Garcia on our tour, and due to the conditions at the time with the brutal murder of--well, I don't even want to get into it--we did not go. We stayed in Singapore and performed. I will tell you that the flight to Singapore was about twenty-three hours, but I would do it again in a heartbeat.

Chase Von: You've opened for the Backstreet Boys, Destiny's Child, Chaka Khan, Earth, Wind & Fire, Maze featuring Frankie Beverly, Pieces of a Dream, and also worked with and recorded a duet with the infamous producer Kashif who has worked with Whitney Houston, Kenny G and Mariah Carey. Is there anyone out there in the entertainment industry that you truly want to work more with or would you love to work with again?

Leah DeVon: I have been so blessed to have had the

opportunity to work with such amazing artists. I learned so much from Kashif. I met him when I was working with a management company in LA. He was, and still is, such a great mentor. He has written a book *Everything You Better Know About the Music Business*. Every artist should own this book.

Chase Von: Who are some of the singers, or just people in general, you truly admire and looked to as role models?

Leah DeVon: *I love, love Celine Dion!* I had a chance to see her show in Vegas last year. She is ridiculously talented and seems like such a wonderful, genuine person. I am also a big fan of Lionel Ritchie. I think he is one of the best songwriters to date.

Chase Von: I couldn't help but notice this huge *rock* on your hand in one of your pictures and what finger it was on. (Smile.) I remember thinking that out of sight of the periphery of the photo, there had to be an armed guard to protect you and the jewelry. (Smile.) But are you married? And if so, is your husband also in the entertainment business? And is your name a stage name or just an attempt to be somewhat like me? Heh-heh :)

Leah DeVon: *You are silly!* I am married to a wonderful man (Kelvin). He is my best friend. (Smile.) He is not in the business, but is so supportive of me and has sacrificed quite a bit to allow me to spread my wings. For *that* I am truly grateful. I will tell him that you like my ring. LOL!

Chase Von: OK, sure...on to other things. (Smile.) You're the face along with supermodel Rachel Hunter for Divas Choice, a fine jewelry line created by award-winning jewelry designer Steven Zale. I also read where *Seventeen*

Magazine and Badgley Mischka also endorse it. When I saw that, I was like... Is that for Zale`s Jewelry? We've all heard of that! And with your exceptional good looks,...

Hey, I'm married--not visually impaired. (Smile.) Do you see any acting in your future?

Leah DeVon: I really lucked out with the jewelry campaign! Steven Zale is a jewel... LOL! He is tied into the Zale line but Zalemark is his company. I appreciate their company for allowing me to have a voice in terms of the people who work with me. They are fantastic, and the jewelry is simply stunning. I would absolutely love to go into acting if the opportunity were offered. My dream is to perform on Broadway.

Chase Von: One of my most recent interviews was with the lovely and amazing actress and model Shawn Richardz, prior to this one. *She is incredible, but then* *again, so are you!* She went from acting to modeling, and it looks like you have gone from being a singer to modeling, as well, But do you see yourself, down the line, producing other artists? Because I have a few I could suggest to you that are off the chain: Dozie, Rachael Bell, Brian O'Neal, Alina, "The Artist" C, Kim Kline, Janice B, Willard Barth, Jena Fair, Alice Marie, Barbara Evans...and all these people are independents, mind you. Least, last I heard. Also, what do you think about the independent artist and is that how you yourself initially started out?

Leah DeVon: I'd love to dabble in working with other artists. I hope that is in the cards for me.

Chase Von: Besides Zales, performing for our troops, and the release of your new hot CD *Come Over* that is climbing the Billboard charts, are there any other future projects you're working on you can share with our readers?

Leah DeVon: I just recently recorded a new dance single and shot a music video for a dance track *What Does It Take.* The song is being warmly embraced, especially overseas. We are getting ready to do quite a few different remixes on the song. I am really looking forward to seeing how they will turn out. I am also heading over to Milan, Italy in October to promote my music--so I can't wait!

Chase Von: I also know you are a proud supporter of Saving Our Children. Can you tell our readers more about that; how you got involved; what wonderful things you see happening because of it, and also share a link where they can learn more?

Leah DeVon: *Saving Our Children is a fantastic organization!* It's crazy that every forty seconds a child is reported missing in this country. What many readers may not realize is that thirty-three percent are African-American children who often don't receive the media attention needed. I guess it's important for us to remember that **ALL** of our children are important! To learn more, please visit: http://www.savingourchildren.bravehost.com/. I'd love to see more supporters of this wonderful organization, or more people getting involved.

Chase Von: How important is family to you, and what is your take on the state of our current world?

Leah DeVon: My family is my number one priority! I have such a close relationship with all of them. I was telling my mother the other day that I always thought that I would have at least three kids. To be honest with you at this point, I would be happy with one healthy child. Right now my husband and I are the proud parents of a little cockapoo named Louie. LOL... He's spoiled rotten! I look forward to starting a family; I just wish my little girl or boy would be able to grow up the carefree way that I did!

Chase Von: What would you say if you were standing in front of a microphone that could be heard by every child on the planet, and regardless of what language it was they spoke, they would understand you? What positive advice would you give the children, if that were possible?

Leah DeVon: I would tell them *to dream big!* That they could do and be anything that they would like. We often give up on our dreams too quickly!

Chase Von: What are some of your different websites and links so that our readers can learn more about lovely singer, Diva, model and spokeswoman for Zales Jewelry Leah DeVon? And also any other music that they can find by you that is available on the net?

Leah DeVon: You can see what's going on in my world at www.leahdeVonmusic.com. You can view my calendar, music videos and hear samples of my music.

Chase Von: Before I close--and...well, hardly anyone reads these interviews...right? (Smile.)--when you wrote *Come Over* was there any possibility that you had me in mind? Heh-Heh:)

Leah DeVon: You were my inspiration! (Smile.) You and the kid that played Napoleon Dynamite, Urkel, Jimmy Walker from *Good Times* and... Well, what was that kid's name that used to always say...."What you talking 'bout... Willis?"...Gary? Please, help me out a little here, Chase. Gary...started with a C right?

Chase Von: I think I get the point, Leah. Can you get back to the other part of the question?

Leah DeVon: (Smile.) I have two writing partners, Michera Clark and Phillip O'Rourke. We work well together because there are no egos, which is nice. *Come Over* was definitely a labor of love for me.

Chase Von: I had to ask, huh? (Looking down, kicking dirt.) (Smile.) On behalf of the *Student Operated Press* and myself, Leah--as well as all the troops worldwide that you were gracious enough to perform for--thanks for finding the time in your busy life to share yourself with our readers. Also wishing you continued success and *love and light.* I'm still waiting on a topic for lyrics because I'm going to hold you to that...if I can catch you again. (Smile.)

Leah DeVon: Thank *you* for sharing your time with me. Also, continued success to you, as well. You are such a beautiful writer. A little birdie told me that your book is killing 'em on Amazon (Smile.) *Be Blessed!*

****

*"Saving Our Children is a fantastic organization! It's crazy that every forty seconds a child is reported missing in this country. What many readers may not realize is that thirty-three percent are African-American children who often don't receive the media attention needed. I guess it's important for us to remember that **ALL** of our children are important!"*
- Leah DeVon, Singer, Model, Songwriter
****

ARMED FORCES ENTERTAINMENT PRESENTS
leahdevon
www.leahdevonmusic.com

DIVA WITH A CAPITAL V

Fresh off the release of her second album *Come Over*, Leah DeVon and her band are coming overseas to share their smooth blend of pop, R&B and soul. Her smooth-as-satin voice, diva stage presence and genre-defying songwriting abilities make her one of the hottest stars to hit the international stage in years.

ARMED FORCES ENTERTAINMENT®

COMING TO A THEATER NEAR YOU.
Tell us how you liked the show at www.armedforcesentertainment.com

****

"I would tell them to dream big! That they could do and be anything that they would like. We often give up on our dreams too quickly!"
- Leah DeVon, Singer, Model, Songwriter

****

Interview with Kiara Hunter

'HUNTER GIRL' - ACTRESS, SINGER, MODEL
by Chase Von

Chase Von: Kiara, hi there again and it was great speaking with you the other night. On behalf of myself and the *Student Operated Press*, I really want to thank you for taking out some time from your hectic schedule to share yourself with our readers. I know you're working on your second CD as well as numerous other things so this is truly appreciated.

Kiara: No problem, Chase. I am happy to be a part of such a wonderful and exciting group you have such as the *Student Operated Press*. (Smile.)

Chase Von: Your list of accomplishments is outstanding. But before we get to the things you've done, what you're currently doing, and your plans for the future, what were your younger years like? And how old were you when you started taking singing seriously as a career, as well as acting? I've had the good fortune to interview some incredible actors and actresses: yourself, Shawn Richardz, Jason Seitz, Jennifer Wilkinson, Darcy Donavan, Barbara Evans, Kimberly Prendez, Kitty "Kitania" Kavey, and Nhojj. Many of them not only act but, like yourself, do a variety of things. Some started later than others but they all *knew* at some point that is what they should be doing. So do you also think that people that enter into this extremely difficult and challenging field just have it in their blood, so to speak?

Kiara: From my earlier years until now, being an *artist* of any sort is who I truly *am* and who I was born to *be*. I was an extroverted child, always dancing, singing and acting in anything that I could find an outlet for. As well, athletic endeavors for me were a great way to express myself and-- well, I very rarely sat still, ever! I didn't start acting professionally until I was in my early twenties, and singing in my early thirties. Additionally, I don't believe age is a definitive prerequisite to starting any artistic endeavor–there are seven-year-olds and seventy-year-olds with careers in both film and music these days, and for that I am thankful. How boring would it be if all artists were between eighteen and twenty-eight? (Smile.)

Chase Von: When we were talking on the phone for the first time, we also had our first disagreement. (Smile.) I said my world was *good people, bad people* and you said there was no such thing as *bad people.* I said, yes there are, you said, no there aren't, I said, yes there are, you said, no there aren't, I said, yes there are, and you said...well, I think the readers get the gist of it. (Smile.) We changed subject but I was really curious after we got off the phone why you felt that way. I've been a correctional officer at one point in my life, and I've also been to two wars. I know people that are permanently injured for life and there are people that I've served with that, sadly, are no longer with us. I myself suffer from PTSD. So I was wondering--since you had a date I hope I didn't make you late for--as you were pressed for time, if you could elaborate on why you feel that way, a bit? And I will say I think if it bleeds, it leads, and that we are often barraged with bad things by the media. And I think that there are perhaps great things that are happening as well, but for some reason, bad stories are what are most often reported on.

Kiara: As a spiritual person, my response came from a place that does not judge good from bad or up from down or right from left–I look at things as they are, without borders. I believe that war is caused by separating ourselves through religion, race, gender, country, and in the many ways we compete to *win.* There are no winners in war and there are no winners in competition; we are all losers, losing ourselves in the process and believing that winning is everything. Everyone is a winner because I believe we are perfect the way we are; and unfortunately, many do not believe that and focus on the negatives of human nature instead of the positives. Competition is best when it is only with myself searching for peace, solace and truth. Truth, to me, does not come from the ego mind but rather from the heart and the soul that connects all of us, including Mother Earth, together as *one*. As oneness, with *love* binding us, there would not be *bad* and *good* people but only a deep connection with our universal knowledge of what is: we are *one*. Good and bad is a judgment based on opinions and experiences through the eyes of the beholder. Who is fighting for peace and who is fighting for freedom? Who is the victim and who is the instigator? Both have their reasons and so neither is right. Without *love* in our own lives and trust in who we really *are*, there will continue to be war and fighting not only among countries, but within our own families and communities. It all starts with ourselves. Together, peace is possible.

Chase Von: What a great answer, Kiara! I don't know if you've seen this, but I saw a video online where a group of people went to places where there was a lot of violence and crime. I believe one of those places was our nation's capital, Washington D.C., and they simply meditated and had good and positive thoughts for a period of time. The crime rates subsequently dropped; and this happened everywhere they went. How much effect do you think our thoughts as a whole have on the way the world is?

Kiara: There is much to be said about meditations and prayers. The *I Am* presence is a very powerful affirmation that can indeed change the world. By filtering our minds with the *love* in our hearts, I know for a fact that miracles happen to those who *believe.*

Chase Von: Now to your many accomplishments, and the readers are going to have to forgive me because I don't think I will be able to mention them all. You're a formidable force in the music world with your internationally popular CD *We Can Play.* You're also working on your second CD as we speak, and you have a truly beautiful voice. You've toured with Atomic Kitten and performed in front of over 60,000 fans, and your hit single "Believe" registered #9 on the European dance/pop charts ahead of music legend and Diva Whitney Houston, as well as Holly Valance. It's also featured on the original soundtrack of the Stephen Baldwin and Peter Gallagher film, *Protection,* for Alliance-Alantis. You wrote it in collaboration with Grammy Award-winning producer Ian Prince, who has worked with music icon Quincy Jones; he's also worked with Joy Enriques and Juno-nominated producer Chin Injeti. The one I personally like the most-- but they are all growing on me--is your soft ballad "With You," but the entire CD is strong throughout. In addition to working on your second release, you are also cast as the lead in a film called *The Plate,* starring opposite David Lewis, who has been in so many things I can't list them all either, but *The X Files, Pay Check, Millennium, The Butterfly Effect II, Accidental Witness, Totally Awesome, Criminal Minds* and *The L Word* just to name a few. You yourself have been in *Alien Incursion, Sub Zero, The Thing Below, Stargate SG-1, Wormhole X-Treme, The Naked and the Dead, The Enemy Within, Timeless Obsession, Bordello of Blood, Mask of Death, Dangerous Prey, The X Files, Madonna: Lost Innocence, Blackmail,* and *L.A.P.D. To Protect and to Serve*--and that's just naming a few as well! Your first lead role was in *Dangerous Prey* but you then went on to star opposite Lorenzo Lamas in *Mask of Death,* and later as a deadly Vampire opposite the amazing Dennis Miller in *Tales from the Crypt: Bordello of Blood,* and with C. Thomas Howell in *Sleeping Dogs.* I remember when I was speaking to you I said that my boss here at the *SOP,* Judyth Piazza, had interviewed Billy D. Williams, and you said you have been in something with him as well.

You're also not only known as a serious actress but as one that can be counted on to handle the more physical roles as well. What has been your most challenging role that you've played to date?

Kiara: I would have to say to say *Alien Incursion* was the most challenging. The reason? It was the lowest budget film I have ever made. So there were no dressing rooms, makeshift everything from makeup to wardrobe areas to sets as well. We were outside for pretty much the whole time (cold and rainy!) and the scripts were changed almost daily so scenes that I had worked out the night before were scrapped and new ones were given literally hours before I had to be on set. Being one of the lead actors, the pressure was hardcore–working ten hours or more and then getting six hours' sleep, and repeating it for days on end. It was horrendous but I was doing what I loved doing, the cast and crew were fantastic, and, well, through it all I had a lot of fun. I have to say, as well, other than the CGI (computer graphics interface) the rest of the movie was really good--and pretty funny too if you ask me! (Smile.)

Chase Von: Who are some of the actresses and actors you most admire as well as--since you are also a singer--those in your other area where you are also excelling? Also, who are some of the people you truly enjoyed working with, and ones you want to work with again? And are there any other people in either field, music or acting, that you haven't worked with but are looking forward to that happening?

Kiara: Wow! There are so many talented actors and actresses out there. Here are some of my favorites: Jack Nicholson, Al Pacino, Robert DeNiro, Tom Hanks, Jeremy Irons. Also Tom Cruise, Russell Crowe, Sean Penn, Gene

Hackman, Will Smith, Forrest Whitaker, Kevin Costner, Leonardo DiCaprio, Clint Eastwood, Heath Ledger, Denzel Washington, Johnny Depp, Christian Bale, Cate Blanchette, Katherine Hepburn, Meryl Streep, Jodie Foster, Judy Garland, Marlene Dietrich, Sally Field, Shirley MacLaine, Jessica Lange, Julia Roberts, Susan Sarandon, Nicole Kidman, Angelina Jolie--to name a few. I would be honored to work with any of these big hitters...lol...I would love to work with Dennis Miller again because I just laughed so much with him on the set of *Bordello of Blood*-- also Thomas C. Howell in *Sleeping Dogs*. Great guy!

Lorenzo Lamas was fun too. In conclusion, I would be honored to work with any actors/musicians out there that are making things happen in their lives and putting out great material with great intentions. Life is grand! (Smile.)

Chase Von: I know when I called you were getting ready to go out to a dinner date. Lucky guy! (Smile.) I hope I didn't make you late. But what are some of your favorite meals? And how do you go about staying in such fantastic shape?

Kiara: Aw, thank you for that. It's not always easy keeping in shape–I struggle sometime because I love my popcorn and butter at movies and black licorice as well, but hey! Being a vegetarian mostly has its perks. I haven't eaten any red meat in over twenty years and I stay away from dairy as I find it indigestible. Bread, pasta and alcohol are all baddies for me so I eat mostly salads, fruit, protein shakes, and nuts, and take tons of supplements since there are not many vitamins in cooked foods. As well, I go to the gym or go for long walks/runs with my dog to stay trim. It's hard, but hey, if it wasn't, everyone would be in fantastic shape, (Smile.)

Chase Von: In a lot of my interviews, I ask people about something a friend of mine, Willard Barth, inspirational singer, songwriter and life coach, calls *expanding your comfort zones*. As for me, I started out as a poet in my younger years, then I branched out into writing song lyrics and quotes; later I took on short stories. After my first book was published I wasn't all that satisfied with how things went, but instead of just looking for another publisher I decided to learn that side of the fence and then became a publisher myself. And as you know, I am now doing interviews as well...You do so many things! You sing, you act, you dance and you even have your own comic book. Judyth Piazza also has her own comic book called *The Reluctant Ghost Hunter*. And she's also got a starring role coming up in a movie called *Horrorween*. What would you say to people about trying new things and expanding their comfort zones?

Kiara: *Stretching,* as I call it, is imperative to growing. Everyone has the ability to go beyond what they *think* is possible, and dreaming about things you want is only a moment away. By believing in yourself and having a clear intention of what it is you want, well, *anything* is possible. The only setback is doing too much and not focusing on one at a time, making sure to nourish all of them and not let them die. Art is all about being spontaneous and creative–stay in the zone and watch your garden grow.

Chase Von: I was checking out your comic book and it looks hot! (Smile.) It's called *Hunter Girl* and it has a picture of you on the cover with a sword, and in what looks like a bathing suit with a pistol tied to your hip. I'd love a signed copy. (Smile.) I myself read comic books and I'm already digging the story line. Can you tell our readers a bit more about that but without giving too much away?

Kiara: Sure, Chase. Here is a brief description: The world has been devastated by Mother Earth. In her fury she has obliterated most of civilization, leaving behind one continent, now known as Kraven, in the year 2204 A.D. Any survivors, as well as those from afar, came to this lone continent looking for peace, safety and salvation. Unbeknownst to them, what they thought as solace in a turbulent, changing time in history, came to them as a horrifying and ultimately sinister demise. Through ignorance and placidity, the remaining millions of humans left to be led by the One World Government (OWL) do not overtly know their true purpose on this Earth. But through the efforts of a courageous and powerful bounty hunter named "Kali" and her traveling companions who meet her on her tumultuous journey, she seeks to find her inner truth as well as those whom she has committed to save from the clutches of an evil empire.

Chase Von: I was thinking when I saw it, maybe you could in future stories introduce a new character that's on your team. He could be a two-time war veteran, but a warrior that also writes poetry. As for character flaws, he could suffer from PTSD--but on the plus side, he thinks women are the most beautiful creation that God ever made. And you're certainly proof of that. He could be called, hmmm, let me think a bit, got it! The Last Panther? heh, heh :)

Kiara: he-he... Well funny enough, she does encounter a rebel boy whom she hunts and falls in love with. She has never felt love before and he could certainly have some poetic in him (sounds good!) that touches her heart. The great thing about writing is that you can make your characters from many sources--and yes, you can be one too. Thank you!

"Hunter Girl,"created by Kiara Hunter

Chase Von: Just from speaking to you briefly, I can tell all the way through you are a deep and caring soul. What are some of the causes you feel most strongly about and charities that you, yourself, support?

Kiara: I have many: World Vision, the Make a Wish Foundation, World Wildlife Foundation, PETA, Conservation International, Ocean Alliance, Center for Food Safety, as well as First Book. There are so many charities that deserve help to assist our world in becoming educated and safe. Please donate or belong to as many as you can. Gratitude is the highest form of abundance. *God bless the world and all of us!*

Chase Von: How important is family to you, and what is your take on the state of our current world?

Kiara: Oh my! You ask many deep questions for me...lol...

****

"I don't believe age is a definitive prerequisite to starting any artistic endeavor–there are seven-year-olds and seventy-year-olds with careers in both film and music these days, and for that I am thankful. How boring would it be if all artists were between eighteen and twenty-eight?"
- Kiara Hunter, Actress, Singer, Model

****

Family, to me, is important, yes, but also so is everyone, as I believe we are *all* a family; my spirituality comes into place here. Everyone that I meet daily is a part of me and I a part of them. Strangers, shop owners, servers, representatives, anyone that I meet belongs to my family.

By believing in this, I treat everyone the same way: with respect, kindness and unconditional love. Everyone deserves to have family–and I, to them, should be no different. My take on this world we live in is that this is how we as humans are accountable with our word and our actions. If you are living a loving and kind way, you will see your world as such. If you are living with blame, judgment, hate and fear, you will see that in your world. Yes, there is crime and murder, but there is also love and peace. It depends on where you want to focus your thoughts and your heart–in the positive or the negative. The choice is truly yours since you are a part of creation. You are responsible for all that comes to you and there are no such things as accidents. I believe we are all meant to assist this planet and all that reside here with unconditional love, peace and courage through our own willingness to know we can indeed make a difference. By doing our part––being honest, truthful, accountable, and honoring our word––the world can become a part of us, as we are a part of it.

Chase Von: What would you say if you were standing in front of a microphone that could be heard by every child on the planet and, regardless of what language it was they spoke, they would understand you? What positive advice would you give the children, if that were possible?

Kiara: I would say, *Know yourself and why you are here in this world.* Without knowing who we are and why we are here, we become recipients of the mass conscious energy without being accountable. We all *can* make a difference by being *conscious* and *awake*. Doing things to better ourselves and then assisting others is a good start. Stay focused on your truth, your purpose, the amazing qualities you bring to this world, and how much you can make a difference just by *caring*. It all starts with yourself first, learning to trust your heart and not your head, focusing on *gratitude* and not gain, learning that abundance is your birthright and you are worthy of anything you want with clear intention and service to others. We are *all one*. And so it is.

Chase Von: Where can our readers learn more about all the amazing things you're doing? Your various websites and links where they can buy your CD? And also find out more information on your coming release and all the other things you are doing...as well as touring dates?

Kiara: I have a website (www.kiarahunter.com) where I will keep my progress and news up to date. Also, I have a MySpace page (www.myspace.com/huntergirlworld). You can Google me as well, as I have many other sites that display many of my songs and pictures. I will be selling my music soon, and will let you know on my website when this will happen.

Chase Von: You're the former Miss Canada...The former Miss Fitness British Colombia...The Former Miss Fitness in Canada Silver Medalist...The former Miss Venus Swim Wear International...The former Miss Venus Fitness Body Pro...as well as the former Miss Ujena of Canada. Are you someone that always challenges yourself?

Kiara: Absolutely. I figure that I've got about one hundred years or so to get at it and, well, there's no better time than *now*. Onwards and upwards is my logo and truly, taking it on is the *passion* that inspires and keeps me in my *happy zone*...lol...Working towards goals and making a difference in this world is my dream coming true-I will continue to go beyond what others may think is impossible and will never stop being who I am here to be: a passionate, creative, inspiring and loving *spirit being of light.*

Chase Von: On behalf of the *Student Operated Press* and myself, Kiara, I thank you for sharing yourself with our readers. I'm going to check out that book by Deepak Chopra you recommended to me called *Jesus,* and I wish you a Happy Thanksgiving and mountains more of success. So thanks again for squeezing this in, and love and light to you.

Kiara: Thank you so much, Chase (I love your name!) for the enlightening and sweet interview. It is my pleasure and honor to be a part of it. Happy Thanksgiving to everyone in the world. I believe this world will change when we find peace, healing and love in our own hearts. We are the creators of our own world--find yourself and celebrate. We are *all* worth it!

Kiara Hunter, "Hunter Girl."

****

"Stretching, as I call it, is imperative to growing. Everyone has the ability to go beyond what they think is possible, and dreaming about things you want is only a moment away. By believing in yourself and having a clear intention of what it is you want, well, anything is possible."
- Kiara Hunter, Actress, Singer, Model

****

Interview with Debra D. Griffin

CANCER SURVIVOR, AUTHOR, PHOTOGRAPHER
by Chase Von

Every day is Christmas for someone like me...who was given the greatest gift of all...LIFE!!

Give the gift of life...donate to the:

Breast
Cancer
Care Research
Fund

6022 Wilshire Blvd.
Suite 201
Los Angeles, California 90036

(310) 927 - 7606
Contact:
Michele Rakoff

Chase Von: Hi, Debra, I want to thank you on behalf of the *Student Operated Press*, for finding the time to do this. I know you have some book signings coming up and various other projects in the works, so we truly appreciate you finding the time. Before I met you, I was asked to proof your initial draft of the book, and through that, although we hadn't yet met, I felt as if I knew you. And now I certainly do! So now, my very brave new friend, thanks you for this interview! (Smile.)

Debra: Chase, anytime I have an opportunity to spend some time with you is a real blessing. I always leave you with more than what I bring and for that, I am truly grateful. *Thank you!*

Chase Von: Before we get into your book, I would like our readers to know more about Debra the woman. What were your earlier years like? Where did you grow up? And what was most important to you when you were younger? And now--having survived what claims so very many lives--how has your outlook and perspectives changed from your previous views?

Debra: My early childhood was a fairytale. My parents and my nine siblings lived just five blocks from the Los Angeles harbor in a small town called Wilmington in Southern California. My father was pastor of Shiloh Missionary Baptist Church and my mother was a stay-at-home mom. One of the most important things I learned early in life was faith-based: *"God is able."* Knowing that my God is a loving and giving God and He is able to carry me through whatever befalls me, took away so much of the fear and dismay concerning my diagnoses, because I knew--and without a doubt--*by his stripes I am healed.*

Chase Von: Now, on to your recent book, *A Journey To Wellness*, you didn't initially want to even keep a journal, if I remember correctly. I also don't think I could blame you. Going through such a traumatic experience is daunting all by itself, but to chronicle it at first must have seemed like not the most enjoyable of things to do. However, you began capturing your thoughts, writing poetry, and positive things that eventually led to your using your skills as a photographer to capture your care providers as well. Looking back on your experience, are you glad that you did write down these events and your feelings? And would you suggest to others, in similar circumstances, to do the same?

Debra: Chase, it wasn't that I didn't want to keep a journal; I just didn't know how to make it a positive thing. So many of the journals I had seen until then seemed to be, in my opinion, grand pity-parties. I just needed to find a way to do it and have it reflect me. When I decided to incorporate the photos is when I found my stride. And yes, I would advise everyone going through a tough time to journal. It's amazing what you find out about yourself. For me, what began as a simple task ended up as my saving grace.

Chase Von: After you beat breast cancer and cancer of the liver, it again returned...and metastasized in your brain. I know the average person might have wanted to throw in the towel at that point. *I mean getting so far, and then what a huge set back!* But you kept fighting! I remember talking to you on the phone a few weeks ago and you telling me, not only that the cancer was gone, but miraculously, it didn't even leave scar tissue. You are an extremely determined woman. How much do you attribute your being able to remain alive to your never-say-die attitude?

Debra: Next to the medications, procedures and surgeries, *everything*... It was that live or-die-attitude that got me up in the morning and pointed me in the direction of the medical facilities. It was the smiles, prayers and well wishes that built my hopes and kept me coming back. *Next round!*

Chase Von: I've mentioned this before when we did the Michele Green radio show together, but I am still so very touched by how--when you were so weak and unable to even bathe yourself--that your daughters carried you to the tub, lovingly washed and dried you, and how deeply that affected you at that time. I also read recently in a book by Joel Osteen, called *Your Best Life Now*, where he relates the story of twins that were born but unfortunately, one had a heart condition. This is not verbatim mind you, but against hospital policy, a nurse asked if they could put both the babies in the same incubator. A doctor finally consented and the healthy baby reached over and put his arm on his sick little sister, and for no apparent reason, her heart stabilized and began to heal. The story later done about it was called *The Rescuing Hug*. I mention this because I am aware how much you feel music helped you, but do you also think that human touch is also essential in healing?

****

"I would advise everyone going through a tough time to journal. It's amazing what you find out about yourself. For me, what began as a simple task ended up as my saving grace."
- Debra D. Griffin, Author, Photographer

****

Debra: Of course, Chase, I do. There have been so many studies on the human touch, but for me and without a doubt, it is my life. I have wonderful family and friends who keep me grounded. They never let me forget that I am loved. Their hugs and kisses nourished my soul and I could feel them with me whenever they couldn't be there in the flesh. Chase, I am so blessed.

Chase Von: Another thing I saw on TV was a young woman whose female relatives had a strong history of breast cancer. Her mother had even had it and survived. This woman, however, didn't want to take any chances, so before it even became a possibility, she had both her breasts removed, and later had plastic surgery to correct the removal. At the end of the program, they stated a figure--and this is from memory, so not exact--that she went from a seventy-five to ninety percent chance of developing breast cancer to a two percent chance. I know that your family also had a history of breast cancer. So would you advocate that those with a strong familial history of breast cancer do the same as that young woman did...to minimize it occurring?

Debra: Chase, *no*--every case of breast cancer is different. There are many types and stages of breast cancer, and for each case the treatment is personalized. What works for some will fail with others, and it is impossible to see the outcome in advance. What I do advocate is finding a good medical staff that will work well with you; who will do all in their power to find the right treatment for you, based on your own set of circumstances. I advocate fighting aggressively and not playing around with time. I advocate not letting fear rule your decisions, but allowing knowledge to be your guide.

Chase Von: Tell our readers--in addition to keeping a positive outlook--how important you believe music was in your eventual recovery?

Debra: *Oh, it's just a matter of life or death, that's all!* Heh-heh... Truthfully, music provides the opportunity to commune with God. When you are listening to music and as it fills your soul, you have no room for discord, worry or concern. For the Lord did say, "Make a joyful noise."

Chase Von: One of the things that struck me about your book was that you told it like it was. You didn't portray yourself or your life prior to cancer as picture perfect. In fact, you had already dealt with some pretty life-altering events prior to learning you had cancer. Do you think, in addition to family history, that stress-related things often do contribute to people developing cancer? The word "disease" if separated comes out as dis-ease or a state of not being at ease. And if so, do you now also practice things such as meditation or yoga or other things to manage your stressors?

Debra: Yes, my life held many distresses prior to cancer and I never took the time to rid my life of them...I just kept heaping them to the pile. After the cancer, I learned I had to purge and get rid of the stress in order for healing to take place. I had to learn to fill my life with positive things and get rid of the drama. Today I do this by dealing with the problems one problem at a time until they are gone. I have also found that doing the things I love to do, such as my photography, my music and prayer, relieves a lot of the day-to-day stress. Today I fight hard and play harder, and I just don't have much time left for worry, fear or doubt.

Chase Von: How receptive has the medical community been to your book chronicling your survival of this dreaded disease? And are the ones listed in the photographs insisting they get signed copies? (Smile.)

Debra: All the doctors and staff who are in it have been quite receptive to the book. Dr. Daniels bought ten copies for his staff and his other breast reconstruction patients. Yes, and all but one of the photographers have been given a copy. The cover photographer was the last to get her copy, and she was so proud of me. Did I ever tell you that she was my instructor when I was attending college?

Chase Von: No, but that certainly makes a very personal book, even more personal and beautiful! My friend Bazhe lost his mother to a form of cancer, which he describes in detail in his book *Damages*. My mother also lost her mother, my grandmother, to cancer, as well. Very few people don't know a friend or a loved one that has not been affected by this dreaded disease. But having survived it, can you tell our readers just a little about some of the medical breakthroughs they have had, and how hearing those ominous words now, doesn't always mean a death sentence?

Debra: I am the first in my family to be diagnosed with breast cancer that has survived. There are no victories before me...so I did hear *death* with my diagnosis. But today there are so many new procedures and drugs--that even with stage IV breast cancer, which has no cure to date--a woman can live with cancer like one would live with diabetes. When my sister Dorothy was fighting, brain metastasis was her demise, yet today with gamma knife surgery, brain mets is now just more than a nuisance. In fact, the girls in my oncologist's office called it a tune-up...today some treatments can be painless--fortunately for me, because I am still here.

Chase Von: Unfortunately, I had your book on a computer that bit the dust. But I remember the part where you were first told you had cancer. Can you share with our readers how you called a friend and what that friend told you, even though he, physically, couldn't be present? There are many parts in your book that touched me emotionally and that was most certainly one of them!

Debra: Chase, that passage reads like this: *When I finally pulled myself together, I called a friend, Dean Dass, and told him about the test. He was working and could not get to me, but what he said to me was quite remarkable. Dean told me that someone who loved me was already with me. I thought he was talking about God until he told me to put my arms around myself and hold on. He also said that no one could love me like I could. So I held myself, and when I felt better, I started my car, said good- bye to my friend, and drove home.*

Chase Von: How important is family to you, and what is your take on the state of our current world?

Debra: My family is the most important thing in the world to me. I am nothing without them. They have kept me afloat through all my struggles...not just the cancer–– all my struggles. I would prefer not to answer the question about our world now; I have to remain positive, (Smile.)

Chase Von: What would you say if you were standing in front of a microphone that could be heard by every child on the planet, and regardless of what language it was they spoke, they would understand you? What positive advice would you give the children, if that were possible?

Debra: Smile, and keep a lot of smiling faces around you. Keep busy; take this time to do all your favorite things. Sing, and make a joyful noise.

Chase Von: How can our readers find out more about you? This interview is certainly not capable of covering all your life-threatening ordeal, so can you share your links and web pages? And when we spoke last, you were telling me you are already working on another book. Can you share something about that one, as well, and a general timeframe when you anticipate it will be available to the public?

Debra: Your readers can find me in several places. First, on my website at namandesimages.com; this is my personal photography site. Then I have two pages on the space as well. www.MySpace.com/serious1cancer and also www.MySpace.com/namandesimages where all are truly welcomed. For those that want to help in this fight for life, they can also donate to The Breast Cancer Care Research Fund at; 6022 Wilshire Blvd. Los Angeles, California 90036, or by contacting Michele Rakoff at (310) 927-7606. Also Chase, my next book will be an anthology, paying homage to the musicians who helped me fight my bout with breast cancer. I hope to have it finished by September in time for Breast Cancer Awareness Month 2008.

Chase Von: On behalf of the *Student Operated Press* and myself, Debra, I truly thank you for taking the time to do this. I also want to extend happy holiday wishes to you and yours, and I am sure we will be in contact with one another really soon. *Love and light* to you, as always, (Smile.)

Debra: Thank *you* so kindly. It is always a pleasure to spend some time with you...as I do enjoy your company. Happy holidays to you and your family, and may God continue to bless.

****

"Smile, and keep a lot of smiling faces around you. Keep busy; take this time to do all your favorite things. Sing, and make a joyful noise."
- Debra D. Griffin, Author, Photographer

****

Debra D. Griffin

Has been called Home to be with our Lord in the
early morning hours of August 21, 2008.

In addition to *A Journey To Wellness*, there are two more titles that
will soon be released by Michele Green, contributing writer to *The
Passion Within* and also the owner of Safe Haven Publishing
Company revealing more of Debra's work.

Additionally, a portion of the profits from *The Passion Within*, a
compilation of various authors also goes towards helping those who
find themselves in domestic violence situations.

INDEX

*"If you think you can do a thing or think you
can't do a thing, you're right."*

- Henry Ford

Kimberly Prendez, reading and reflecting on another "Dream Reacher."

Inspirational Singer, Songwriter, Life Coach Willard Barth

Willard Barth is a singer and songwriter whose music and soulful delivery is often compared to Seal, Journey and Michael Bolton. Combining his passion for music and his passion for life, Barth's life revolves around inspiring, educating and empowering people through his music, facilitating seminars, doing keynote speeches and one-on-one success coaching.

At the age of eight, Barth lost his left leg to cancer. In an attempt to show the world and himself that he was no different than anyone else, he lettered in junior high wrestling, in varsity football as a place kicker, and was one of the first known licensed amputee motorcyclists in central Pennsylvania. But underlying all the heroics was pain and resentment over his situation. Alcohol and drugs became the controlling substances in his life. Barth, however, was one of the lucky ones, and eventually he reached out for help. In an effort to reevaluate his life, he made his first attempts at songwriting. Since that time, he has been on a quest to carry his music and his message to whomever will listen, hoping it will help them through their own pain.

Barth has performed on numerous occasions with the legendary Les Paul and has also played his music as a featured guest at events that included presenters Mary Manin-Morrissey, Wayne Dyer, Dr. Michael Beckwith, Bob Proctor and Larry Wilson. Barth is not only actively involved in promoting his music, he is also a nationally recognized inspirational speaker, author, success coach and founder of The Neuro-Dynamic Institute, Inc., a New Jersey-based Personal Development Company.

Willard Barth, Lou Pallo, Pappy Kay and the Legendary
Les Paul Performing at the Iridium Jazz Club in NYC

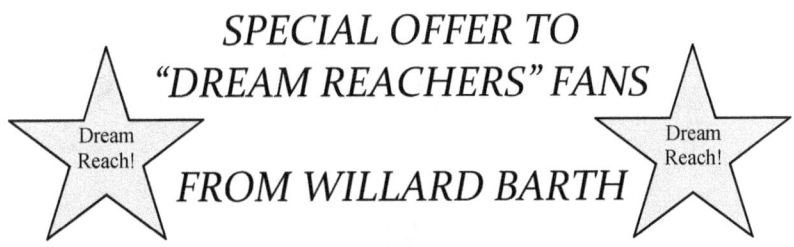

SPECIAL OFFER TO "DREAM REACHERS" FANS

FROM WILLARD BARTH

"Elevate Your Own Self-Awareness Through Inspiration, Education & True Personal & Professional Empowerment."

To receive your free copy download of

"Wind Dancer"...

Email Willard at:

DreamReachersOffer@willardbarth.com

To assist in response speed, put in your subject line:

Purchased "Dream Reachers"

Blessings to everyone from all involved in this creation...and Dream Reach!

Because dreams aren't meant to just be dreamed; they can, if you really reach, be attained.

The Amazing Judyth Piazza
Radio Host, Journalist, CEO/SOP

Judyth Piazza, known as "The Italian Oprah," was born in Florida and knew she wanted to be a journalist at a very young age. Life, however, stirred her away from that pursuit until she endured a failed marriage. She then went back to school, undaunted by her age, and is now the host of the immensely popular radio show, *The American*

Perspective--a cutting-edge radio program that is full of inspiration and information. It's intended to help people succeed in life.

Each week the *American Perspective* features celebrity guests from around the nation, such as Maya Angelou, Zig Ziglar, Yolanda King, Billy D. Williams, Tony Little, Mark Victor Hansen, Dave Ramsey and many, many more. The *American Perspective* can also be heard on WTTB 1490am http://www.wttbam.com/ "It's the next generation of Inter-tainment"

Award winning journalist Judyth Piazza is also the founder of the *Student Operated Press* (www.thesop.org) and content Manager/Editor for *Newsblaze* (www.newsblaze.com) and *Vero Beach Local News* (www.verobeachlocalnews.com). For more information, visit: www.thesop.org
or www.myspace.com/thestudentoperatedpress

Piazza and her two lovely children currently reside in Florida.

About the Author
Chase Von

Chase Von was born in Japan to a military family. He is a retired United States Marine and also served in the US Army as an air traffic control tower operator. He has also been a county correctional officer, a human services assistant in a mental health facility and is a veteran of Desert Shield and Desert Storm, as well as OIF one and two.

Von is also the author of *Pink, Blue and Green* and *Your Chance To Hear The Last Panther Speak*. Additionally, one of his short stories is included in the 2007 *American Review Literary Journal Vol. One*, created by Bryant H. McGill, world-famous author, poet and consultant to the stars. Pieces of his work have also been included in *Songs of Hope*, a compilation by Sachel. Von also is owner of VonChase Publishing Company, with a number of authors in his stable. One of his poetry books, written by Ed Roberts, has been submitted for a Pulitzer Prize in Verse.

Von currently resides in California with his beautiful wife and three lovely children. For more about him visit:
http://www.exposweb.net/ExposedWebPages/ChaseVon/Layout.html
http://www.myspace.com/chase77777
or http://www.nextcat.von/ChasevonTheLastPanther and www.thesop.org

About the Author
Betty Dravis

Betty Dravis was born in Hamilton, Ohio where her natural writing ability was nurtured by a "great school system, caring teachers, and a loving family." She is a sensitive writer, adept in many genres. Dravis, a former newspaper publisher and long-time California journalist, also hosted a Cable TV talk show.

She has written three novels, *Millennium Babe: The Prophecy*, *The Toonies Invade Silicon Valley*, and *1106 Grand Boulevard*, and has published short stories in an anthology and has best-selling shorts on Amazon Shorts. She's also fine-tuning a horror story, a serial-killer thriller and writing a sequel to *"Toonies,"* titled *The Toonies Rock New York.*

Dravis is an Honorary Kentucky Colonel; listed in several Who's Who books; recipient of many California city, county and state awards; is a former member of Sigma Delta Chi; and is a U.S. Amazon Top Reviewer...no. 36 in Canada.

Dravis has four lovely adult children, two angels in Heaven, nine grandchildren and three "greats." A thirty-year resident of her beloved Silicon Valley, she now resides in the Central Valley of California. Her main website is: http://bettydravisauthor.googlepages.com/

*"The interviews are enlightening, but it's the dual writers'
stories of preparation, excitement and nervousness--
in meeting the celebrities--that
make this an oh-so-fun read. And who wouldn't
be nervous interviewing 'Dirty Harry?'"*

- Paul Kyriazi, Hollywood movie director,
audio book producer, author and
"James Bond" motivational speaker

*"At last, a book for people like me who crave the voyeuristic
glimpse into the lives of Hollywood personalities
but who keep their curiosity a secret.
'Dream Reachers' is crammed full of the private thoughts of
those people who--through talent, cunning or attrition--
have risen high into the sky of stardom. Author and career
journalist Betty Dravis and star interview meister Chase
Von combine to tease the real lives from the glossy facades
of our most loved and despised celebrities. The result
is a rare view into the lives of the people who have become
like gods and goddesses, saints and
demons to a world enamored of stardom.
In 'Dream Reachers,' those superstars are made human
again, filled with fears and folly, love and loss
--just like the rest of us."*

- Mark LaFlamme, award-winning Maine crime reporter,
author of "Dirt: An American Campaign,"
"The Pink Room" and other horror novels.

"The word 'dream' is not an abstract noun; it's a concrete verb defined by zealous action. My album includes a song that begins: 'There's reality in whatever you dream, you can have whatever your mind's eye can see...' 'Dream Reachers' realize the truth in these words and they know if they can perceive the dream then the dream is reality, which makes it attainable. This book is a source of confirmation and encouragement, spoken by a collection of free thinkers who refused to look back on their dreams and wonder 'What if...?' Assembling these achievers is ingenious literary artistry on behalf of Chase Von and Betty Dravis. Hat's off to you both!"

- Gem Avery, The Pioneeress of Ambient Soul, Internationally recognized debut album "Gas Money," vocalist and songwriter

"Betty Dravis and Chase Von dazzle the reader with charm as they reach deep into each celebrity, bringing their humanity to the surface with questions we would all have loved to ask if we were lucky enough to meet them. Grand celebrities open up to reveal their souls and dreams, and through Betty and Chase we get the privilege of peeking into their glamorous lives unlike never before. There's something for everyone in this book––for fans big and small––and best of all it comes in a paperback I can carry around with me and a stunning hardcover to keep on my bookcase for years to come."

- Kasia Sienkowska, fashion designer, NYC

"I was so thrilled when my pal, Betty Dravis, disclosed that she met Clint Eastwood. I love him... always have. I think he's one of the sexiest men on the planet...even at his "elder" age, he's fabulous. I can't believe all the fascinating people Chase Von has interviewed: Darcy Donavan, Shawn Richardz, MT Robison, Dawn Huffaker, Kitania "Kitty" Kavey, Barbara Evans, Aberjhani, Kiara Hunter... the list goes on. Can't wait to read 'Dream Reachers.'"

- Carol Engan Borrelli/Florida, author of
"Cinagro Farm" cookbook, www.cinagrofarm.com

"'Dream Reachers' combines the best of yesterday and today all in one. At once there is the charming reflections of Betty Dravis's encounters with high profile stars of a bygone era out of enchanting Hollywood and powerful Washington. As well, we see the ground-breaking interviews of Chase Von's up-and-coming stars of today. This book will make you smile and, indeed...dream."

- Meesh, Founder of Mixeddna and
The Group for Sexy Mixed People

"'Wow! 'Dream Reachers' is legit! There's no hocus-pocus formula here to a better life. It's about real people; some are living in the public eye on a large scale, while others are living their dreams, even if it isn't worldwide knowledge...yet! What strikes me about this book is the honesty and the fact that people that do 'Dream Reach' generally have a belief or a point in their lives where they make a decision to go for it––and determination that they won't be swayed by the naysayers. I could have been a statistic myself, but I reached a point where I knew if I stayed on the same path, I would end up behind bars...or worse. When we realize that we have the ability to choose, we can put our energy in any direction. So follow your dreams! Put your energies in a positive direction! I think this book will be the catalyst for a lot of people who just need that extra 'nudge' to give them the courage to go for their own dreams. I wish it had been available to me‒‒BEFORE my life of crime."

- Glenn Brandon Burke, M.Ed., motivational speaker, business coach, CEO of Burke Advantage Incorporated, author and frequent "inspirational speaker" in colleges and prisons across the nation

"I have a dream that my four little children will one day live in a nation where they will not be judged by the color of their skin, but by the content of their character."

- Dr. Martin Luther King, Jr.

"Faith is taking the first step even when you don't see the whole staircase."

- Dr. Martin Luther King, Jr.

Sweet Dreams, Dream Reachers

If the universe
Is big enough
To hold countless stars
And uncountable galaxies
Is it really a stretch
Of the imagination
To believe within it
It can also hold
Your dreams?

By Chase Von
tlp
The Last Panther